Chef!

20 Great British Chefs
100 Great British Recipes

Chef!

20 Great British Chefs
100 Great British Recipes

James Winter and James Bulmer
with a foreword by James Martin

First published in Great Britain
as *Yes Chef!* in 2009 by

Absolute Press
Scarborough House
29 James Street West
Bath BA1 2BT
Phone 44 (0) 1225 316013
Fax 44 (0) 1225 445836
E-mail info@absolutepress.co.uk
Website www.absolutepress.co.uk

This paperback edition first published
in 2010

Text copyright
James Winter and James Bulmer
Foreword copyright James Martin
Recipes copyright of the chefs

Photography copyright
Cristian Barnett

Publisher Jon Croft
Commissioning Editor Meg Avent
Editor Joanna Wood
Art Direction Matt Inwood
Design Matt Inwood and
Claire Siggery
Publishing Assistant Andrea O'Connor
Photography Cristian Barnett

A catalogue record of this book is
available from the British Library

ISBN 9781906650391

Printed and bound in China on behalf
of Latitude Press

A note about the text
This book is set in Sabon MT. Sabon
was designed by Jan Tschichold in
1964. The roman design is based on
type by Claude Garamond, whereas
the italic design is based on types by
Robert Granjon.

FOREWORD BY JAMES MARTIN

I still remember a day – and it wasn't so long ago – being in a French two-star Michelin kitchen, aged 16, standing in my tall chef's hat and starched white jacket and eager to learn from some of the world's best.

This was the only way to learn how to cook great food back then. Years have passed, times have changed and thankfully the young chefs of today don't have to travel across the Channel in search of the best... they're right here in the UK.

We Brits are on a roll! Our gastronomic revolution is gathering pace and chefs with passion and skills to rival anyone have helped to change the way we feel and think about food. This book is an insight into the minds of some of them and showcases how they will continue to shape and influence the way we eat. It's also a great food guide for people who want to search out these chefs and try their food for themselves.

It will become clear as you browse through these pages that you don't have to venture far from your home in search of the best restaurants. And while you sample the amazing food these people produce, just pause for a minute to remember that 16-year-old in the kitchen, who only gets to say two words... 'Yes Chef!'.

JAMES MARTIN, SEPTEMBER 2009

INTRODUCTION

There are an estimated 25,000 restaurants in the UK. The majority of these are chain outlets selling the same food to the same sorts of people day-in-day-out. But hidden amongst this sea of mundanity are a small number of glistening jewels – restaurants in which you'll get an exceptional experience thanks to the superlative skills of their chefs.

Each one of the 20 chefs included in this book fall into that category. All are cooking at the highest level – in layman's terms, theirs is premiership cuisine. Each one is unique in his (and her) style and each one cooks with passion and pride.

Never before in the history of Britain's restaurant scene have there been so many technically skilled artisans. Many have learnt their craft in the original and great kitchens of Britain run by legendary chefs like Raymond Blanc, Marco Pierre White, Gordon Ramsay and the Roux Brothers. Some have even cut their culinary teeth in America, Spain or France. It goes without saying that they are all able to recreate the dishes of their teachers but what makes them shine is their desire to evolve, to move their cooking on to a new level and to create a dining experience that surpasses anywhere else in the world.

If you are so inclined then you can have a go at any of the 100 recipes in this book. They are of varying levels of difficulty ranging from the incredibly technical, like Jason Atherton's BLT or Nigel Haworth's chocolate and cherry dessert, to the amazingly simple spiced poached pear with gorgonzola and honey comb from Matt Tebbutt. Some involve equipment and apparatus that you may not have, like water baths, Thermomixes and Pacojet machines, but remember that each recipe is a starting point, an opening salvo for you to interpret and change if you wish and better still, to improve.

It has been a task of great joy to travel this 'sceptred isle' of ours to meet these men (and woman) and talk food and life and recipes. Between us, we've been lucky enough to have been involved in the world of food for over 25 years and we can say without any hesitation that we are in a golden age for British cuisine. Every region of Britain has a great British chef in it, go and find them and let them take you on a journey of discovery. As a nation we produce some of the finest ingredients on this earth and now, finally, our chefs know how to prepare and cook them and extract the very best out of them.

We are both in the very lucky position of spending a great deal of our working time sitting at restaurant tables and talking to, and about, chefs. It was during one such lunch that we realised that it has been some years since anyone did a stock take of the state of British cooking. Yes, there are guide books and awards but there was nothing out there that brought these places to life, that recreated that personal feeling you get from having a terrific meal in a terrific place, thanks to a master craftsman.

There's a common perception of a chef as a firebrand, barking orders to a team of frightened underlings then tearing shreds off the owner of any dissenting voice, whether it be a waiter or even a paying diner. The reality is often very different. Most professional kitchens are dedicated and focused places, where seriously skilled people go about the task of creating very complicated works of art under extreme time-pressure. To work in a hot kitchen you have to control your passions but still inspire your staff.

It has been a privilege to get to know each and every one of the chefs in this book: and each and every one of them we would both be proud to call our friend (they, on the other hand, would probably call us something very different!). Their cooking reflects who they are and the dishes contained within this book tell their story. Once you have drooled over the stunning photos and studied the recipes we hope you will glance over the words and get to know these people as we have. We have tried to give you a real sense of who they are and hope we have, to some measure, succeeded. At this point we must credit our amazing editor, Joanna Wood, who has given our inane ramblings a sense of purpose.

Essentially, what we've tried to do with this first volume (take note Mr Publisher) is to give you a broad slice of what's out there in the big, wide, wonderful world of UK restaurants. A bit like cutting into Mark Hix's stargazey pie, we want to make sure that whoever reads this book – or cooks from it – gets a taste each of the 'goodies' contained inside.

We definitely eat with our eyes and Cristian Barnett was the photographer tasked with bringing to life the joy that these chefs give to their diners on the plate. We hope (in fact we know) you will agree as you turn the pages that he is a genius and that you will wallow in the sheer self-indulgence of looking at beautiful food – and salivate over the exquisite photographs in these pages.

Finally, we'd urge you, as you go through this book, to carry one very important thought with you. All the chefs we have featured are British and cook with a British heart. Their recipes may involve some techniques and ingredients borrowed from France, India or even Italy but their dishes have a British sensibility. This country has always embraced the best that other cultures have to offer and ever since we first set sail and headed off to explore the world there have been men, like Sir Walter Raleigh, who knew a tasty vegetable when they saw one.

It means that Britain is a fertile hot pot of produce and culinary styles. So, be proud of your food, be proud of your chefs and most of all try the recipes contained within these beautiful pages. Better still, though, go and book a table at any of the restaurants and let these chefs cook you the meal of your life!

JAMES WINTER & JAMES BULMER, SEPTEMBER 2009

20
GREAT BRITISH
CHEFS

100
GREAT BRITISH
RECIPES

JASON ATHERTON

The modern dining experience can be a full-on affair. The fashion is for tasting menus ranging from six-to-eight courses, with the chef throwing in an *amuse-bouche* and a pre-dessert. It can take you hours to eat and days to digest, but Jason Atherton had the bright idea of changing all that. Within plain, simple frontage and occupying the northern corner of Grosvenor Square in Mayfair lies Maze, one of the most modern and revolutionary restaurants in Britain. A smart restaurant where you can pop in for just a plate of food and a glass of wine, or blow out on a full multi-course multi-plate meal.

Climb the steep steps to the restaurant and walk through the tall, glass doors and you find yourself faced with not one, but two restaurants. Right takes you into Maze Grill where the best steaks in town are served with chunky chips and various sauces and you can chew down on anything from

the Aberdeen Angus to the revered Wagyu beef. Turn left and you find yourself staring at the deceptively large dining space that is Maze. Created by New York-based designer David Rockwell, it's sleek and chic. Banquette tables in the foreground lead up to a circular dining space with tables edging a round, raised platform. Leather-backed pale, mustard seating and natural woods are in abundance, while a high ceiling makes the space feel exciting.

The most exciting thing, though, about Maze is Jason's food. It's heavily influenced by his time spent cooking in Spain, where grazing on small plates of food at one's own pace is common. At Maze he's translated this concept to tasting dishes arranged in starters and mains – and diners are requested to select a few from each in order to pull together their own menus.

To understand the menu you have to look at the man. This 38-year-old can cook any style of cuisine to the highest level. Like many chefs, he had a basic understanding of food as a child. Having grown up in Skegness, he approached the catering world without much direction but found the daily grind surprisingly comforting. Jason's parents broke up when he was just three and although he describes his Lincolnshire childhood as 'pretty tough', he says that his stepfather provided a strong moral compass. When Jason's mother and stepfather decided to buy a guesthouse, they realised that it made commercial sense to make their own food from scratch to serve to their guests.

Despite this backdrop, Jason's first vocation was the navy and only the failure of his English exam prevented him from sailing the Seven Seas. Study was never his strong point – something he was reminded of recently when he decided to take a higher-education business qualification. So instead of the navy, he joined the Army Catering Corps. It was a rude awakening. He hated the regiment and its strict rules and timetables. He found himself battling against his superiors and, after just four months, was booted out. His stepdad intervened. 'He told me that things had to change and I had to sort myself out or move on. It really got through to me and I asked him to give me one week. That was it, I was back on track.'

The track was a local Skegness hotel where Jason got a job as a commis chef and found his calling. Armed with a new found confidence and, finally, some catering qualifications from Boston College, he soon headed to London. Never one to do things the conventional way he did it without telling his family, knowing that his mum would think he was too young to leave home at the tender age of 16. By the time she tracked him down, he was working in a restaurant in Kensington and finally starting a career.

A series of work experiences, or *stages* in culinary speak, around London followed and one particular job interview even led to him working a shift as a waiter at Bibendum, one of London's most influential restaurants. 'They just gave me the uniform and told me to get out there. I was too scared to say I was there for the chef's job!' He didn't get the job.

He had much better luck at the celebrated La Tante Claire under its legendary chef-patron Pierre Koffmann, and, later, with it's equally legendary chef Nico Ladenis at Chez Nico. A short stint in France followed, before he returned to the UK to work for restaurateur Oliver Peyton (these days famous for his judging role on the Great British Menu) at the latter's London restaurant Coast, then at the new all-in-one entertainment experience that was Mash & Air in Manchester.

But Jason's life was about to change. Aged 27 with just a rucksack on his back, he headed, uninvited, to Spain to work at arguably the greatest restaurant of them all, Ferran Adrià's El Bulli. He found himself mixing curry with bananas and making ice cream from avocados. Not all of it worked for him and he still recalls his uncertainty at the seawater foam he had to make for one scallop dish.

And then Gordon Ramsay entered his life. Jason was back in England, running the hobs at a Kensington restaurant called L'Anis, owned by restaurateur Claudio Pulze, and attracting a lot of notice for his food. Spotting his talent, Gordon contacted Jason, said that his stable of restaurants was 'going places' and that he wanted Jason's help. And that was that – Jason became part of Gordon Ramsay Holdings, starting off at the company's restaurant, Verre, in Dubai before coming home to launch Maze.

Jason's touch is felt across every element at Maze. The dining room runs to his exacting standards, the food is cooked to his detailed spec. He has written every recipe and designed a kitchen that allows him to create anything he can dream up. It operates on a line system with a huge number of chefs, but no-one but Jason is responsible for a complete dish and

he watches his food like a hawk as it leaves the hot pass on its journey to the diner's table.

He is always looking for ways to open up familiar dishes, to break them down and reform them. Be it a version of macaroni cheese with truffle oil and Parmesan foam and an egg yolk slowly poached at 65C; or a John Dory carbonara where the pasta is steamed and served in a ball with a quail's egg yolk at the heart of it and accompanied by a button mushroom sauce served, for a bit of theatre, at the table. The dish looks so simple, but boy is it not!

Jason loves to experiment – not in the way that Heston Blumenthal might do – but his menu is a delightful

playground. Take his reconstructed BLT. Normally the stuff of supermarket sandwiches, Jason has transformed the combination of bacon, lettuce and tomato into a superstar dish – a green and fresh lettuce purée, topped with the cleanest of tomato jellies and a healthy splash of bacon cream. Served in a cocktail glass, you would have to be made of stone not to smile when it arrives. It's a dish that turned him into one of the most talked-about chefs in London and is the most popular dish on the menu – and one that Jason is resigned to serving forever.

Maze is the perfect ego-less restaurant – an antidote to many other Michelin-star places in its neighbourhood. It is a brilliant concept and one that has global potential –

currently it has four outlets in three international cities, London, New York and Cape Town. Jason runs a smooth ship and is hands-on at every level, even down to designing the chinaware. But there is no trace of chef swagger at all within Maze, no trumpeting of horns when a dish is served and no waiters pushing truffles on you like a Tunisian beach trader. In some ways, this is not Jason's restaurant at all – it is our restaurant, the people's restaurant. 'They can come in torn jeans or a tuxedo, as long as they enjoy my food, I really don't care!'

Maze
13–15 Grosvenor Square, London W1K 6JP
Phone 020 7107 0000 **www.gordonramsay.com/maze**

BLT

This dish has got the flavour profiles of a BLT without the bread. I did it for the BBC2 series the Great British Menu in 2008 and it's been such a huge success that I don't dare take if off the menu. I love smoked Alsace bacon, but if you can't get hold of any, substitute it with some smoked Cumbrian ham. The key thing is the smokiness.

SERVES 4

For the tomato jelly
2kg plum tomatoes, peeled
2-3 tablespoons olive oil
100g leeks, thinly sliced
50g celery, thinly sliced
100g carrots, thinly sliced
100g shallots, thinly sliced
2 tablespoons tomato paste
2 bunches basil stalks (one for clarifying)
1 garlic clove, chopped
2 bay leaves
250ml tomato juice
100g sugar
50g salt
3 egg whites
5½ leaves per litre gelatine

For the bacon and onion cream
1 tablespoon olive oil
1kg white onions, finely sliced
100g Alsace bacon
200ml double cream
Pinch of salt

Ingredients for the lettuce soup
2 heads iceberg lettuce
Salt

For the garnish
200ml vegetable oil, for deep frying
2 onions, sliced into rings
120g thick-cut bacon, roughly chopped
100ml milk
50g plain flour

For the cheese mixture
825g Cheddar cheese, grated
215ml milk
60g plain flour
60g fresh breadcrumbs
2 free-range eggs
2 free-range egg yolks
1 teaspoon English mustard
Good splash of Worcestershire sauce

For the sandwich
1 loaf brioche
8 large slices prosciutto ham
1 black truffle, thinly sliced

Tomato jelly
Deseed the tomatoes over a bowl and sieve so that you catch their juice – and keep the juice to one side but discard the seeds. Heat the olive oil in a saucepan over a medium heat, add the vegetables and cook for a few minutes so they are softened but do not colour. Add the tomato paste and continue to cook for a further two minutes, then add one bunch of basil stalks, the garlic clove and the bay leaf. Add the flesh from the plum tomatoes and cook for 10-15 minutes. Now add the tomato juice and the juice extracted from the fresh tomatoes, then the sugar and salt. Bring the mixture to the boil and then turn down the heat and simmer it gently for 1 hour to reduce it down. Remove the saucepan from the heat and cool the mixture.

Once it is cool, pour it into a muslin cloth over a bowl large enough to collect the strained juices. Transfer the liquid to a clean saucepan and place over a medium heat, adding in the egg whites and remaining basil stalks. As the tomato stock heats up, the egg whites will congeal and soak up any impurities – you need to simmer the stock for about 20 minutes, stirring it continuously. Once you have a clear consommé take it off the heat and pass again through a clean muslin cloth, then place the stock in a clean saucepan over a medium heat, bring it to a simmer and reduce the liquid volume by a third. Transfer it to a measuring jug to establish the volume of the clear stock and calculate how many gelatine leaves you need to use.

Soak the gelatine leaves in cold water until softened, squeeze out any excess water, then mix them into the warm tomato stock and dissolve. Strain the stock a final time into Martini glasses and place these into the fridge to set.

Bacon and onion cream
Heat the olive oil in a saucepan over a low heat. Add the onion rings and bacon and fry until the onions are softened but not coloured and infused with the flavour of the bacon. Continue cooking over a low heat for one hour, then remove the bacon and transfer the onions to a food procesor with 100ml of the double cream and blend until smooth. Whip the remaining 100ml of double cream to soft peaks and fold in the onion purée.

(Continued on page 18)

(Continued from page 16)

Lettuce soup

Bring a saucepan of water to the boil over a medium heat, place in the lettuce leaves and cook for 1 minute, then remove them, put them in iced water and drain them off. Blitz the leaves in a food processor and pass the resulting 'soup' through a fine sieve into a clean bowl. Season the 'soup' to taste with salt and pour it into small shot glasses, then chill these in the fridge.

Garnish

Heat the oil in a deep, heavy-based pan until a breadcrumb sizzles and turns brown when dropped in it. Do not leave the oil unattended. Dip the onion rings into the milk, then coat them in the flour. Drop them in the hot oil in batches to deep-fry until they are just turning golden-brown, then remove with a slotted spoon and drain them on kitchen paper. Heat an extra teaspoon of oil in a frying pan over a medium heat and add the bacon pieces. Fry these until golden brown, then remove them with a slotted spoon and drain them on kitchen paper. Keep them warm until you serve the dish.

Cheese mixture

Place the Cheddar and milk into a large heavy-based pan and heat, stirring regularly, until the cheese has melted and combined with the milk. Add the flour and breadcrumbs and cook for a further 5 minutes, stirring constantly. Remove the mixture from the heat and cool it down. Once cool, transfer it to a food processor and blend until smooth. Add the eggs, one at a time, and blend them in until combined, then repeat the procedure with the egg yolks. Add the mustard

and Worcestershire sauce, blend again, then cool the mixture in the fridge.

Sandwich

Preheat the oven to 180C/gas mark 4. Cut 8 very thin slices from the brioche and spread the cheese mixture onto one side of each slice. Place 2 slices of prosciutto ham onto 4 of the brioche-and-cheese slices and sprinkle a few slices of fresh truffle over the top. Place a second slice of brioche on top of each to create 4 sandwiches. Next, place each sandwich into a non-stick frying pan over a medium heat and fry for 2-3 minutes, or until golden-brown on each side. Transfer the sandwiches to a baking tray and place this into the oven to cook for a further 2-3 minutes, or until the cheese has melted. Once this has happened, remove the sandwiches from the oven, cut off their crusts and cut into 'soldiers'.

Serving

Place a glass of tomato jelly onto each plate. Add a layer of onion cream to each jelly. Top with the deep-fried onion rings and the cooked bacon pieces. Place a shot glass of lettuce soup alongside and arrange the sandwich 'soldiers' around.

OX CHEEK AND TONGUE, RAISIN PUREE AND GINGER CARROTS

You can't get more British than ox cheeks and tongue, and I've had them on the Maze menu since we opened. If you've got the time I'd advise cooking your own ox tongue. Just poach it with some root vegetables in a little chicken stock for about 2½ hours.

Horseradish pomme purée is a combination of creamed horseradish and mashed potato – very easy, very delicious!

SERVES 6-8

4 ox cheeks, trimmed of fat and sinew
375g mirepoix (chopped onions, carrots and celery)
6 black peppercorns
Small handful of thyme
1 bay leaf
1 sprig of rosemary
300ml port
600ml red wine
2 teaspoons olive oil
500ml veal stock
500ml light chicken stock
125g capers
125g raisins
Cold water
125g baby carrots, blanched
1 teaspoon ginger
1 teaspoon sea salt, finely ground
25g unsalted butter
¼ of a poached ox tongue
185g horseradish pomme purée, to serve
Sea salt and black pepper

Place the ox cheeks, mirepoix vegetables, peppercorns, herbs, port and red wine into a bowl, cover with clingfilm and put in the fridge to marinate overnight. The next day, remove the ox cheeks from the marinade and pat them dry on some kitchen paper. Strain the marinade liquor through a sieve and keep the marinade and veg, separately, on one side to use later. Heat the olive oil in a large heavy-bottomed saucepan, add the marinated ox cheeks and fry them until golden-brown all over. Remove them from the pan and set aside.

Add the chopped vegetables to the pan and gently fry for 3-4 minutes. Add the marinade liquor and bring it to the boil over a high heat until the volume of liquid has reduced by half. Return the browned ox cheeks to the pan. Add both the stocks and bring everything to the boil again, then reduce the heat and simmer for 3½ hours, or until the ox cheeks are meltingly tender. Turn off the heat and allow the ox cheeks to cool in the stock. Once cooled, remove them, cut into portion sizes and place them into individual Vac Pac bags, if you have them, ready for reheating later.

Pass the cooking liquor through a sieve lined with a muslin cloth into a small saucepan. Boil over a high heat until reduced to a sauce consistency that coats the back of a spoon. Pour a small amount of the reduced liquor into each of the bags containing the ox cheeks and seal the bags. Keep the remaining sauce warm.

Raisin Puree
Place the capers and raisins in separate saucepans with enough water to cover them and boil them until they are soft. Strain both through a sieve, place in a food processor and mix them until they're smooth before passing them through a fine sieve.

Ginger Carrots
Mix together 1 teaspoon each of ginger and finely ground sea salt, then heat this and the butter in a frying pan over a medium heat, add the carrots and cook them until golden.

Serving
Place the Vac Pac bags with the ox cheeks in a pan of simmering water and gently warm through (or just gently warm them through in their sauce in a saucepan). Slice the ox tongue to 6mm thickness and pan fry them in a little olive oil. Season if necessary. Arrange the ox tongue on your plates, put a dollop of the caper purée on top of them, then add the glazed ox cheeks. Arrange the carrots around the plate with a little horseradish pomme purée on the side.

ROASTED HAKE, SQUID, PEPPER AND CHORIZO PUREE

Some years ago I spent a brief but inspiring time working in Spain and this dish is a homage to the classic fish dishes of the Basque region, where they love hake and invariably use peppers and chorizo – which means the dishes are always bursting with big flavours. I've used French fleur de sel salt, but Maldon is fine if you can't get it. And if you can't get hold of pomace oil – which is a blend of olive oil and soya oil – just mix your own 50:50 blend of olive oil and a neutral vegetable oil.

SERVES 4

500g hake fillets, skinned
Juice and zest of 1 lemon
4 or 5 slices Parma ham
Fleur de sel, to taste
3 shallots, roughly chopped
Sprig of thyme
1 chorizo sausage, roughly chopped
2 x 125g tins of roasted piquillo
  peppers, drained and roughly
  chopped
3 baby squid (50g)
4 bunches of curly parsley, stalks
  removed
50ml squid ink (removed from the
  fish)
Splash of chicken stock
Pomace oil, for frying
Deep-fried parsley crisps, for garnish
Olive oil, for cooking

Cut the hake fillets into even-sized strips, lay them on a baking tray and season them well with the fleur de sel (salt) and the lemon zest. Roll the strips tightly in Parma ham and then chill them in the fridge. Once chilled cut the strips into portions, the size is up to you.

Heat a little olive oil in a saucepan over a medium heat, add the shallots and thyme and cook until the shallots are translucent and soft. Add the chorizo and cook it through, then add the piquillo peppers. Continue cooking until any liquids or oils have been absorbed, then remove the mixture from the heat, place everything in a food processor, combine them thoroughly together and pass the purée through a sieve.

Remove the ink sack from the squid and put it to one side for later use. Rinse the squid in water, pat it dry and cut into fine dice. Put a little water in a saucepan, bring it to the boil over a medium heat, drop the parsley into it for 10 seconds, then remove the herb and refresh it in iced water to set the colour. Repeat the process, this time cooking the parsley for around 10 minutes. Once you have refreshed it in iced water again, drain and dry the parsley, then put it into a Thermomix (or liquidiser) and blitz it until smooth. Finally, pass it through a sieve to get a smooth purée.

Remove the squid ink from the sack, place it in a bowl together with a touch of chicken stock. Whisk in 10ml of olive oil until a smooth paste is achieved.

Heat some pomace oil in a frying pan over a medium-high heat, add the hake and pan-fry it for about 3 minutes. At the same time, heat another frying pan until it is very hot, add a little olive oil and quickly fry the diced squid in it. Add the parsley purée and lemon juice and salt to finish.

Serving
Warm the chorizo purée in another pan and while you are doing so, take a pastry brush – or better still a small, broad paintbrush – dip it into the squid ink paste and then paint a stripe of it onto your serving plates. Next put the purée and the diced squid onto the plate and add the hake. Garnish with deep-fried parsley crisps.

ROAST RACK OF LAMB WITH SHEPHERD'S PIE

Who hasn't grown up with roast lamb and mint sauce – and shepherd's pie? I certainly did and as a chef it excites me now to take traditional rustic dishes like these and refine them for Maze. The key as ever is to start off with great ingredients and our mutton mince for the pie comes from Orkney sheep grazed on seaweed, which gives their meat an almost gamey flavour.

SERVES 4

For the mint jelly
600ml water
540ml vinegar
150g sugar
150g mint leaves
1½g agar agar
100g mint, finely chopped

For the shepherd's pie
Knob of butter for cooking
3 swedes, finely diced
100-150ml chicken stock
2 hispi cabbages, shredded
Drizzle of olive oil for frying mince
1kg mutton mince
2 onions, chopped
1 head of garlic, roughly chopped
3 carrots, finely diced
20g rosemary, finely chopped
1 heaped tablespoon of tomato purée
50ml Worcestershire sauce
1 litre lamb stock
300g ratte potatoes
300g butter
75ml each of milk and cream, mixed together
2 braised lamb tongues, peeled and sliced
2 tablespoons capers
50g pancetta
2 shallots, finely chopped
1 large rack of lamb
Salt

First make the mint jelly. Put the water, vinegar, sugar and mint leaves in a large saucepan, place it over a medium heat and bring to the boil, stirring to dissolve the sugar at first. Remove from the heat once the liquid hits a rolling boil and allow the mint to infuse until the liquid is cold. Once cool, strain the mint through a sieve, measure out 750ml of the liquid into a clean saucepan and add 1½g of agar agar. It is essential that the liquid is cold when you add the agar agar otherwise the jelly will not set. Put the saucepan over a medium heat and bring the mixture to the boil and simmer for 1 minute, whisking constantly throughout the process to ensure the agar agar is cooked properly. Take the saucepan off the heat and allow the liquid to cool down before adding the chopped mint. Now pour it into a shallow tray lined with clingfilm and put in the fridge for 45 minutes to set.

Melt the butter in a saucepan over a medium heat, add 2 of the swedes and cook gently until soft. Add a dash of chicken stock if it gets too dry. Once cooked, remove from the heat and put to one side.

Bring some salted water to the boil in another saucepan, drop in the hispi cabbage and blanch it for 30 seconds. Take it off the heat, drain and put the cabbage in some iced water to refresh it and set its colour.

Heat a very small amount of olive oil in a saucepan over a medium high heat, add the mutton mince and cook until nicely browned. Don't put too much oil in as the lamb will render off a lot of fat. Once the mince is cooked, take it off the heat and drain its fat off through a colander.

Heat a little oil in another saucepan, add the onions and garlic and cook until translucent and soft. Add the remaining swede and the carrots and cook out until soft. Add the rosemary and tomato purée and continue cooking the vegetables until they caramelise. Add the mince, Worcestershire sauce and lamb stock and cook over a medium heat until the meat has absorbed the liquid. It should take about 2 hours but don't overcook the meat – you don't want a dry, rubbery mince, it should have a rich, thick sauce.

While the mince is cooking, boil the potatoes in salted water over a medium heat until soft. Remove from the heat, drain and put through a potato ricer into a bowl. Add the butter and then, gradually, the milk and cream (mixed together), beating vigorously until you have a velvety smooth mashed potato. Put to one side and keep warm.

Roast the rack of lamb in the oven at 200C/gas mark 6 for about 25 minutes until cooked but still pink in the centre.

Heat a knob of butter in a frying pan over a medium high heat, add the slices of lamb's tongue and fry until nicely golden, adding in the capers, pancetta and shallots as you do so. Put some mince into individual serving pots and top with the mashed potato. Gently reheat the cabbage and swede. Cut 2 cutlets of lamb per person from the rack and arrange on your plates. Add some cabbage, then a slice of tongue, some swede and mint jelly. Serve with the shepherd's pie on the side.

LEMON MERINGUE PARFAIT WITH GREEN BASIL SORBET

I always like to have a citrus-based dessert on the menu and this one looks back to those lemon meringue pies we all ate when we were kids. It's got all the essential lemon meringue flavours, plus an extra twist – a basil sorbet. If you haven't got access to a Pacojet ice-cream machine, then you need to replace the basil sorbet with a strawberry sorbet, because the basil will go black and look horrid. Trimoline is a sucrose-based syrup which you can buy on the internet.

SERVES 6

For the lemon meringue
250ml lemon juice
6 egg yolks
500g sugar
6 egg whites
Splash of white wine vinegar
500ml cream

For the lemon sorbet
500ml lemon juice
200ml water
100ml milk
100g trimoline
100g icing sugar

For the lemon curd
270g lemon juice
270g egg (approx 10 medium eggs)
270g sugar
4g agar agar
350g butter

For the green basil sorbet
200g glucose
400ml water
200ml sugar syrup (made with equal
  amounts of sugar and water)
Juice of 2 lemons
80g fresh basil, stalks removed

For the garnish
Micro basil leaves
Grated lime
Candied lemon and orange zest, cut
  into very thin strips

Lemon meringue
Put the lemon juice, yolks and 250g of the sugar in a saucepan over a medium heat and cook until the mixture thickens, stirring to prevent it from becoming lumpy. Whisk the egg whites and vinegar until you have doubled their volume, then slowly add in the remaining 250g of sugar till the mixture is stiff. Fold the meringue into the lemon and yolk mixture, whip the cream until it thickens and then fold this into the lemon meringue mixture.

Lemon sorbet
Mix all ingredients together in a suitable bowl until smooth, then transfer it to an ice-cream machine and churn for about 15-20 minutes until the mixture has a slushy texture. If you don't have an ice-cream machine, place the mixture in the freezer, taking it out every few minutes to stir. When the sorbet is slushy put it into a freezer-proof bowl and put it in the freezer to set completely.

Lemon curd
Put the lemon juice, eggs, sugar and agar agar in a saucepan and bring them to the boil, whisking continuously. When the mixture has thickened – it should take around 10 minutes – transfer it to a Thermomix machine and blitz in the butter. If you haven't got a Thermomix, then add the butter over the heat, beating vigorously to incorporate it with the other ingredients.

Green basil sorbet
Put the water into a saucepan over a medium heat, add the glucose and continue to heat until the glucose has dissolved and the liquid is smooth Add the sugar syrup and incorporate well. Remove the mixture from the heat, cool it down and add the lemon juice. Place 500ml of this base syrup into a Pacojet ice-cream machine container and add the basil leaves. Freeze the mixture at minus 21C until it has set solidly. Once set, churn the sorbet in the Pacojet, then reset it in the freezer. Churn in the Pacojet again until you get a smooth sorbet. If you don't have a Pacojet, don't go for a basil sorbet (you need a machine like this because it is fast and stops the basil from going black). Try a strawberry sorbet instead and make in the same way as the lemon sorbet.

Serving
Spoon a meringue onto each plate, then quickly colour it with a culinary blowtorch. Alongside the meringue put a small swipe of lemon curd and top this with some basil sorbet, micro basil leaves and some grated lime zest. Finally, make a circle of lemon curd, pop a scoop of lemon sorbet on top and one strip each of candied orange and lemon zest on the sorbet.

GALTON BLACKISTON

Most directions to the village of Morston tell you to drive in a straight line until you hit the sea. That's because this small Domesday Book village with its stone-walled houses and red-tiled roofs sits on the most northern tip of Norfolk – a geographical stroke of fortune for smugglers who once used to ferry fish, brandy, gin and tobacco through the waters here. These days the village is famous for food not contraband, thanks to the hidden jewel of Morston Hall. Yet it would be easy to drive straight past this blissful restaurant-with-rooms – just a single, simple sign marks the entrance to its gastronomic paradise.

The beauty of Morston Hall is in its understated confidence. It simply knows its place. It's neither flash nor showy and as you enter the property you immediately see a reception covered in children's drawings of the main building, each and every one of them a testament to great

and happy memories made possible by chef-proprietor Galton Blackiston and his wife, Tracy. Galton is tall, fast-bowler tall – cricket was even a possible career before cooking took over – and he exudes contentment, someone who understands when things are right and who knows when to leave them be.

Galton was born, and spent his early years, in Norfolk, but his parents relocated the family to Kent after his father's job took a turn for the better. One of five boys, he was a keen sportsman and soon found himself at the Kent Cricket Academy and in with a shout of being signed for the main team. Sadly, he didn't make the grade. He had left school to pursue his sporting dream and not knowing where else to direct him, his mother suggested catering. Galton was already a keen cook – he had a small market stall in Rye selling homemade 'goodies' to hordes of hungry people three days a week and his cakes sold out every time. So his mother arranged for him to visit a chef she had met up in the Lake District.

That chef was John Tovey of the renowned Miller Howe hotel in Windermere. The flamboyant Tovey was as famous as a chef could be at that time, with television shows and books to his name, but, more importantly, he ran a good hotel. He treated dinner as a piece of theatre with all his diners eating in unison off the same menu. Young Galton hadn't prepared too much for the interview, but his mother had suggested he at least learn a pastry recipe. Tovey challenged the 17-year-old to make him a simple, sweet, short-crust pastry and Galton walked the interview and became part of the brigade.

He spent two years in the pastry section, then moved into the main kitchen and eventually spent 10 years there ending up as head chef. Tovey taught Galton the importance of doing things the right and proper way. An error in Tovey's kitchen usually resulted in an object being flung at the offender and Galton quickly learned never to make the same mistake twice. The food was very classical and when Galton eventually left in 1991, he had an armoury of treasures in his culinary repertoire. He also left Miller Howe with another treasure, Tracy, who had been working as part of the hotel's front-of-house team while he was backstage in the kitchen.

Galton had always dreamt of going back to Norfolk and it was his parents, who had returned to the county on their retirement, who first spotted Morston Hall. They lived nearby and noticed that although it was being run as an exclusive restaurant, it wasn't making money. They believed it was there for the taking. So Galton and Tracy teamed up with another colleague from Miller Howe who had some finance available and together they bought Morston Hall.

That was 17 years ago and Galton and Tracy now own all of Morston Hall. The intervening years have seen it flourish, but success didn't come overnight. Galton's food has evolved gradually, as he freely admits. Dishes such as roasted potatoes with lavender got him a pummelling from the critics in the early days and he quickly adapted. 'One food writer described them as smelling and tasting like the drawers of a National Trust wardrobe! I shall never forget it.'

So Galton literally retaught himself from books and trips abroad, merging this newly found knowledge with the principles of Miller Howe and his passion for Norfolk. One thing that hasn't changed is having a set menu at every dinner – one menu for all – although it alters every night of the week. Choice can be a highly overrated ideal: why wouldn't you choose sweetcorn soup with Cromer crab followed by a slow-braised neck of lamb – so tender it's almost mousse-like – with fresh peas and a light, mint foam?

The menu is always dripping in local influences and when so much grows or lives on Galton's doorstep it's easy to see why. Being on the coast means simple, stunning fish dishes are a speciality – like grilled black bream with a buttery lobster sauce – and Galton's always on the lookout for new ways to showcase local produce. He's recently installed a smoker at Morston Hall, so now he is able to offer home-smoked kippers and even smoked mashed potato.

Awards have come regularly over the years and Morston Hall has held a Michelin star since 1999. These days, too, Galton runs cookery courses for all ability levels, even one just for men. He is the perfect teacher, calm and caring with a culinary compass stuck squarely on the correct path. This paternal attitude has inspired great loyalty in his staff and his two head chefs have been with him for an impressive 30 years, combined. Things don't change quickly at Morston Hall, not because Galton fears change but because, to use a cricketing analogy, he is building a big innings. He is the kind of player who steadies the ship – no fireworks or barnstorming sixes, just clear, controlled hundreds.

Galton prefers to tread his own path, quietly, through the food world and has always shied away from the hustle and bustle of the London food scene. He has calmly written three cookbooks and notched up numerous television appearances but his ambitions are firmly fixed to Morston Hall. Any spare time he has is spent on the golf course or at cricket matches. He himself, at 46, is considering hanging up his pads but he takes great pride watching his eldest son play the 'gentleman's game'.

Morston Hall itself mirrors Galton's gentle confidence. As you sip pre-dinner drinks in the cosy dining room, surrounded by soft, light colours, olive-green walls and pictures of Norfolk scenes, watching rabbits hop on the lawn, with, if you're really lucky the evening sun streaming through a glass conservatory, it's difficult to imagine a more serene scenario. There's nothing for it but to sit back with a big smile on your face and tuck in to the delicious, freshly made bread.

The fact that everyone eats the same menu creates a shared buzz with your neighbours. A joyous union of voices bubbles up, discussing treats like guinea fowl slowly roasted with a rich truffle sauce, or pannacotta with gooseberry sorbet, or a strawberry and mint summer pudding.

Many of the herbs and some of the vegetables come from Morston Hall's very own herb and kitchen garden, hidden among the wisteria and honeysuckle. This is the kind of place you always hope still exists in Britain, but rarely does. Luckily, as long as Galton can keep standing, it will remain. But you do suspect that if there was room for a cricket pitch at Morston Hall there would be one right in front of the main reception door.

Morston Hall
Morston, Holt, Norfolk NR25 7AA
Phone 01263 741041 **www.morstonhall.com**

SWEET CORN SOUP WITH SEA BASS FRITTERS

We live on the Norfolk coast, so I make a point of only using fish caught in the North Sea (scallops excepted). I've used sea bass for the fritters in this dish, most white fish will work easily as well – sea bream and plaice are good and, actually, mackerel works really well. If you can, use wild, line-caught fish and a species that isn't over-fished.

SERVES 6

For the soup
50g salted butter
1 clove of garlic, sliced
3 medium-sized English onions, roughly sliced
1.2 litres water
The kernels of 6 whole sweet corn
150g double cream
Salt and pepper

For the sea bass fritters
500g whole sea bass – skinned, pin bones removed, filleted and cut into 6 pieces
Tempura flour (see below)
Plain flour, to coat the sea bass
Sunflower oil for shallow frying
Sparkling mineral water, cold

Note: make the tempura flour by mixing 25g cornflour, 100g self-raising flour, ½ teaspoon baking powder, ½ teaspoon salt.

Soup
Heat the butter and garlic in a large saucepan over a medium heat. Add the onions and cook them until they are translucent and soft. Next add 1.2 litres of water and a good pinch of salt, bring the liquid to the boil, throw in the sweet corn kernels and cook until they are just softened. Remove the stock from the heat, add the cream and blitz the stock in a liquidiser, then pass it through a fine sieve, taste to check the seasoning and add a little salt and pepper if necessary.

Fritters
Pour the sunflower oil to a depth of about 2½cm into a deep-sided saucepan and heat up to 160C/gas mark 3. You can test the temperature of the oil by dropping in a small blob of batter, if it sizzles and rises to the top then the oil is hot enough.

Place some tempura flour into a bowl and using a fork add in and mix enough sparkling water to make a runny batter. Make sure you don't overbeat it, you want the batter to have lumps in it. Coat the pieces of sea bass in a little plain flour, then dip into the tempura batter before lowering them into the hot oil. Be careful not to overfill the pan as it will prevent the fritters from cooking quickly and crisply. Fry the fritter for about 2 minutes then take them out and place on kitchen paper to drain.

Serving
Bring the oil back up to temperature and then quickly fry the pieces of sea bass in it again for a couple of minutes. Drain on kitchen paper, then serve alongside the re-heated soup.

ROSTI POTATO BAKE WITH SAMPHIRE, COCKLES AND BROAD BEANS

You can buy ready-cooked cockles but it's always much nicer to prepare them yourself. Just remember, in their shells you'll need about 450g of fresh cockles to get the right amount of meat.

At Morston Hall we cook them with a splash of oil, chopped onion, sliced clove of garlic and a glass of white wine over a high heat until all the cockles have opened (discarding any that have remained closed). The bonus is that if you do this you also get a lovely stock that makes a wonderful base for a fish soup.

SERVES 6

225g samphire
450g King Edward potatoes, coarsely grated
150g cockles
125g broad beans, blanched, refreshed and skins slipped off
50ml butter, melted
50ml olive oil
Salt and pepper
6 rashers of bacon
6 large organic eggs
110g Gruyère cheese, grated

Preheat the oven to 180C/gas mark 4. Bring a saucepan of water to the boil over a medium-high heat. Strip the fronds from the main stalks of the samphire, wash it thoroughly and then blanch it by plunging into the boiling water for 30 seconds. Remove from the heat, drain and refresh the samphire in iced water. Drain thoroughly again and set aside.

Place the potatoes in a clean tea towel and wring out as much moisture as possible before putting them into a bowl together with the samphire, cockles and broad beans. Add half the melted butter, season with salt and pepper and mix well. Heat a 20cm non-stick frying pan over a medium-high heat, add the olive oil and the remainder of the melted butter, then put the grated potato mixture into the frying pan and cook on a fairly high heat until the underside is browned. Shake the pan occasionally so the potatoes do not stick. Next, turn the potato rosti over, and continue to cook until the other side is browned. Remove from the heat and place it in the oven for 15-20 minutes, or until the potato is cooked right through. Remove from the oven and keep warm.

Serving
Pan fry or grill the bacon and fry the eggs. Slip the rosti out of the pan and cut it into 6 wedges. Top with bacon and a fried egg before finishing with some grated Gruyère cheese.

STRAWBERRY, CHERRY AND MINT SUMMER PUDDING WITH STRAWBERRY AND BLACK PEPPER ICE CREAM

Summer pudding is a British classic usually made with summer berries but you can use any summer fruit and in this recipe I've stuck with cherries and strawberries. I like to use brioche instead of white bread: it absorbs liquid much better, is easier to work with and I like its sweetness. The pudding is best made the day before so that it soaks up all the lovely fruit juices.

SERVES 6

For the pudding
350g stoned cherries
800g strawberries, hulled
150ml water
175g caster sugar
Sunflower oil to grease the basin and
*   a little extra caster sugar*
2 tablespoons of chopped mint
12 medium slices brioche, crusts
*   removed.*

For the strawberry and black pepper
ice cream
450g hulled ripe English strawberries
1 tablespoon strawberry jam
300ml double cream
150g caster sugar
1-2 tablespoons lemon juice
Freshly ground black pepper

Summer pudding
If the strawberries are very large, cut them in half. Place the fruit and sugar together with 150ml of water into a large saucepan and cook over a low heat for about 5 minutes, just enough time to allow the sugar to melt and the juices to start to run. Be careful: the idea is not to cook the fruit, it is important to keep the individual flavours and to keep them as whole as possible. Lightly grease a 1.2 litre pudding basin with the oil and sprinkle over a little caster sugar.

Quickly soak the bread in the liquid from the fruits, then line the inside of the basin with the bread, overlapping the slices to ensure that there are no gaps.

Add the chopped mint to the fruit and then spoon it into the bread-lined basin until you have filled it to the top. Now cover the fruit with some more soaked bread, making sure that there are no gaps, and if you have any spare juice pour it over the top and allow it to seep through the pudding. Place a snugly-fitting saucer on top then a heavy tin, jar or stone. Put the pudding in the fridge for at least 24 hours.

Strawberry and black pepper ice cream
Place the strawberries, jam, cream and sugar into a liquidiser and blitz really well. Add the lemon juice and freshly ground black pepper to taste and blitz well again. Pass through a sieve and churn in an ice-cream maker. If you don't have an ice-cream maker, place the mixture in the freezer, taking it out every 30 minutes to stir. The ice cream is ready when it holds its shape after scooping.

Serving
Remove the saucer from the summer pudding and gently press down round the top rim of the pudding to allow a little air around the sides, then run a knife carefully around the edge between pudding and basin and dip the basin briefly in hot water. Place your serving dish face-down on top of the basin and quickly turn the pudding over. It should pop out easily. Spoon over any spare fruit and serve with a scoop of the strawberry and black pepper ice cream.

CRAB, PINK GRAPEFRUIT AND AVOCADO COCKTAIL SERVED WITH GAZPACHO SORBET

If you want quantity in your crab, head to the West Country; if you want quality stick with the ones from Cromer! They're best May-September and this is an easy way to showcase them, particularly in the summer. I've used grapefruit in the cocktail because it gives sweetness as well as acidity and just seems to complement the crab. It's best served with thinly sliced French bread cut on the diagonal and toasted.

SERVES 4

For the cocktail
2 large Cromer crabs, cooked and with white and brown meat kept separate (175g white and 100g brown crab meat)
1 large ripe avocado, roughly chopped
A good squeeze of lemon juice
A splash of olive oil
1 pink grapefruit, peeled and segmented
A few handfuls of watercress
Sea salt flakes and freshly ground black pepper

For the dressing
½ teaspoon Dijon mustard
1 tablespoon white wine vinegar
½ teaspoon clear honey
150ml olive oil
1 lime, juiced
1 large shallot, finely chopped
1 large mild red chilli, deseeded and finely chopped
Salt and pepper

For the gazpacho sorbet
1 large garlic clove
3 tablespoons extra virgin olive oil
1 tablespoon wine vinegar
1 small onion, finely chopped
300g ripe tomatoes, roughly chopped
1 red pepper, de-seeded, finely chopped

40ml sherry
150ml tomato juice
½ cucumber, finely chopped
A splash of Tabasco
A splash of Worcestershire sauce
150ml stock syrup, see recipe below
Salt and pepper

For the stock syrup (makes about 570ml)
275g caster sugar
275ml water
1 vanilla pod, split
1-2 tablespoons lemon juice

Cocktail
Carefully go through the crabmeat to ensure that there is no shell in it. Place the white crabmeat into one bowl and the dark into another. Season both with sea salt and freshly ground black pepper. Place the avocado in a blender with the lemon juice, a seasoning of salt and pepper and a splash of olive oil, then whiz to a fine purée. If not using straight away, transfer to a bowl, then place a piece of clingfilm on top of the purée and another piece tightly over the bowl to prevent discoloration. The purée will keep for a day – but remember to stir it before use.

Dressing
Whisk together the mustard, vinegar and a good seasoning of salt and pepper in a bowl, then add the honey and continue to whisk well. Keep whisking slowly and add the olive oil and then some lime juice to taste. Stir in the shallot, chilli and 1-2 spoonfuls of the brown crabmeat. Taste and season with salt and pepper and more lime juice if necessary.

Take 4 cocktail glasses and put a quarter of the avocado purée into the bottom of each one. Arrange the

grapefruit segments on top. Next flake the white crabmeat over the grapefruit segments. Sprinkle a few more flakes of sea salt over the crab meat, then arrange some of the watercress over the top. (You can prepare to this stage up to 1 hour before serving and store in the fridge.)

Gazpacho sorbet
Blitz everything except the stock syrup in a blender. Strain through a sieve into a bowl and then add enough of the stock syrup until you have the sweetness you desire (you may or may not wish to use it all). Season with salt and pepper if necessary. Chill and then churn in an ice-cream machine. If you haven't got an ice-cream machine place the mixture in a shallow dish in the freezer, taking it out every few minutes to stir. When the sorbet is slushy put it into a freezer-proof bowl and place it in the freezer to set completely.

Stock syrup
Put the sugar and water into a saucepan. Scrape the seeds from the vanilla pod then add these to the sugar and water. Over a low heat, allow the sugar to dissolve then bring it up to a light simmer for 10 minutes. Remove from the heat and allow to cool, then stir in the lemon juice. The syrup will keep in the fridge for up to a week.

Serving
Give the dressing a good stir, then spoon some of it over the crab cocktail already in the glasses (you probably won't need it all) and then pop a small scoop of gazpacho sorbet on the top. Serve the cocktail with toasted French bread – these can be spread with some of the remaining brown crab meat if you like.

ROAST WHOLE FILLET OF BEEF WITH ROASTED SHALLOT PUREE AND EASY BEARNAISE SAUCE

This is a great way to serve a lovely cut of beef – and you can make the shallot purée and Bérnaise sauce in advance, so it's a very easy dish. At Morston Hall we like to source locally and our beef comes from Melton Constable, 5 miles away. It's Aberdeen Angus, but you can use any breed – just make sure the quality is first class.

SERVES 6

For the roasted shallot purée
450g shallots, ends trimmed
60ml olive oil
1 fresh thyme sprig
Knob of butter
3 tablespoons double cream
Salt and pepper

For the béarnaise sauce
3 egg yolks
½ teaspoon caster sugar
1 tablespoon lemon juice
1 tablespoon white wine
1 tablespoon tarragon vinegar
1 shallot, finely sliced
12 white peppercorns, cracked
175g salted butter
1 good tablespoon of fresh tarragon, finely chopped
Salt and pepper

For the beef
700g whole fillet of beef, get your butcher to tie it for you
Splash of vegetable oil
Salt and pepper

Roasted shallot purée
Preheat the oven to 180C/gas mark 4. Lay two large sheets of foil on top of each other on a work surface. Place the shallots in the centre of the foil, pour over the olive oil, add the thyme and season well. Draw the sides of the foil up to the centre and crinkle the edges to seal and form a parcel. Place on a baking tray and bake in the oven for about 1½ hours, until the shallots are really soft.

Remove the papery skin from the shallots and then place the shallots in a liquidiser with the butter and cream. Blitz really well and pour into a bowl. Check the seasoning and add salt and pepper if necessary.

For the béarnaise sauce
Place the egg yolks, salt and sugar in a food processor and give them a quick whiz. Heat the lemon juice, wine, tarragon vinegar, shallot and peppercorns together in a small saucepan over a medium heat and simmer until the liquid has reduced by half. Meanwhile, in another saucepan melt the butter and allow it to bubble but not colour. Turn on the food processor again and gradually strain in the hot reduced liquor, followed slowly by the hot butter. Once all the butter has been added, pour the sauce into a bowl and keep it warm, covered with clingfilm, until needed.

Beef fillet
Preheat the oven to 200C/gas mark 6. Heat a heavy-based frying pan until it's smoky hot, add a splash of olive oil and then the fillet of beef, turning the meat to colour and seal. Remove the fillet from the frying pan, season well and place it on a trivet in a roasting tin. Put it in the oven and roast for

20 minutes, then remove and allow it to rest in a warm place for 5 minutes before serving.

Serving
Gently reheat the shallot purée over a low heat. Add the tarragon to the béarnaise sauce. Slice the beef and serve it with a spoonful of purée and drizzle of béarnaise sauce.

MICHAEL CAINES

The minute you arrive at the entrance to Gidleigh Park you know you are somewhere out of the ordinary. Signs saying 'do not lose heart you are on the right road' punctuate the winding mile-and-a-half drive leading up to the hotel's Tudor-style facade. The reassurance is needed because the truth is that Gidleigh is hidden away in a secretive hollow of the North Teign river in the middle of Dartmoor. Surrounded by 107 acres of secluded woodlands, gardens and parkland, it's the equivalent of a gentle sigh of relief after the wildness of the Devon moors; relaxing and comforting at the same time, it also holds the promise of one of the finest dinners in Britain.

The dinner comes courtesy of its long-time executive chef, Michael Caines, who has been at Gidleigh since 1994. Gidleigh already had a name for culinary excellence even then, thanks to Michael's predecessor Shaun Hill. But

Michael slipped into Shaun's shoes with ease and was soon sprinting away to his own culinary fame, gaining the hotel's restaurant two Michelin stars in 1999.

Making such an impact at Gidleigh was immensely satisfying to Michael who is the epitome of the 'local boy made good'. Adopted as a baby, he grew up just down the road in Exeter in a large, close family where everyone did chores. Michael took to lending a hand with the cooking, because 'it beat doing the washing up,' but was soon baking cakes and helping his mother turn produce from the family's vegetable patch into tasty meals. He went on to train at Exeter College, graduating as its best student in 1987 before landing a job in London's famous Grosvenor House hotel and, eventually, heading for Le Manoir aux Quat'Saisons in Oxfordshire to work for the charismatic French chef Raymond Blanc.

The Frenchman's taste buds are legendary in the cheffing world and he is incredibly passionate about produce – Le Manoir has a famous kitchen garden – so he soon inspired Michael to think about food in a very different way. Once Raymond became his mentor, the young Devon chef made flavour the number-one requirement in anything he cooked and committed himself heart-and-soul to the stove.

Michael work for three years with Raymond, then, at the latter's suggestion, took himself off to France to finish his culinary education. He spent a year apiece working in the kitchens of two of France's most renowned chefs: – firstly with the late, great Bernard Loiseau at La Côte d'Or in Saulieu then with the phenomenal Joël Roubechon at Jamin in Paris.

Raymond, though, didn't forget his protégé, whose skill he had always admired. When he heard on the grapevine that Shaun Hill was leaving Gidleigh Park he suggested to the hotel's then owners – Paul and Kay Henderson – that they should take a chance and hire Michael, despite the fact that Michael had never headed up a kitchen. They did, and soon Michael was heading back home to Devon.

Over the years, Michael enjoyed a healthy, sometimes abrasive, relationship with the Hendersons. But the job suited him and his cooking took flight, its modern classicism earning him newspaper column inches and netting that cherished second Michelin star in 1999. His success has been all the more remarkable because he achieved it after losing his right arm in a horrific car accident only weeks after taking up his job at Gidleigh. Michael had always been right-handed and had to totally rethink his entire cooking technique on the job.

Never one to stand still, Michael used his success at Gidleigh to launch himself as a restaurateur, setting up his own company and taking over responsibility for the food at Exeter's Clarence Hotel. He never left Gidleigh, though; the ties were too strong and the Dartmoor haven was where he cooked. Yet it was a chance meeting at the Clarence in 2003 with businessman and hotelier Andrew Brownsword that changed the course of Michael's career and the future of Gidleigh.

Andrew already owned the Bath Priory hotel. The two men got talking, clicked and ended up founding a company, ABode, which not only bought and revamped the Clarence but quickly set about launching a string of food-led boutique hotels around the country. And when the Hendersons decided to call it a day and retire, Brownsword's pockets were deep enough to buy Gidleigh Park, too.

The two men now share the same drive to make Gidleigh the finest dining experience in the West of England and they are having fun doing it. They gave the hotel a multimillion-pound refurbishment in 2006. Every wire, every plug was changed and Michael's kitchen was totally refitted. And, much to his delight, he acquired a kitchen garden in which to grow and harvest his own produce. There are plans, too, for a cookery school and food development centre in the future.

The whole set-up at Gidleigh has resonances of Le Manoir aux Quat'Saisons and Michael's food is a testament not only to his time with Raymond, but also to the years he spent in France. Everything he cooks is impeccably presented and intensely flavoured, showcasing great Devon ingredients with immense technical skill and passion.

Dinner starts promptly at 7.30pm every evening with canapés served in Gidleigh's cosy drawing room. These can range from sautéed foie gras in a Madeira sauce, to a delicately poached quail's egg in herb and truffle oil. The main meal takes place in the hotel's wood-panelled dining room, which abounds in natural surfaces and colours. Every table has a view of Gidleigh's idyllic gardens and the sound of the rushing North Teign river outside floats through the window and mingles gently with the intermittent hubbub that bursts out of the kitchen every time the doors to the latter swing open.

The quick 'in' to Michael's food is through his classic tasting menu which reads like a Michael Caines greatest-hits collection. Here you'll find his trademark Cornish duckling with apple, star anise and apple galette; and his Dartmoor lamb with fondant potato, vegetable niçoise and tapenade jus. Michael's dishes push you towards new flavour dimensions but his skill is in knowing when to stop. He never forces you to lose your connection with the familiar or your joy of eating it.

A starter of langoustine with smoked bacon foam, asparagus, pea purée, pork belly and pea shoot salad coated in truffle oil is a perfect example of how he pulls off that particular trick. One beautiful langoustine tail curls seductively over a small piece of slow-cooked pork that melts away satisfyingly in the mouth. The purée is rich and fresh and there's a distinctive British-ness to the asparagus and bacon flavours, despite the modernity of the foam, which just makes you smile.

These days, in addition to Gidleigh, Michael is executive chef for its sister hotel the Bath Priory, so he makes regular trips to check-up on its progress as well as undertaking monitoring calls to ABode hotels around the country. But he's never really been tempted away from Devon, preferring to keep his home and business offices in Exeter. Perhaps because of this, the people of Devon are fiercely proud of him. He's a big deal in Exeter – everyone, from cabbies to weekend gourmands, shouts hello when they see him and children run across the street to get his autograph. And it's not only the locals of Exeter that love him: in 2006 he was awarded an MBE by the Queen for his services to the hospitality industry.

He's come a very long way, this 'Exeter Lad'. And yet not far at all. But who can blame him for staying put in Devon when he has the jewel of Gidleigh to inspire his culinary creativity? Gidleigh is one of those special places that everyone deserves to visit just once – and Michael gets to cook here and spread a little of his brand of culinary genius through the ever-expanding ABode hotels and the Bath Priory. If you can, get yourself to Gidleigh. If you can't, get to the Bath Priory or one of the six ABodes dotted around the UK. They'll give you an inkling of what this man is all about.

Gidleigh Park, Chagford, Devon TQ13 8HH
Phone 01647 432367 **www.gidleigh.com.**
Bath Priory Weston Road, Bath BA1 2XT
Phone 01225 331 922 **www.thebathpriory.co.uk**
www.abodehotels.co.uk

DEVON QUAIL, TRUFFLED EGG YOLK, POTATO GNOCCHI AND TARRAGON JUS

Quail are not indigenous to England, but there are some great producers rearing them in the country. I was introduced to my local producer, based in the Teign Valley, when I appeared on the Great British Menu television programme. Quail are easy and fun to cook – I often use them in starters or salads. At Gidleigh we butcher our own quails, but you can get your butcher to do this for you.

SERVES 4-6

For the herb purée
4 small shallots, sliced
30g butter
300g spinach
30g chervil, stalks removed
75g parsley, blanched and refreshed
16g garlic purée
150g cream
Salt and freshly ground pepper

For the quail jus
40ml vegetable oil
1kg chicken winglets, chopped small
4 quail carcasses, chopped small
1 small onion, sliced
1 small head of garlic, cut in half
5 sprigs of thyme
500ml water
1½ litres chicken stock
1 teaspoon white peppercorns
A good handful of tarragon
Salt

For the poached quail's eggs
1 litre water
30ml white wine vinegar
10g salt
20 quail eggs

For the potato and Parmesan gnocchi
50g unsalted butter
100g onions, finely chopped
10g rosemary, finely chopped
300g Binje potato, cooked and passed through a potato ricer
200g plain flour
50g grated Parmesan (plus a little extra for coating)
3 egg yolks
Salt and pepper

For the truffled egg yolk
9 egg yolks
1-2 drops of black truffle oil
A few slices of fresh truffle, finely chopped
Splash of Champagne vinegar, to taste
Salt and freshly ground black pepper

For the potato crisp
1 large King Edward or Maris Piper potato
4 tablespoons clarified butter, melted
Salt

For the quail
4 quail, oven ready and legs removed
2 sprigs of thyme
2 garlic cloves
20g butter
30ml vegetable oil
Freshly ground black pepper

For finishing
A knob of butter
2 tablespoons of chopped parsley
A few slices of black truffle

Herb purée
Heat the butter in a stainless-steel saucepan over a medium heat, add the shallots and cook until they are translucent. Add the spinach and chervil and continue to cook until the spinach is wilted. Place the mixture in a blender or food processor with the blanched parsley and garlic purée. Meanwhile, bring the cream to the boil over a medium heat, and then also add this to the herb purée and blend everything until you have a smooth purée. Check the taste and add a little salt and pepper if necessary, then decant the purée into a container and cool it down over a bowl of ice.

Quail jus
Heat the oil in a roasting pan over a medium heat until it starts to haze, then add the chicken bones and lightly colour. Add the quail carcasses and continue to roast until light brown. Then add the onions and lightly colour them before adding the garlic and the thyme. Next, add the water and deglaze the pan by reducing the liquid volume by one-third. Then add the chicken stock, white peppercorns, a pinch of salt and the tarragon. Bring the broth to the boil and skim, then reduce the heat and gently simmer for about 1 hour. Now remove the broth from the heat, pour it through a colander, catching the liquid in a bowl, then strain through a fine sieve into a saucepan. Put the saucepan over a medium heat and slowly reduce the liquid to a sauce consistency. Once you've achieved this, season with salt and pepper and strain it, again, through a fine sieve.

(Continued on page 44)

(Continued from page 42)

Poached quail eggs

Place the water, 20ml of white vinegar and salt into a saucepan over a medium heat and bring to the boil. Crack 10 quail eggs into a small bowl filled with water and 10ml of white wine vinegar, leave for 30 seconds and then add them to the boiling stock.

Bring the stock to the boil again and then reduce it to a simmer until the eggs are cooked, then remove them from the saucepan with a slatted spoon and put them into iced water. Repeat the process until all the eggs are poached. Trim and tidy the eggs, place them on to a tray and cover them with a cloth.

Potato and Parmesan gnocchi

Melt the butter in a saucepan over a medium heat, add the onions and cook until they are soft and transparent. Put the rosemary into a bowl, add the cooked onions, stir well and leave on one side to cool.

In a bowl, mix the potato, flour, Parmesan cheese, onions, rosemary and egg yolks and season well with salt and pepper. Roll out and shape into little gnocchi dumplings, using a little flour to stop the dough sticking.

Truffled egg yolk

Whisk all the ingredients together in a bowl, except the chopped truffle and the Champagne vinegar. Next, pass the mixture through a fine sieve then add in the chopped black truffle. If you can, Vac Pac in three equal amounts (approx. 110-115g each), and cook in a water bath at 68C for 16-17 minutes, depending on how thick you require the egg yolk to be, then refresh the yolks in the bag in some iced water.

If you haven't got a Vac Pac machine or water bath then place the mixture in freezer bags, squeeze out all the air and put the bags in a saucepan heated to 68C for 16-17 minutes, then refresh the yolks in iced water.

Open a bag of the egg yolks and mix in the Champagne vinegar to taste. Once opened, you must use the truffled yolks on the same day. You can store any you don't use in the fridge but it must be used within 3 days of making.

Potato crisp

Shred the potato using the finest shredder attachment on a food processor. Season it with salt, making sure you mix the seasoning through evenly, then rest the potato for 10 minutes to draw out the water. Squeeze out excess moisture with a tea towel, then evenly coat the potato with clarified butter and finally cook it in a non-stick saucepan over a high heat until golden brown and crisp.

Quail

Preheat the oven to 200C/gas mark 6. Fill each quail cavity with a sprig of thyme, a garlic clove and a little of the butter. Heat the vegetable oil and remaining butter in a roasting pan, add the quail and the quail legs and cook for about 6 minutes, turning the meat on each side for 2 minutes. Remove from the oven and rest for 10 minutes.

Serving

Warm up the jus, herb purée and truffled yolks. Cook the gnocchi in salted boiling water for 3-4 minutes or until it has doubled its size – then drain and keep warm. Heat up some butter in a saucepan until foaming, pop the quail breasts and legs into the butter and crisp up the skin. Now toss in the gnocchi and finally the chopped parsley. Put a swipe of herb purée on each plate. Add on the quail, potato crisp and gnocchi and finish with the quail jus, truffled egg yolks and, if you want, a slice of black truffle.

RIVER DART WILD SALMON, OSCIETRA CAVIAR, SALMON JELLY, CUCUMBER, HONEY AND SOY VINAIGRETTE, WASABI AND GREEK YOGHURT VINAIGRETTE

This recipe is inspired by two cooking cultures, Chinese and Norwegian. The dill and salmon come straight from gravlax, and five-spice powder, honey and soy are pure Chinese. The salmon jelly just melts in the mouth and adds another texture to everything. I like to finish off with micro leaves and herbs from our kitchen garden at Gidleigh: dill, purple basil and borage flowers are particularly good.

SERVES 4

For the salmon
600g wild salmon fillet, skin on
15g sugar
15g sea salt
Lemon – zested, peeled and segmented
   (the segments reserved for
   garnishing)
Pinch of freshly ground pepper

For the cucumber
1 cucumber – peeled, deseeded and cut
   into 7cm lengths
1 tablespoon of chopped dill
A splash of groundnut vinaigrette
Salt

For the honey and soy vinaigrette
50ml clear honey
Pinch of Chinese five-spice powder
1 teaspoon Dijon mustard
10ml balsamic vinegar
100ml white wine vinegar
10ml soy sauce
200ml extra virgin olive oil
Salt and pepper

*For the wasabi and Greek yoghurt
vinaigrette*
25ml double cream
1½ teaspoons wasabi
50ml Greek yoghurt
Salt and pepper

For the salmon jelly (stock)
1 salmon carcass
50g onion, chopped
35g leeks, chopped
1 cloves of garlic, crushed
250g tomatoes, chopped
75g fennel, finely chopped
2 parsley stalks
½ star anise
1 small sprig of thyme
¼ stick of celery
1 tablespoon white peppercorns,
   crushed
50ml Noilly Prat
100ml white wine
700ml water

*For the stock clarification (for salmon
jelly)*
125g salmon trimmings
2 egg whites
30g ice
3 leaves of gelatine
Salt and pepper

For garnish
4 lemon segments, cut into 5 equal
   pieces
A handful of micro herbs (eg purple
   basil)
18 borage flowers
Keta caviar (salmon roe)
Oscietra caviar

Salmon
Prepare a marinade by mixing together the sugar, salt, lemon zest and pepper. Place the salmon on a tray and cover with the marinade, then leave it for 8 hours. After this wash and skin the fillet, trimming off any brown meat. Cut the fillet in half lengthways, then cut in half twice more, wrap the fish in clingfilm and place it in the fridge for several hours to firm up, ideally overnight.

Slice the cucumber on a mandolin into 2mm x 3mm strips. Trim evenly then place the slices in a colander over a dish and scatter salt over them. The slices should be left for 10 minutes to draw out the water, then rinsed thoroughly with water and dried off with a clean cloth. Place the strips on a tray and freeze the cucumber briefly, then take out and defrost. Cover with a pinch of chopped dill and some groundnut vinaigrette and marinate until ready to serve.

Honey and soy vinaigrette
Put the honey, Chinese five-spice powder and mustard together in a bowl and mix well until blended. Then whisk in, separately, the balsamic vinegar, white wine vinegar and soy sauce. Once the ingredients have been blended together, using a hand blender, gradually add the olive oil slowly until it is completely mixed. Season with salt and pepper to taste.

Wasabi and Greek yogurt vinaigrette
Whisk the cream and wasabi together until stiff. Pass the mixture through a fine sieve into a bowl then fold in the Greek yoghurt and season with salt and pepper.

For the salmon jelly
Put all the stock ingredients together in a large saucepan over a medium heat and bring to the boil. Reduce to a simmer and cook for a further 30 minutes, then strain the stock through a colander and then a fine sieve. Pour it back into the saucepan and simmer over a medium heat until it has reduced its volume by one-third.

(Continued on page 47)

MICHAEL CAINES   45

(Continued from page 45)

Next clarify the stock. Blitz the salmon trimmings with the egg whites and salt in a liquidiser. Once mixed together, blend in the ice and put to one side. Bring the stock back to the boil, then whisk in the clarification mixture and bring the stock back to the boil again, stirring constantly with a wooden spoon. Reduce to a simmer and leave to cook for 10 minutes, then remove the stock from the heat and pass it through a fine sieve into a clean saucepan. Put this over a medium heat and bring the strained stock back to the boil. Correct the seasoning and add the leaves of gelatine. Line a tray with clingfilm and pour in the stock to a depth of 1cm. Put in the fridge to set. Once set, take out and cut into small cubes.

Serving
Remove the salmon from the fridge. Heat up a saucepan of water to 40C over a low heat, drop in the salmon (still in its clingfilm) and poach for 10 minutes. Meanwhile, place some of the cucumber slices on your plates and sprinkle these with some keta caviar. Dot some blobs of the honey and soy vinaigrette around the plate, add the lemon segments and fill in the gaps with some blobs of wasabi and Greek yoghurt vinaigrette. Add some salmon jelly cubes and then the salmon – three pieces per person – and finish with the micro salad leaves, borage flowers and keta and Oscietra caviar.

CORNISH DUCKLING, CABBAGE, BRAISED TURNIPS, ROAST GARLIC AND A SPICED JUS

This is inspired by the classic Chinese crispy duck – the flavours of honey, five spice and duck just seem to work really well. I like to use local duck from the Cornish Duck Company, but you just need to make sure you get a good quality bird. Depending on the season you can change what you serve the duck with. If you want a more classic French style of dish then garlic purée works well, or celeriac purée in the autumn and winter.

SERVES 4

For the duckling
2 x 2kg ducklings
1 tablespoon vegetable oil

For the honey and spice jus
1.25kg duck carcasses, chopped small
1 teaspoon Chinese five spice
2 medium onions, cut into thick rings
½ head of garlic, cut in half
A handful of thyme
725ml chicken stock
100g clear honey
50ml Xeres (sherry) vinegar
350ml reduced veal stock
1 teaspoon white peppercorns
50ml double cream
Pinch of salt

For the roast garlic
24 garlic cloves
30g unsalted butter

For the turnips
100ml chicken stock
225ml water
25ml reduced veal stock
15g honey
½ teaspoon white peppercorns
1 sprig of thyme
1 bay leaf
16 baby turnips
Pinch of salt

For the Savoy cabbage
50g rindless smoked streaky bacon, roughly chopped
25g unsalted butter
80g Savoy cabbage, shredded, blanched and refreshed
1 teaspoon garlic purée

Duckling

Remove the legs and wings from the ducks, keeping the wings for the sauce and retaining the legs for use in another dish. Blast chill the breasts on the bone (or crown) in the freezer until the skin is slightly frozen, then take out and score the meat with a serrated knife, ensuring that you are scoring three quarters of the way through the fat.

Heat up the oil in a saucepan over a medium-high heat and cook the duck crowns in it for approximately 1 minute on each side until golden, then remove and chill them in the fridge. Once chilled, remove the breasts from the bone and cook them skin-side down, ensuring that the skin gets crispy and the flesh is pink in the middle. Take off the heat and keep to one side.

Honey and spice jus

Preheat the oven to 200C/gas mark 6. Place the duck carcasses on a roasting tray and roast them lightly in the oven for about 20 minutes, taking them out after about 10 minutes and sprinkling the bones with the Chinese five-spice powder.

Remove the tray from the oven, take out the carcasses and add in the onions and garlic. Lightly colour the onions, then add the thyme and a splash of water to gather any residues. Strain through a fine sieve into a clean saucepan, add the chicken stock and reduce by a third over a medium heat

Meanwhile, put the honey in another saucepan and place it over a low heat until you achieve a rolling boil, continue to cook for 3 minutes, but be careful not to burn the honey. Add the vinegar and reduce the liquid to almost nothing, then add the duck carcasses with the chicken stock, the veal stock, peppercorns and cream. Bring the mixture to the boil and skim off the scum, then reduce back down to a steady simmer and cook it for 30 minutes. Next, strain it – firstly through a colander and then through a fine sieve. Pour the liquid into a clean saucepan, then bring it to the boil over a medium high heat and reduce to a sauce consistency; adjust the seasoning with salt, if necessary.

Roast garlic

Blanch the garlic cloves 3 times – by plunging them into boiling water, then refreshing them – until soft but not completely cooked. Then, in a saucepan, slowly roast the garlic cloves in butter over a medium heat until golden on all sides.

Turnips

Place all the ingredients except the turnips into a saucepan over a medium heat and bring to the boil. Remove from heat and allow everything to cool a little, then add the baby turnips and replace the saucepan over a medium heat and bring the mixture back to the boil before reducing it to a simmer. Cover with parchment paper (cartouche) and leave to cook for about 20-30 minutes until the turnips are soft and tender. You may need to top up the liquid back up with water during the cooking time. Once the turnips are cooked, remove them from the heat and allow to cool in the liquid.

Savoy cabbage

Heat the butter in a frying pan over a medium heat, add the bacon and cook it gently – but don't colour it – then add the cabbage and the garlic purée and cook the cabbage until it is wilted and coated in butter but not soggy.

Serving

Reheat the duck and warm the remaining ingredients. Carve the duck, then arrange down the middle of a serving plate with the turnips and some Savoy cabbage scattered around. Finally drizzle some of the sauce over the top. You can serve any extra cabbage and sauce at the table if you want to.

CHERRY PARFAIT

Chocolate and cherries are a classic match – if I can get them I prefer to use English cherries from Kent, but the season is very short, only about eight weeks in the summer, peaking in July. This parfait is a great way to showcase them and it's got more than one texture going on, so there's always something to keep you interested when you eat it. At Gidleigh we finish the dish with a biscuit, a cherry dipped in chocolate and a thin rectangle of cherry jelly – but they're not essential!

SERVES 8

For the poached cherries
600g fresh stoned cherries
30ml kirsch
½ lemon, juiced
80g caster sugar
1 teaspoon arrowroot

For the marinated cherries
125g poached cherries, chopped fine
25ml kirsch

For the cherry parfait
100g sugar
30ml water
6 egg yolks
200g cherry purée
125g marinade cherries
½ lemon, juiced
200ml double cream, whipped
8 tempered dark chocolate tubes

For the cherry chocolate mousse
3 egg yolks
75ml stock syrup
50ml griotte cherry liquor
100g griotte cherries, finely chopped
160g dark chocolate (75% cocoa solids), melted
300ml double cream

Note: you buy preserved griotte cherries in a jar – strain them through a sieve before use, catching their preserving liquor and use this in the mousse.

For the cherry jelly
1-2 leaves (2g) of gelatine
150ml cherry juice (from the poached cherries)

Poached cherries
Place the cherries, kirsch, lemon juice and sugar into a stainless-steel saucepan and bring to the boil over a medium heat. Cook for approximately 5 minutes at a gentle simmer until the cherries are soft. Add a drop of water to the arrowroot and then whisk it into the cherries. Bring back to the boil then remove from the heat, strain off 150ml of juice through a fine sieve to use later for the jelly and leave the rest of the cherries to cool down in any remaining juice.

Once the cherries have cooled, separate out 125g of them, chop finely and put them into a bowl with the kirsch to steep (or marinate) for 12 hours before using them in the parfait. Weigh out another 200g, place in a liquidiser and blitz to a purée – also to use in the parfait.

Cherry parfait
Place the sugar and water into a saucepan over a medium heat to make a stock syrup and cook until it reaches 120C. Place the egg yolks into a bowl and pour on the hot syrup, whipping all the time until the eggs are cold. Add the cherry purée and blend with the cooked egg yolk, then add the steeped cherries and the lemon juice. Now carefully fold in the whipped cream and then pour the mixture into the dark chocolate tubes until the tubes are ¾ full and place them in the freezer.

Cherry chocolate mousse
Place the egg yolks, 25ml of the stock syrup and 15ml of the griottes' liquor into a bowl, put the bowl over a pan of gently simmering water (making sure the water doesn't touch the bowl) and whisk continuously as it cooks until it thickens and turns frothy and forms a sabayon. Meanwhile, heat the remaining 50ml of stock syrup in a saucepan over a medium heat until it reaches 120C. Place the sabayon in a food mixer and quickly whisk in the warm stock syrup until the mixture is cold. Then mix in the chopped griotte cherries and the remaining 50ml of griotte liquor. Fold in the melted chocolate and double cream and mix until you have a smooth mousse. Transfer the mousse into moulds and put in the fridge to set for 2 hours.

Cherry jelly
Soften the gelatine leaves in cold water. Meanwhile, heat up the cherry juice in a saucepan over a medium heat. Once the gelatine is soft, remove it from the water, squeeze out the excess water and then add it to the juice to dissolve, stirring a little to help the process. Once the gelatine has dissolved, carefully spoon the mixture on to the set mousse, then replace the moulds in the fridge to set the jelly.

Serving
Take the chocolate tubes filled with cherry parfait and top them up with the remaining poached cherries. Serve with the cherry chocolate mousse alongside and if you want, garnish with a dipped cherry and a tuille (biscuit).

TRIO OF CHOCOLATE

Chocolate desserts are surefire winners and this particular one has become a bit of a signature dish for me. The best thing about it is that it's got a great balance of bitter, milk and white chocolate in its different elements, plus some classic flavour matches like hazelnut and chocolate which is underlined by the Frangelico, the famous Italian liqueur also made of hazelnuts. It's a fairly tricky dish, but worth all the effort. The key thing is to always use good-quality chocolate – make sure the dark chocolate has 72% cocoa solids – and to have a sugar thermometer to hand.

SERVES 8

For the hazelnut nougatine
400g hazelnuts
1kg caster sugar
500g liquid glucose

For the pâté à bombe
150g caster sugar
60ml water
12 egg yolks

For the Italian meringue
75g caster sugar
75g liquid glucose
30g water
10 egg whites, whipped to a stiff peak
50g Frangelico
200g hazelnut praline milk chocolate, melted
150g double cream, whipped
100g milk chocolate, roughly chopped
125g hazelnut nougatine (see above)
8 chocolate tear moulds

For the chocolate sablé
250g plain flour
15g cocoa powder
Pinch of salt
200g unsalted butter, softened
100g icing sugar
2 egg yolks
30g dark chocolate, melted

For the chocolate ganache
2 eggs
160g milk
400g cream
400g dark chocolate, melted

For the white chocolate ice cream
5 egg yolks
50g sugar
500ml milk
25g milk powder
100ml whipping cream
200g white chocolate, melted

Note: always melt chocolate in a bowl placed over a saucepan of simmeing water (a bain marie) but don't let the water touch the bowl.

Hazelnut nougatine
Preheat the oven to 200C/gas mark 6. Place the hazelnuts on a tray in the oven and roast until golden. Remove, place them in a cloth and rub to remove the skin. Once the skin is removed, keep warm on one side. Heat the sugar and the glucose in a saucepan over a medium heat until the sugar starts to turn golden, then add the hazelnuts and mix thoroughly. Pour the mixture into a non-stick tray and leave to cool. Once cooled, place the mixture in a food processor and blitz until you get a coarse texture.

Hazelnut parfait
Make the pâté à bombe first. Put the caster sugar and water into a saucepan over a medium heat and bring to the boil, stirring occasionally to help the sugar dissolve. Continue to boil until it reaches 120C. Meanwhile, whisk the egg yolks in a bowl until they turn creamy. Take the sugar syrup off the heat and pour in the egg yolks, whisking all the time. Continue to whisk while the mixture cools, then decant it into a large mixing bowl.

Now make the Italian meringue. Put the sugar, glucose and water together in a saucepan and heat until it reaches 120C, stirring occasionally to help the sugar and glucose dissolve. Remove from the heat and pour steadily on to the whipped egg whites, continuing to whisk until the mixture has cooled.

Next add the Frangelico and the melted hazelnut chocolate to the pâté à bombe mixture. Fold in the whipped cream and then the Italian meringue. Now, sprinkle and fold in the chopped milk chocolate and the hazelnut nougatine. Place the mixture into a piping bag and fill the chocolate tear moulds with it. Put in the freezer until it is ready to be served.

Chocolate sablé

Preheat the oven to 150C/gas mark 2. Sift the flour, cocoa powder and salt into a mixing bowl, then add the butter and rub in until the mixture resembles fine grains of sand. Add the icing sugar and egg yolks and then pour in the melted chocolate. Mix and bind together, then remove from the bowl and place in the fridge in some clingfilm for 2 hours, before rolling out and cutting into 6cm x 4cm biscuits. Place the biscuits onto a baking sheet lined with baking parchment then pop into the oven to cook for 20 minutes. When cooked take out and cool.

Chocolate ganache

Place the eggs into a jug. Put the milk and cream in a saucepan over a medium heat and bring to the boil. Then, using a stick whisk, pour the boiling milk and cream onto the eggs, blending as you do so. Stir the mixture into the melted chocolate, using a whisk at first and then a wooden spoon. Line 8 x 4cm rings with clingfilm, pour the warm ganache mixture into these and put them in the fridge for a minimum of 2 hours until the ganache has set.

White chocolate ice cream

Put the egg yolks and sugar into a bowl and cream together using an electric hand whisk until they are white and stiff. Put the milk, milk powder and cream, into a saucepan over a medium heat and bring to the boil. Once the boil is reached, pour a little of the milk and cream mixture onto the creamed eggs and sugar, whisking continuously. Add the rest of the mixture, then return it to the saucepan, place back on the heat and make a custard, stirring continuously until it has reached 85C. Take the custard off the heat, strain through a fine sieve and then add in the white chocolate. Mix thoroughly, then pour the mixture into an ice-cream machine and churn until frozen. Transfer the ice-cream to the container and keep in the freezer until ready to use. If you don't have an ice-cream machine, place the mixture in a container in the freezer, taking it out every 30 minutes to stir until it is set. The ice cream is ready when it holds its shape after scooping.

Serving

Take the ganache rings out of the fridge and leave to one side until they reach room temperature. Then take the parfait out of their teardrop moulds and put one on each of your plates. Loosen the ganache from the rings (either by heating the outside of the rings, briefly, with a culinary blow torch or by carefully running a knife around the edges of the ganache), then pop them out and place each one on a sablé biscuit. Transfer the biscuits to the plates, add a scoop of white chocolate ice cream and serve.

ANTHONY DEMETRE

Eating is a classless occupation. Rich or poor, everyone has to eat. But it takes a truly great chef to be able to cook for all walks of life successfully, especially in the territorial food landscape that is London.

The West End of our capital city is divided geographically by the shopper's heaven of Regent's Street. It meanders from Oxford Circus, heading south, gently twisting and turning to the neon paradise of Piccadilly. It is a beautiful street, full of glorious shops and commercial icons such as Hamley's and Apple's flagship media store.

However, in the food map of Britain, it has another more significant purpose – it separates the high-flying, gold-cufflinked world of Mayfair from the more bohemian delights of Soho. The areas may be less than 100 yards apart, but the gulf between them is immeasurable. In the

normal order of things, as a restaurateur, you would set up shop in either one or the other.

Mayfair is fine dining and Soho tends to be a less formal foodie hangout, the home of bistros and trendy brasseries. Anthony Demetre, however, straddles both areas like the great Colossus of Rhodes. He and his business partner Will Smith have two restaurants – Arbutus in Soho and Wild Honey in Mayfair – and, impressively, both have Michelin stars. This makes 42-year-old Anthony something of a trailblazer.

Both Arbutus and Wild Honey are modelled on the great tradition of French bistros, but, amazingly, they feel British. Yes, there is bouillabaisse on the menu, but there are also mackerel and squid burgers, beautifully constructed patties of seafood with the firmness of the traditional beef variety but the flavour of the seashore. Bistro in Britain has long meant endless chain restaurants with soulless cooking and stale bread. Here, there is passion in every dish. As a diner, you can enjoy steak and chips, of course, but also pig's head and an elderberry trifle.

Having grown up in Stratford-upon-Avon to a Greek Cypriot father and an English mother of Irish extraction, Anthony's first love was not food but the Royal Navy, which he joined straight from school at the age of 18. He craved discipline and the Armed Forces gave him the secure environment which mirrored his school days at Selly Oak Boys school. A persistent knee problem cut his service short and he was faced with a dilemma of what to do with his life. However, Anthony had always had an interest in food and cooking. Childhood holidays in Greece, and his grandparents' passion for the culinary arts, had given him an inkling that he might enjoy a career in food.

But it was an old school friend who first suggested he should try cheffing. The friend was working at a Stratford-upon-Avon restaurant in the Ettington Park hotel, under a chef called Michael Quinn. Michael was an influential figure in the world of food and had been awarded an MBE after becoming the first British man to be made head chef at the Ritz in London. He ran a strict brigade, the kitchen was heavily structured and disciplined. Anthony went along to fill in – and fell in love with the job.

After a while, he decided to expand his knowledge and took *stages* at Marco Pierre White's celebrated Harvey's in

Wandsworth, the renowned Le Manoir aux Quat' Saisons in Oxfordshire and the Castle Hotel at Taunton (when Gary Rhodes was heading the kitchen) to gain experience and more technical know-how. However, it was his time working with a gifted French chef called Bruno Loubet that was to prove his biggest inspiration.

Anthony worked for him, initially, at the Four Seasons restaurant and when the Frenchman struck out on his own he joined him at his new restaurant, Bistrot Bruno, which, coincidentally, was on the site that Arbutus now occupies. He spent six years as Bruno's right-hand man, first at Bistrot Bruno then helping the French chef open the Regent's Street hotspot L'Odeon in 1996.

He stayed on at L'Odeon after the French chef departed in 1997, eventually parting company with the restaurant in 1999 when he was offered a job across the river in Putney. This district of south-west London was a very different place from the parts of town he was used to working in, but Anthony needed to get out of Bruno's shadow. Putney Bridge restaurant, which had opened with a great fanfare in 1997 but had failed to make a culinary impact, was in need of inspired leadership. It was his big chance.

The restaurant – a modern architectural landmark – sat right on the banks of the Thames, just at the spot where the historic university boat race begins, and Anthony soon made his mark. Accolades came quickly and Michelin handed him a star within a year. But awards don't pay the bills and Putney Bridge had a massive rent and often struggled for lunchtime custom. The challenge this presented meant that Anthony earned his stripes in the world of business. Helping him was Will Smith, his current business partner, who Anthony had brought in from L'Odeon to manage the restaurant. Between them, the duo tried every way possible to make the restaurant work, but eventually the rent was just too much and they decided to move on.

Disillusioned with fine-dining, Anthony, wisely, took some time out of the restaurant world. He started a family with his wife, Frédérique, and slowly, slowly fell in love with food again. Time spent in New York, and also working at the Kayser bakery in Paris, renewed his enthusiasm for cooking – and then he heard that the old Bistrot Bruno site was free. It seemed fortuitous and he and Will grabbed their

chance. In 2006, Arbutus was born, with Anthony at the stove and Will front-of-house.

The restaurant's rise was meteoric. It won every award going and in less than a year was joined by its sister restaurant, Wild Honey, which like Arbutus, quickly picked up a Michelin star. Wild Honey's is a direct 10-minute walk westwards from Arbutus, just off Hanover Square on the posh side of Regent's Street. At first, the Mayfair crowd were shy of the unfamiliar cuts of meat and slices of tripe that litter Anthony's menus, but they soon got the hang of things and the restaurant does a roaring trade, even at the weekends.

Anthony's skill at extracting every ounce of flavour from his ingredients is hard to resist. It rests on slow cooking, sous vide style: that is, popping ingredients into a vacuum-sealed plastic bag and cooking in a pot of low-temperature water

for hours on end. It's a strangely precise technique, with dishes cooked for exactly so many hours and so many minutes at something between 40C and 60C, but the results are brilliant with amazing depths of flavour. And it allows Anthony to offer his customers really good price deals on his food because sous vide is the perfect way to transform inexpensive cuts of meat into something wondrous.

Like Anthony's food, both Arbutus and Wild Honey are chic but unfussy – with natural wood, simple colour schemes and textures framing the plain, linen-free tables. The waiters are dressed comfortably, in black, and both restaurants have a relaxed bar on entry. The only real difference between the two restaurants are the dining booths at Wild Honey.

The restaurants' main beauty, however, is their accessibility. Plats du jour fill the menus and carafes of wine are plentiful. In fact, the wine lists at both are a major calling card. Not only have they been carefully constructed with a wide range of unique and very quaffable wines, but serving by the carafe means people can try out great wines without having to fork out for a full bottle. It's a simple notion, but as with all of Anthony and Will's ideas, it opens up the dining experience to everyone.

When you come across restaurants like Arbutus and Wild Honey, you can't help but ask yourself 'why has no one done this before?'. The simple answer is: they have and they are; the difference is, they just don't do it as well.

Arbutus 63-64 Frith Street , London W1D 3JW
Phone 020 7734 4545 **www.arbutusrestaurant.co.uk**
Wild Honey 12 St George Street , London W1S 2FB
Phone 020 7758 9160 **www.wildhoneyrestaurant.co.uk**

CHILLED ORGANIC CARROT SOUP WITH PINK GRAPEFRUIT, HAZELNUTS AND OLIVES

This summer soup is a complete fluke. We were on holiday in France, it was raining and I had to cook something for the kids' lunch, so I did the classic – opened up the cupboard, used the ingredients that were there and ended up with a surprisingly tasty carrot soup. I tweaked it of course when I got back to London, did it on the BBC1 weekend show *Saturday Kitchen* and then couldn't make enough of it for my customers – and I still can't.

SERVES 4

500g carrots
50g butter
1 garlic clove, crushed
750ml water
1 sprig of fresh thyme
1 sprig of fresh rosemary
150ml milk
2 pink grapefruits, segmented and the segments halved
1 handful of green Gordal olives, stoned and halved
1 handful of hazelnuts, crushed and toasted
1 punnet fresh micro coriander cress
4 tablespoons hazelnut oil
Salt and freshly ground black pepper

Slice the carrots as thinly as possible, using a mandoline. Heat a large saucepan over a medium heat until hot, then add the butter, sliced carrots and garlic and gently cook for 2-3 minutes until the vegetables are just beginning to soften. Add the water, thyme and rosemary, then season with salt and freshly ground black pepper. Bring the stock to a simmer, then cover it with a lid and cook for 5-6 minutes, or until the carrots are tender. Remove the pan from the heat and stir in the milk. Allow to cool slightly, then transfer the mixture to a blender and blend until smooth. Place into the fridge to chill for at least 30 minutes.

Serving
Divide the soup among four serving bowls. Arrange the grapefruit segments, olives, nuts and coriander cress on top of the soup, then drizzle over the hazelnut oil.

BLANQUETTE OF VEAL WITH SEASONAL VEGETABLES

The breast of veal is, I find, the best cut for this dish and one which we often use at Arbutus. For me, its cartilaginous texture and silky richness lends itself to slow cooking and produces incomparable results. However, if you have trouble finding the breast or belly, the shoulder is a good alternative. English rose or French Limousin veal is best, and I like to serve it with seasonal vegetables and some freshly baked brown bread.

SERVES 4-6

1kg veal breast, cut into 2cm square
   cubes
2.5 litres chicken stock
6 garlic cloves, peeled and crushed
1 teaspoon black peppercorns
1 sprig of sage
1 bay leaf
1 lemon, zested and juiced
6 medium Maris Piper potatoes, cut in
   half and trimmed
2 bunches of young carrots
2 medium-sized leeks, cut into 2cm
   lozenges
A handful of spring greens
50g butter
50g flour
1 tablespoon chopped parsley
50ml whipping cream, whipped to soft
   peaks
Salt and pepper

Put the diced veal into a saucepan and cover it with stock. Bring to the boil over a medium heat, simmer for 1 hour and skim all the scum from the surface. Add the garlic, peppercorns, a pinch of salt (not too much), sage, bay leaf and lemon zest, then continue to simmer gently for 1 hour.

Add the potatoes, carrots, leeks and greens and cook until soft. They will cook at different stages, so lift them out when ready and leave to cool naturally. By the time these are done the veal should be tender or just yield under pressure, so lift it out and cool naturally. If it's not quite done, simmer a little longer, checking to prevent overcooking but once you have removed the veal, keep the stock on the simmer.

Take another saucepan, ideally the same size, melt the butter until it foams, add the flour, and make a roux. Now strain the simmering stock onto the roux, stirring constantly. Lower the heat and simmer for 20–30 minutes, this allows the flour to cook. Correct the seasoning with salt and pepper and lemon juice if necessary. Add the meat, vegetables and parsley into the broth, then add the whipped cream to finish.

Serving
You don't need to be fancy with this dish – just serve it in a soup bowl with freshly baked brown bread on the side.

ROAST HALIBUT WITH CRUSHED JERSEY ROYAL POTATOES, BRAISED YOUNG GEM LETTUCE

Although Atlantic halibut has been over-fished, Pacific halibut is abundant so you can use it with a clear conscience. Cooking baby gem lettuce in this way, rather like the Italians do with radicchio, brings out their sweetness and makes them perfect to serve with fish.

SERVES 4

500g Jersey Royal potatoes
100g butter
A splash of extra virgin olive oil
4 x 200g halibut steaks on the bone
4 whole baby gem lettuce, halved
   lengthways
Splash of Noilly Prat or dry vermouth
1 sprig of rosemary, chopped
2 cloves garlic, finely chopped
2 tablespoons double cream
Squeeze of lemon
Maldon sea salt and freshly ground
   pepper

Put the Jersey Royals into a saucepan of water and gently cook them over a medium heat. Drain and peel them whilst still warm, then put them into a stainless-steel bowl, add a knob of butter, drizzle with olive oil, season with a little sea salt and crush with a fork or old-fashioned potato masher, adding more butter and olive oil as you go. The aim is to create a smooth, homogenous texture. The quantities of olive oil should be greater than the butter. The potatoes should be rich but also have hints of fruitiness from the oil. Put to one side and keep warm.

Preheat the oven at 150C/gas mark 2. Season the halibut steaks with the sea salt. Take a large non-stick frying pan and melt a knob of butter and a splash of olive oil in it over a medium-high heat, add the seasoned fish and lightly colour it on both sides, basting as you go. Lower the heat and continue cooking, gently basting. When cooked, leave the fish to rest in the warm but take it off the direct heat. Take another non-stick frying pan, melt a knob of butter with a slug of olive oil, then pop in the baby gems on their split, flat sides. Add a splash of Noilly Prat, then the rosemary and garlic. Season and bake for 10-15 minutes in the oven until tender.

Serving

Lift out the fish from its liquor and place it, together with the baby gems, onto your serving plates. Keep hot while you add some of the fish cooking liquor into the gem cooking liquor, put in the double cream and reduce quickly to a sauce consistency. If you need it, add a little more seasoning, a squeeze of lemon juice then spoon over the fish and serve.

SQUID AND MACKEREL BURGER, SEA PURSLANE AND PARSLEY JUICE

When we first opened Arbutus I put brochettes of squid and mackerel, a favourite combination of mine, on the menu but they weren't popular. So I thought I'd try using the fish to make a pâté and, by accident, ended up making these burgers, which are now synonymous with our restaurants. You need to remember to soak and wash the razor clams in plenty of water as they'll be full of sand – and don't forget to dry them before you use them.

SERVES 4

300g razor clams (enough to get 100g clam meat)
1 glass of white wine
1 bunch of flat leaf parsley, stalks removed
100g sea purslane
2 medium whole mackerel
200g squid, frozen then defrosted to tenderise
1 tablespoon chopped coriander
1 tablespoon grated ginger
1 tablespoon chopped garlic
1 teaspoon lime zest
Salt and pepper
Olive oil for cooking

Heat a good splash of olive oil in a saucepan with a tight-fitting lid. Add the razor clams in their shells (they'll sizzle, but don't worry) and a glass of white wine, cover quickly with the lid again and steam the clams over a medium heat until they are just open, then take them off the heat and put to one side. It should take about 3 mintues. Drain the juices through a colander over a bowl, pull the meat from the shells and put the clams to one side.

Blanch the parsley and a handful of the sea purslane in a litre of boiling water, then drain and refresh them immediately in iced water to set their colour. Drain again and liquidise them with a little of the clam cooking juice. You need to end up with the consistency of a vinaigrette. Season with salt and pepper if necessary and set to one side.

Finely chop the mackerel and squid, mix them together in a large bowl and then add all the remaining ingredients, and then leave the mixture to set in the fridge for 2 hours.

Mould into 4 burgers, using clingfilm to hold their shape if you want.

Serving
Blanch the remaining sea purslane in some boiling water, then drain and refresh immediately in iced water. Drain again and dress with the parsley and vinaigrette juice. Pan fry the burgers in olive oil until they are nice and golden then pop them onto your plates and garnish with the cooked razor clams and some dressed sea purslane.

ENGLISH SUMMER BERRY TRIFLE WITH ELDERFLOWER AND FRESH ALMONDS

Trifle is a British classic and this one is a lovely light and fragrant summer version, particularly if you happen to have an elderflower tree in your garden. It's nice to finish off the trifle with some fresh or toasted almond flakes (just toast the flakes on a baking tray in the oven at 175C for about 5 minutes until they're golden). If you can't get hold of either, pink sugared-coated almonds are another good option. Almond milk should be available through delicatessens.

SERVES 4-6

For the sponge
50g butter
4 eggs
100g caster sugar
100g flour

For the elderflower syrup
125g elderflowers, stems discarded
500ml water
150g caster sugar

For the custard
250ml full fat milk
2 egg yolks
65g sugar
20g cornflour
½ vanilla pod, scraped

For the almond cream
175ml whipping cream
50ml full fat milk
15g sugar
20g almond milk

For garnish
A handful of almonds (flaked or fresh)

Sponge
Preheat the oven at 175C/gas mark 4. Melt the butter in a small saucepan over a medium heat then leave it to cool. Meanwhile, whisk the eggs and sugar until light and fluffy. Gently fold in the flour and butter then pour the mixture into a non-stick container and bake in the oven for 15-20 minutes.

Elderflower syrup
Put the flowers, water and sugar together into a large saucepan, bring them to a gentle simmer over a medium heat, then remove from the heat and leave the flowers to infuse the water until it is completely cold. Strain the syrup through a fine sieve.

Custard
Bring the milk to the boil in a saucepan over a medium heat. Whisk the eggs, sugar, cornflour and vanilla together to form a custard base then pour a little hot milk onto this, mix it in and return the mixture back to the remaining milk. Place the custard back over a low to medium heat and stir continuously until it thickens. It is done when it is thick enough to coat the back of a spoon. Pour into a bowl, cover with clingfilm to prevent a skin forming and chill in the fridge.

For the almond cream
Warm all the ingredients together in a saucepan over a medium heat until the sugar has dissolved. Pour this into an iSi soda siphon bottle and put on one side to chill completely before adding the siphon canisters.

Serving
Dice the sponge into 2cm cubes and put into individual glass bowls, add a handful of raspberries and strawberries, and pour over enough syrup to saturate the sponge. Add a decent layer of custard, then shake the iSi bottle and gently discharge a generous amount of almond cream on the top. Finally add your almonds.

MARCUS EAVES

Once upon a time, Marylebone was a bit of a backwater in London. Nice, polite – but not exactly rocking. Then, about 12 years ago, everything changed. Stylish shops and chic, big-hitting restaurants moved in and the area began to buzz. Places like Orrery and The Providores upped the culinary tempo initially, but a relative newcomer has given it a new beat. Walk southwards down Marylebone High Street, about halfway, hang right into Blandford Street, cross over the road and you'll find it, L'Autre Pied, the home of a ridiculously talented young chef called Marcus Eaves.

Marcus looks like he should be fronting an indie band. A sharp, artfully dishevelled haircut, cleft chin and laid-back manner give him, seemingly, an aura that could easily carry

a full-on pop gig. Actually, he's rather self-conscious when he chats, until you get him waxing lyrical on food. Then it becomes clear that he's one of the hottest young chefs on the London foodie scene, having, when he was just 27, netted a Michelin star for his restaurant a mere 14 months after it opened in November 2007. That culinary confidence comes from the fact that he's been around food all his life.

He was born in Leamington Spa in 1981, to a father who was – and is – himself, a head chef in a country house hotel in Banbury. As a boy, Marcus often used to sneak into his father's work kitchen and help him prepare for the evening service; it was sometimes the only time he would get to see his Dad because of the long hours that Eaves Senior worked.

It wasn't long before Marcus was experimenting by himself in the kitchen at home. One day he tried to cook a strawberry sablé from the Roux brothers' famously challenging book on pâtisserie. There were no strawberries in the fridge, so he used tinned peaches instead and then came up against the challenge of making crème pâtissière. 'I didn't know what that was, and I just got deeper and deeper into a hole…the kitchen ended up like a bombsite,' he remembers.

The sense of adventure that led to the sablé disaster can still be seen in Marcus' food at L'Autre Pied. His cooking is based on classic foundations, but his dishes often have exciting and quirky ingredient matches that just beg to be tried out. Things like a pinenut and tarragon dressing on a salad of young autumn vegetables; or saddle and herb-crusted leg of hare with pumpkin and orange purée and a bitter chocolate sauce.

Marcus' classic culinary foundations can be traced back to his father and to his first job at one of Warwickshire's most prestigious restaurants, Simpson's (then located in Kenilworth), whose chef-proprietor Andreas Antona's cooking has always been renowned for its modern classicism. Here, not only did Marcus acquire the essential craft skills of his trade, but he also discovered the addictive buzz of working in a fine-dining kitchen. And he soon struck up a friendship with another talented young chef who was on the team, Glynn Purnell (see xx). The two of them spent hours together, in and out of the kitchen, reading as many cookbooks as they could get their hands on in an attempt to further their knowledge of food.

Simpson's was only the start of Marcus' training. Fuelled by a desire to broaden his horizons, the next three years saw him acquire finesse and culinary know-how at a series of Michelin-starred restaurants. First, with Martin Blunos at Lettonie in Bath (at the time one of the most acclaimed restaurants in the country), then after that with John Burton Race at the latter's short-lived eponymous restaurant in London's Landmark hotel. When the restaurant folded, Marcus found himself out of work, but he used his enforced leisure time well, maxing-out his credit card by eating at all the top restaurants in London. One meal in particular stood out – at Michelin-starred Pied à Terre owned by restaurateur David Moore and chef Shane Osborn. So Marcus plucked up the courage to pick up the phone and ask Shane if he could do a *stage* – or work experience – at the restaurant.

Shane's answer was 'yes', and it wasn't long before Marcus proved his worth and was offered a full-time job, joining Shane in 2003, just after Pied à Terre won back its prized second Michelin star. Without knowing it, Marcus had sealed his future because five years down the line Shane and David set him up at L'Autre Pied as a chef-proprietor. However, sandwiched between his first time at Pied à Terre and the adventure of L'Autre Pied was one final cuilinary finishing school; that of Claude Bosi in the latter's acclaimed kitchen at Hibiscus in Ludlow. The Frenchman's cuisine was challenging and modern without being too alien and his kitchen was incredibly intense, its standards faultless. Marcus soaked up its lessons, inadvertently preparing himself for the challenge that lay ahead.

The first inkling of that challenge came when, one evening after service, Shane drove him through Marylebone, paused outside what was then the Blandford Street restaurant and casually asked him what he thought of his, Marcus', new restaurant. Once he'd got over his astonishment, Marcus' first thought was that he was still too young and inexperienced to be able to handle being torn between the creativity required to be a top fine-dining chef and the management skills necessary to be a top restaurateur.

Shane and David had greater faith in him, though, and he rose spectacularly to the responsibility they invested in him,

bringing home plaudits and rave reviews from restaurant critics almost from the word go. Both critics and L'Autre Pied's diners, both, liked the fact that the restaurant wasn't Pied à Terre's 'mini-me' and applauded its convivial elegance and lack of tablecloths. Most of all they appreciated Marcus' culinary vision and ability to bring his ideas off.

Those ideas often included bold flavours and always had texture layers, frequently provided by the judicious use of various nuts. They were also often imaginative expansions of classic dishes like baked Alaska, only Marcus' one, in the autumn at least, comes with a lemon thyme ice cream,

poached plums and damson consommé: a veritable sweet-and-tart fruit-fest.

The great thing about Marcus, however, is that he is also comfortable enough with his own culinary identity to know when he can't improve a classic. He knows that a piece of succulent, juicy Cornish lamb just needs some perfect root vegetables and maybe a herb or two and a nuance of spice to show it off.

And what is truly refreshing about Marcus is that, even with all his early success at L'Autre Pied, he's focused on evolving his

cooking. Despite his fashionable looks he has no interest in following other chefs into the media bear pit. For the moment, he is happiest in the kitchen taking charge of service. 'I am a young guy running my own Michelin-starred kitchen. This is something I've dreamed of since being a boy. Is it tough? Naturally, but that's the fun of the challenge.' With an attitude like that, he's going to be around for a long time to come.

L'Autre Pied
5-7 Blandford Street, London W1U 3DB
Phone 020 7486 9696 **www.lautrepied.co.uk**

SEARED FOIE GRAS, PEAR AND STAR ANISE SORBET, SOUSED BABY ARTICHOKES, STAR ANISE CRISPS

When we first opened L'Autre Pied we didn't put luxury ingredients on the menu, but once we got to know our customers we tried this dish out and it's been on ever since. Always remember that you need to use the best foie gras – and if you've not come across isomalt, it's basically a very dry type of sugar which when you use it in biscuits and sugar crisps keeps them from going soft much longer than ordinary sugar does. You can buy it on-line at www.msk-ingredients.com.

SERVES 4

400g premier duck foie gras, cut into 4
   x 100g pieces with a hot knife

For the pear discs and sorbet
400g water
200g caster sugar
1 vanilla pod
1 star anise
½ cinnamon stick
2 Williams' pears

Note: Slice 1 Williams' pear into discs. Halve the second Williams' pear, then finely cube ½ and roughly chop ½.

For the artichokes
4 baby artichokes
1 teaspoon coriander seeds
1 teaspoon white peppercorns
50ml white wine vinegar
100ml good quality sweet wine
150ml water
1 fresh bay leaf
Splash of olive oil
Sea salt

For the star anise crisps
300g isomalt (see introduction above)
170g glucose
2g ground star anise

For the garnish
50g toasted pistachio, crushed
A pinch of ground star anise
A handful of red amaranth and rocket
   cress micro herbs

Pear discs and sorbet
Put the water and sugar in a saucepan and bring to the boil over a medium heat to make a sugar syrup (sometimes known as a stock syrup), stirring occasionally to help dissolve the sugar. Add the vanilla pod and spices and simmer for 5 minutes. Add the pear discs and infuse them for 15 minutes, then remove the discs and keep to one side. Repeat the same process with the chopped pear, but this time once it has infused put it into a food processor or blender with the stock syrup or blender and blitz until smooth. Transfer to an ice-cream machine and churn according to its instructions. Once churned, put the pear mixture in a freezer-proof container and place it in the freezer. If you haven't got an ice-cream machine, then place the mix in a shallow dish in the freezer, taking it out every few minutes to stir. When the sorbet is slushy put it into a freezer-proof bowl and put it in the freezer to set completely.

Artichokes
Prepare the artichokes by breaking down the leaves and peeling away the outer skin until you get to the heart. Then heat a splash of oil in a saucepan, add the artichokes and cook them for 3-4 minutes, making sure you don't colour them. Add the coriander seeds, white peppercorns and white wine vinegar and simmer until the wine vinegar has reduced to a glaze. Once the vinegar has almost disappeared, add the sweet wine and reduce to a glaze again. Add the water and bay leaf, bring to the boil and then season

with a little sea salt. Simmer for 5 minutes then remove from the heat.

Star anise crisps
Preheat the oven to 180C/gas mark 4. Place the isomalt and glucose in a saucepan over a medium heat and bring up to 158C. Use a sugar thermometer to check the temperature. Once the sugar mix has reached the correct temperature, take it off the heat and stir in the ground star anise. Place the mixture onto a non-stick silicone mat or tray and cool until it becomes firm and brittle. Then take a 30g piece of this, put it on a baking tray lined with greaseproof paper and warm it through in the oven until it is soft and pliable. Remove it from the oven and place it, while still warm and pliable, between two sheets of greaseproof paper, then roll it out as thinly as possible and divide into 4 pieces. Chill, then store somewhere cool.

Serving
Heat a non-stick pan over a high heat and then quickly sear the foie gras pieces in it until they are caramelised on both sides – about 30 seconds on each side. Then place the seared foie gras on a baking tray and put in the oven for 2 minutes at 180C/gas mark 4. When the foie gras is cooked, take it out and it place on a clean cloth to drain away any excess fat. Once this is done, put a piece of foie gras on to each serving plate, together with a pear disc and soused artichoke. Sprinkle a bit of toasted pistachio on to the plate. Add a scoop of pear sorbet and a pinch of ground star anise. Finally stick a star anise crisp in to the pear sorbet and scatter a few red amaranth and rocket cress leaves around the plate.

BREAST OF CORNISH LAMB, CARROT AND CUMIN PUREE, GLAZED BABY CARROTS, PUY LENTIL AND THYME JUS

This summer lamb dish came about as a way of using up some breast of lamb which was in the kitchen as an off-cut from making another dish. When it went on the menu we suddenly found ourselves with a hit on our hands – not bad for something thrown together quickly! I like to use grelot onions – a type of large spring onion – when they're in season between April and September, but you can use little button onions if you can't get them. The same goes for ratte potatoes, a type of new potato – if you can't get this variety use another new, preferably organic, potato.

SERVES 4

2 x medium breasts of lamb, deboned

For the pomme purée
500g ratte potatoes
125g unsalted butter
70g milk
A pinch of sea salt

For the carrot and cumin purée
25g butter
4 large carrots, chopped into 2cm pieces
5g cumin seeds
100ml white chicken stock
1 tablespoon honey

For the garnish
50ml white chicken stock
25g butter
8 baby carrots
8 new season grelot onions
A pinch of salt

For the sauce
500ml lamb stock
1 teaspoon thyme leaves
30g Puy lentils
Lemon oil

Preheat the oven to 110C/gas mark ¼. Place a sheet of clingfilm flat on the work surface. Put one of the lamb breasts on it and roll it into a cylindrical shape, making sure there are no air pockets. Next get a sheet of kitchen foil and roll the breast in this. Then repeat the whole double-wrapping process again with the second breast of lamb. Put the lamb on a baking tray and cook in the oven for 6-8 hours. Once the lamb is cooked and tender, remove the clingfilm and kitchen foil. Then remould the lamb breasts, once again using clingfilm and making sure there are no air pockets. Put the lamb in the fridge to firm up.

Pomme purée
Bring a saucepan of salted water to the boil over a medium heat. Add the ratte potatoes, with their skins on, and cook them until they are soft. Once the potatoes are cooked, remove them from the heat, drain and peel away their skins, then push them through a potato ricer back into the still-warm saucepan. Slowly add the butter, mixing it in thoroughly, then add the milk – again incorporating thoroughly. The potato needs to stay hot while you are doing this. Next, push the potato through a drum sieve. If you don't have one pass it twice through a fine sieve. Season with sea salt.

Carrot and cumin purée
Melt a knob of butter in a non-stick saucepan over a medium heat. Once the butter is slightly coloured, add the chopped carrot and cumin seeds and cook until the carrots have caramelised a golden brown and are beginning to soften. Drain off any excess butter, then cover the carrots with white chicken stock, add the honey and cook for a further 5 minutes. Once the

carrots are cooked all the way through, remove them from the heat, drain and blitz them in a food processor for 3-5 minutes or until you get a smooth purée.

Garnish
Put the chicken stock in a saucepan and bring to the boil over a medium heat. Add the butter and a pinch of salt, then drop in the baby carrots and onions and poach them for about 4 minutes. Once they are cooked, remove from the heat and drain, keeping a little of the stock to reheat them up in before you serve the dish.

Puy lentil and thyme sauce
Put the lamb stock in a saucepan over a medium heat and simmer until it reduces back down to a sauce consistency. Add the thyme leaves and lentils and cook gently over a low heat for 15 minutes.

Serving
Remove the lamb from the fridge and slice into 2.5cm-sized pieces. Heat a large non-stick frying pan over a medium-high heat and caramelise the lamb slices in it. Once the lamb is golden brown, turn the heat down and ladle over the sauce to warm it through, basting the lamb continuously to ensure the meat stays moist. Meanwhile, reheat the carrots and onions in some of their cooking liquor. Next spoon some carrot purée onto your serving plates, add some of the baby carrots and onions, then top with slices of lamb and a few coriander leaves. Finally, add the pomme purée, and drizzle some of the puy lentil and thyme sauce and a little lemon oil around the outside of the plate.

OPEN RAVIOLO OF POACHED LANGOUSINTES, TURBOT, SUMMER TRUFFLE

This is another lovely summer or early autumn dish which began life as a starter without the turbot. After a while I wanted to move it to the main section so I added the turbot to give it a bit more depth. Depending on the time of year, I change the mushroom garnish. In early autumn fantastic Scottish girolles are in season, but morels are just as good. Just adapt to whatever is around.

SERVES 4

200g pasta dough
1 medium turbot fillet
1 medium summer truffle
   (approximately 80g)
1 shallot, finely chopped
50ml good quality cooking wine
50ml water
100g unsalted butter, chopped into
   small cubes
8 wild rocket leaves, roughly chopped
20g mixed soft herbs, finely chopped
15 small Scottish girolle mushrooms,
   sautéed
4 large langoustine tails
A splash of olive oil

Using a pasta machine, roll out the pasta dough to its thinnest setting. Make sure the pasta is a uniform thickness. Next, cut out some pasta discs using a 70mm pastry cutter. Bring a large saucepan of salted water to the boil and blanch the pasta discs in it for 45 seconds. Cool the discs down in iced water.

Put the shallot into a small saucepan, cover it with the white wine, then bring it to a simmer over medium heat and reduce the wine to a glaze – it shouldn't take more than 2-3 minutes. Now add the water and bring to the boil, then slowly add the unsalted butter, whisking continuously so that it emulsifies and forms a sauce. Once all the butter is incorporated, take the sauce off the heat.

Put a splash of olive oil in a non-stick frying pan over a moderate heat and once hot, place the turbot inside and cook for 2 minutes on either side.

Serving
Warm the pasta discs in hot water. Warm a saucepan over a medium heat, add in the shallot and butter sauce and warm it through, then finish the sauce by adding in the rocket, chopped herbs, and sautéed girolle mushrooms. Next, drop the langoustines into the sauce for 30 seconds. Then put a disc of pasta at the bottom of each serving dish, followed by a layer of langoustine, another pasta disc, a layer of turbot and a final pasta disc. Finish with some sauce and a little bit of shaved truffle.

MARINATED HAND DIVED SCALLOPS, HORSERADISH CHANTILLY, NATIVE OYSTERS AND LIME VINAIGRETTE

I like to use classic ingredient and flavour combinations in different ways. Scallops and horseradish, scallops and oyster – they're both no-brainers. I've just used them differently to provide a bit of a surprise with the dish. If you can't get hold of native oysters, then Pacific – also known as rock – oysters are fine: and you might find salmon roe sold as keta caviar. I've finished the dish with a few micro herbs but they're not essential. However, if you do use some, red amaranth and red-veined sorrel work well with the other flavours in the dish.

SERVES 4

8 large hand-dived scallops
4 native oysters
2 limes, juiced
1 lemon, juiced
80g salmon roe
50g dill
A small handful of micro herbs (optional)
Sea salt and freshly ground black pepper

For the pickled cauliflower
1 tablespoon olive oil
50g cauliflower florets
50ml champagne vinegar
50ml good-quality cooking wine

Note: 1 cauliflower is enough to make the cauliflower pickle and the purée. Detach the florets and keep the rest for the purée.

For the cauliflower purée
125g cauliflower, roughly chopped
75g double cream
35g milk
Salt

For the horseradish cream
100g double cream
10g grated horseradish
1 lemon, juiced
Salt and freshly ground black pepper

Scallops

If you have fresh scallops in their shells, open the shells then take a reasonably sharp knife and run it down the back of the shell, releasing the scallop flesh. Remove the excess muscle along with the roe. Rinse the scallop briefly in ice-cold water, drain and pat dry with a little kitchen paper. Place the scallops in the fridge to firm up. Once firm, slice them as finely as possible with a sharp fish filleting knife and place the slices on a flat plate, making sure they are not over lapping. Cover with clingfilm and put the scallops back in the fridge.

Oysters

Open the oysters using an oyster shucking knife. Do this over a bowl so that you catch their natural juices, then wash the oysters in their juices. Pour the juices through a very fine sieve, twice, to remove any bits of shell. Put the oysters back in the strained juices and place them in the fridge.

Pickled cauliflower

Heat 1 tablespoon of olive oil in a saucepan over a medium heat, add the cauliflower florets and gently cook for 1 minute until just beginning to go soft. Next, add the champagne vinegar and continue cooking until it is reduced to a glaze, then add the white wine, and again reduce down to a glaze. – each reduction shouldn't take more than 1-2 minutes. Make sure the cauliflower is well coated in the pickling glaze, then remove the saucepan from the heat and cool the cauliflower.

Cauliflower purée

Put the cauliflower, double cream, milk and a pinch of salt into a saucepan over a medium heat and bring to the boil. Simmer for 5 minutes, stirring from time to time, until the cauliflower is cooked, then remove, drain and blitz the cauliflower in a blender or food processor until you get a smooth purée.

Horseradish cream

Put the cream into a bowl and whip until it starts to thicken, then slowly add the grated horseradish. Add a touch of lemon juice and season with a little salt and a touch of black pepper.

Serving

Take the scallops and oysters out of the fridge. Add some lime juice to the scallops and drain the oysters through a sieve over a small bowl so that you catch their juice. Cut the oysters in half, then make a dressing with 3 tablespoons of the oyster juice and 1 tablespoon of lemon juice. Next, put some of the scallop slices on to your serving plates and lightly season them with sea salt and black pepper. Scatter some of the oysters over the scallops, sprinkle the salmon roe on top of the scallops and add some pickled cauliflower, dill, micro herbs, cauliflower purée and horseradish cream around the plate. Finish with with some of the oyster and lemon juice dressing.

WHITE CHOCOLATE TART, VANILLA ICE CREAM, ENGLISH RASPBERRIES

Bitter chocolate tart is a classic dessert – and this is a spin-off from that, inspired by a white chocolate crème brûlée I once had. The tart works well served with lots of different fruit, so long as the fruit has a bit of acidity to cut through the chocolate's richness. Just change the fruit with the seasons: in autumn, pear and blackberries are perfect, in the summer, blackcurrants or raspberries. I like to have an element of surprise in my dishes as well, so we often finish the dish with smalll 'cannelloni' of ice cream wrapped in a fruit jelly.

SERVES 6-8

For the pastry
500g plain flour
250g unsalted butter
70g caster sugar
4 free-range eggs, lightly beaten
A pinch of table salt

For the tart filling
800ml double cream
450g white chocolate
10 egg yolks
30g caster sugar

For the vanilla ice cream
200ml milk
300ml double cream
½ vanilla pod, split
6 egg yolks
100g caster sugar

For the raspberries
500g ripe English raspberries
100ml sugar syrup
A splash of lemon juice

For the garnish
Caster sugar
A handful of mint

Pastry
Mix the flour and butter together in a food processor until they are like a fine breadcrumb texture. Mix in the salt and sugar, then add 3 of the beaten eggs, one by one, working and kneading as little as possible, but doing just enough to form a dough. Wrap the pastry in clingfilm and rest it for 45 minutes in the fridge.

Preheat the oven to 180C/gas mark 4. Take the pastry out of the fridge, roll it out on a cool, floured surface and line a 25cm tart ring. Rest it again for 1 hour in the fridge, then take it out, line it with ovenproof clingflim and fill it with baking beans, before blind baking it in the oven for 35-40 minutes. Remove from the oven and brush the pastry case with some of the remaining beaten egg to seal it.

Tart filling
Preheat the oven to 110C/gas mark ¼. Put the cream and white chocolate in a saucepan over a low heat, stirring occasionally to make sure the chocolate is incorporated properly as it melts. Meanwhile, mix the egg yolks and sugar together in a bowl. Add the cream and chocolate mixture slowly to the egg yolks and sugar, stirring continuously. Once the mixtures are combined, pass through a fine sieve and then pour the mixture into the pastry case. Place the tart on an oven tray and cook in the oven for about 1 hour. Once it is cooked take it out and put into the fridge to cool for 45 minutes.

Vanilla ice cream
Put the milk and cream in a saucepan, add the vanilla pod and bring to the boil over a medium heat. Meanwhile, mix the egg yolks and sugar together in a bowl, then remove the milk and

cream from the heat and slowly pour the mixture over the egg yolks and sugar, stirring continuously, to make a custard. Once all the ingredients are combined, pour the custard back into the saucepan, put it back on the heat and cook, still stirring, until it begins to thicken. When it is thick enough to coat the back of a wooden spoon, remove from the heat and chill over a bowl of ice. When the custard is cool, churn it in an ice cream machine until it begins to set, then transfer it to a container and put it in the freezer. If you don't have an ice-cream machine, place the mixture in the freezer, taking it out every 30 minutes to stir. The ice cream is ready when it holds its shape after scooping.

Raspberries
Put the sugar syrup in a bowl together with a splash of lemon juice, then mascerate the raspberries in the syrup for 5 minutes.

Serving
Cut the tart into 8 portions. Sprinkle its surface lightly with caster sugar and then caramelise this using a culinary blowtorch. Place the tart on to your serving plates and add some raspberries. Drizzle some of the sugar syrup that the fruit has mascerated in around the plates, then add a scoop of vanilla ice cream and a few sprigs of mint.

MARK HIX

The modern British restaurant scene is thriving and the range of food you can eat has never been greater. Even our national cuisine is undergoing a miraculous revival. Yet when you look for a central soul behind the resurrection of British cooking, one name keeps cropping up. Mark Hix. An understated, 47-year-old man who's never sought celebrity (or notoriety), he's quietly become one of the leading evangelists of this country's traditional, often forgotten, cuisine. However, until relatively recently, apart from his customers only foodies and journalists really knew about him.

That all changed in 2007 when Mark appeared in the second series of BBC2's highly successful *Great British Menu* and ended up cooking two dishes – a version of stargazy pie and a perry jelly with summer fruits – at a culinary-star-studded gala dinner at the British Embassy in Paris. From that day onwards, his fame spread beyond his

Saturday food slot in the *Independent* magazine and his, then, day-job as chef-director of Caprice Holdings, which saw him overseeing some of the most loved and exclusive dining spots in London (including The Ivy and Le Caprice restaurants, both beloved of actors and royalty).

Mark didn't start out his culinary career cooking up-market versions of traditional British dishes, however, even though his credentials are thoroughly British. Nor was he always destined to be a chef. Born in Weymouth in Dorset, Mark muddled his way through school until he made the life-changing decision to opt out of metalwork and transfer to domestic science in his final year. The lessons ignited a latent passion for food and he signed up to train as a chef at Weymouth College. After bagging his basic qualifications, he was soon heading off to London, aged 18, to take up a job as a commis (trainee) chef in the staff canteen at the London Hilton on Park Lane.

It wasn't long before he jumped ship and headed a bit further up Park Lane to work for two of London's great hotel chefs. Initially, Anton Edelman, at the Grosvenor House Hotel, then, two years later, for the revered Anton Mosimann (the chef often credited with introducing nouvelle cuisine to London) at the famous Dorchester Hotel. By the time he left the Dorchester, a further two years down the line, he had moved the next rung up the career ladder, to become a chef de partie.

That position was bettered with his next move to a small restaurant group called Mr Pontac's, where lady luck really rolled a double six for Mark. After just two months working as second-in-command at the group's City eatery, The Candlewick Room, his head chef left and Mark was in charge of his first kitchen. He was just 22 years old. What's more, it was an enviable job. Being in the City meant the dining room only served lunches from Monday to Friday and because of the income level of his customers Mark was able to use the very best ingredients to feed his hungry diners.

But the West End had left its impression on Mark and he yearned for its bright lights and more glamorous clientele. So when, in 1990, his fishmonger, Tony Allen, told Mark he'd heard the position of head chef at West End hotspot Le Caprice was up for grabs Mark put his hat into the ring. Le Caprice was a London legend, a favoured haunt of the rich and famous. After a series of interviews with its owners

Chris Corbin and Jeremy King, Mark got the job – and with it, changed the way he cooked.

His style altered radically from its hybrid of classic and nouvelle cuisine to the sophisticated but simple food that he was to become famous for. Mark gives Chris and Jeremy the credit for this fortuitous evolution because, he says, the duo taught him that the most important thing about being a chef is giving diners the food they, not you, want to eat. At Le Caprice, everything from risottos to sticky toffee pudding was the order of the day.

Overnight Mark became the much-loved chef to the stars, cooking for politicians and princesses alike. Then, in 1990, Corbin and King expanded their business, acquiring the famous Ivy restaurant in Covent Garden. When they reopened it, they did so with Mark as their executive chef. A favourite theatrical-spot in its early life back in the 1920s and 1930s, The Ivy now became the most famous celebrity restaurant of them all and soon both it, and Le Caprice, picked up awards for Mark's West End version of good home cooking.

The accolades came as no surprise to the restaurants' fans. Mark's food evoked a sense of home for nomadic celebrities that was comforting and understandable. His shepherd's pie, fish cakes and burgers were all executed with a sophisticated Hix touch that became the adopted calling card of modern British cuisine.

That calling card was present when the Le Caprice group expanded over the next 17 years to include J Sheekey, Daphne's, Bam Bou, the Rivington Grill, Scott's and Urban Caprice. Mark oversaw them all and by 2007 he was the undisputed King Midas of the London food world. He had won award after award for the restaurants from all sorts of bodies – everyone from food guides Michelin and Harden's to the *Tatler* magazine – written numerous books and even netted a prestigious Glenfiddich award for his writing in the *Independent*.

However, nearly two decades is a long time working for one company if it isn't yours and Mark decided to fly solo. He parted from the Caprice group at the end of 2007 to concentrate on setting up his own restaurants. Typically, while he was getting these off the ground, he took on another project and helped hotelier Rocco Forte revamp the food at Mayfair's much-loved Brown's hotel. Mark's new menu for the hotel's Albemarle restaurant was a delight of long-forgotten British gems like Brown Windsor soup and favourites like whole Dover sole and potted shrimp. At lunchtime a laden carving trolley now roams the room full of joyous pieces of Corwen lamb, Goosnargh duck and Hereford beef. It is all gloriously traditional but done with modern flair.

Mark's own restaurants are, naturally, also skilled at giving a modern-edged sense of the past. The Hix Oyster and Chop House in the buzzy Smithfield district of London and the Hix Oyster and Fish House in Lyme Regis, in his home county of Dorset, both opened in 2008. The former – a bread roll throw from the old Smithfield meat market – occupies a former sausage factory.

Porterhouse and hanger steaks, ox cheek, Barnsley chop, even a nibble of homemade pork scratchings are all typical temptations on its menu: and, in summer, the perry jelly.

It serves oysters, too, of course. But if you can, save these as a treat for when you eat at Hix's Lyme Regis outpost. Perched like a stork's nest above the fishing town's famous Cobb, where the French Lieutenant's Woman pondered her misfortunes, there's no more enticing place than its sun-drenched terrace on which to enjoy a plate of native shellfish, or lobster and chips with a glass of fizz.

And now, there's another restaurant, Hix. It's just opened in London's bohemian Soho area. And its clubby bar, Mark's Brit food and art work by Tracey Emin and Damien Hirst on its walls will undoubtedly score a hit in London's artistic community and with Mark's loyal army of fans.

Those fans have become avid disciples of Mark's plates of praise to British producers and culinary traditions. It's not exaggerating to say that the current celebration of our nation's food owes a lot to him – he's helped us become proud again of our once rubbished cuisine. As Tracey Emin has said: 'Every time I eat with him, it's like coming home.' That, in a nutshell, is the secret to Mark's success.

Hix Oyster and Chop House
37 Greenhill Rents, Cowcross Street, London EC1M 6BN
Phone 020 7017 1930 **www.hixoysterandchophouse.co.uk**
Hix Oyster and Fish House
Cobb Road, Lyme Regis, Dorset DT7 3JP
Phone 01297 446 910 **www.hixoysterandfishhouse.co.uk**
Hix
66-77 Brewer Street, London W1F 9TR
Phone 020 7292 3518 **www.hixsoho.co.uk**

FILLET OF SILVER MULLET WITH COCKLES AND SEA VEGETABLES

Good-quality fish that play in the culinary second division still deserve their place on restaurant menus and fishmongers' slabs. A few years ago I renamed grey mullet, silver mullet (it sounds better and it helps the humble mullet get out there.) A good, large silver mullet that's spent a bit of time at sea instead of muddy rivers and estuaries has a great flavour, on a par with bass.

SERVES 4

*4 x 200g grey mullet fillets from a
    large fish, boned and skinned
200-250g cockles, washed
50ml white wine
120-150g sea vegetables, prepared and
    washed (eg sea purslane, sea beet,
    sea aster)
175g unsalted butter, cut into cubes
Vegetable oil for cooking
Sea salt and freshly ground black
    pepper*

Lightly season the mullet with sea salt and black pepper. Heat a little oil in a large non-stick pan over a medium heat and fry the mullet fillets in it for about 3 minutes on each side, until they are nicely coloured (if the fillets are very thick you will need to finish them in a hot oven for another 5-10 minutes).

Meanwhile, give the cockles a final rinse. Put a large saucepan over a high heat, add the cockles, pour in the white wine and cover immediately with a tight-fitting lid. Cook the cockles until they begin to open, shaking the saucepan from time-to-time and giving them an occasional stir. Once cooked, drain the cockles through a colander over a bowl to catch their cooking liquor, then pour the liquor back into the saucepan. Add the sea vegetables and butter and keep stirring until the butter has melted. Return the cockles to the pan (they will not need seasoning as the sea vegetables will do that) and stir well.

Serving
Carefully remove the mullet from the pan with a fish slice and place it on to your serving plates. Spoon the cockles, sea vegetables and butter over the top.

RABBIT AND CRAYFISH STARGAZY PIE

Like everyone else, I'm keen to do my bit for the environment and sustainability was the thinking behind this pie. Rabbits and crayfish are doing their fair share to ruin crops and destroy other water life, so it makes sense to eat more of them to keep them under control. You might remember seeing me prepare this dish on the *Great British Menu*. It's traditionally served with pilchards peeping out of the pie crust.

SERVES 4

The legs of 4 wild rabbits, boned and
    cut into rough 2cm chunks
2 tablespoons vegetable oil
2 good knobs of butter
1 small onion, finely chopped
2 tablespoons flour
100ml cider
1 litre hot chicken stock
40 freshwater crayfish, cooked
250ml water
3-4 tablespoons double cream
1 tablespoon chopped parsley
Salt and freshly ground black pepper

Note: buy the crayfish live and cook them for 2 minutes in boiling salted water flavoured with fennel seeds, black peppercorns, some sprigs of thyme, star anise and a bay leaf. Once cooked, refresh them in iced water.

For the pastry
225g self-raising flour
1 teaspoon salt
85g shredded beef suet
60g butter, chilled and coarsely grated
2 medium eggs, lightly beaten
150-175ml water

Pie filling
Put the flour and a little salt and pepper in a dish and roll the pieces of rabbit in it. Heat half the vegetable oil in a heavy-based frying pan over a high heat and fry the rabbit in it for 2 minutes until it is lightly coloured. Meanwhile, melt the butter in a medium-sized frying pan over a medium heat and gently cook the onion for 2-3 minutes. Next stir in the 2 tablespoons of flour and gradually add the cider and hot chicken stock, stirring constantly to prevent any lumps forming. Transfer the rabbit to the sauce and simmer for about 1 hour, or until the rabbit is tender.

Meanwhile peel the crayfish, reserving 4 whole ones to finish the dish with, and put the meat to one side. Break up the shells and fry them in the remaining oil in a heavy-based pan. Add about 250ml water and about 200ml of the sauce from the rabbit and simmer gently for 30 minutes.

Blend about a third of the sauce (including the shells) in a liquidiser until smooth and then add it back to the pan. Stir well, then strain all of the sauce through a fine sieve into the rabbit mixture. The rabbit sauce should now be a thick consistency that coats the back of a spoon. If it isn't, remove the rabbit and simmer the sauce until it has thickened, then replace the rabbit in the sauce, add the cream and parsley and add a little more salt and pepper, if necessary. Leave to cool.

Once the rabbit and its sauce have cooled, stir in the crayfish meat and transfer everything to a pie dish, placing a pie bird in the centre.

Pastry
Mix the flour, salt and suet in a bowl. Rub in the butter until you obtain a fine breadcrumb texture.

Mix in 1 egg and about 150-175ml water and bring the mixture together to form a smooth dough, kneading it for 1 minute. Roll the pastry on a floured surface to about 1cm thick and cut out a piece to fit over the pie dish, making sure you cut it about 2cm larger than the pie dish actually measures.

Brush the edges of the pastry with some of the remaining beaten egg and then lay the pastry on top of the pie dish, pressing the egg-washed sides against the rim of the dish. Cut 4 holes around the pastry and insert the tails of the 4 reserved crayfish into them, facing the centre, and brush the top of the pastry with beaten egg so that it will produce a nice golden glaze as it cooks. If you like, you can put a trim around the edge of the dish with a strip of leftover pastry. Leave the pie to rest in a cool place for 30 minutes.

Preheat the oven to 200C/gas mark 6. Put the pie in the oven and bake for about 45 minutes, or until the pastry is golden.

Serving
Serve the pie at the table with greens or mashed root vegetables, such as celeriac or parsnip, and/or small, boiled parsley potatoes.

FISH HOUSE SALAD

As you can probably see, this is my take on a Salade Niçoise. With the recent scares about mercury levels in tuna, the mackerel, being a distant relative of the mighty tuna, may have to step in on a few classic dishes. Cooked in this way, there are similarities in flavour between mackerel and canned tuna generally used for a run-of-the-mill Salade Niçoise. I actually think that mackerel cooked like this tastes better than some of the bog-standard canned tuna.

SERVES 4-6

150ml rapeseed oil
1 small onion, halved and finely
   chopped
2 cloves of garlic, finely sliced
1 small chilli, deseeded and finely
   chopped
½ teaspoon cumin seeds
A few sprigs of thyme
2 tablespoons cider vinegar, plus a
   little more for the dressing
½ lemon, juiced
4 medium or 8 small mackerel fillets
4 free-range hens' eggs
100-120g podded broad beans,
   cooked
200-250g ripe tomatoes
2 little gem lettuces
80-100g green beans, cooked
6-12 new potatoes, cooked in their
   skins and halved or quartered
Salt and freshly ground black pepper

Heat 2 tablespoons of the rapeseed oil in a saucepan over a medium-low heat, add the onions garlic, chilli, cumin seeds and thyme and gently cook for 2-3 minutes, until the onion and garlic are soft and translucent. Add the rest of the rapeseed oil, cider vinegar and lemon juice and bring to a gentle simmer. Meanwhile, lightly season the mackerel fillets with salt. Heat a little more rapeseed oil in a non-stick frying pan over a high heat, add the mackerel, skin-side down first, and fry for 2-3 minutes on each side. Next, drop the fillets into the oil mixture, remove this from the heat and leave to cool.

Bring a small saucepan of water to the boil over a medium heat and semi hard boil the eggs in it for 5 minutes. Cool the eggs under a cold tap, then carefully peel them and rinse under a cold tap again to remove any little bits of shell.

Remove the mackerel from the oil and strain the liquid through a fine sieve into a bowl. Whisk the oil up and add a splash more vinegar to make a dressing.

Serving
Cut the tomatoes into wedges or chunks. Put the little gem leaves together with the beans, potatoes and tomatoes in a bowl, add some dressing and mix. Season with a little salt and pepper, then arrange the salad in serving bowls. Break the mackerel into chunks and arrange on top of the leaves, then halve or quarter the eggs and add these. Finally, spoon over a little more dressing before you serve the salad.

JELLIED HAM HOCK WITH PICCALILLI

Ham hock is one of my favourite cuts. I remember my gran used to cook a couple every week and I can still remember the smell of them simmering on the stove top – and the soup she used to make from the cooking liquid which seemed to last for days. This dish is a great way to use some of those bits that get left on the hock. Just remember, you need to make the piccalilli a week ahead of the rest of the dish – and if you can't get ham hock use a ham joint instead.

SERVES 6-8

For the piccalilli
1 medium cucumber, halved lengthwise and deseeded with a teaspoon
½ large head of cauliflower, cut into small florets and then each halved
1 onion, roughly chopped
1 tablespoon salt
150g caster sugar
65g English mustard
1½ teaspoon ground turmeric
1 small chilli, deseeded and finely chopped
150ml malt vinegar
125ml white wine vinegar
1 level tablespoon cornflour
150ml water

1 x 1kg ham hock (or 1 x 700g ham joint), soaked overnight in cold water if very salty
A few sprigs of thyme
1 bay leaf
2 medium onions, quartered
3 celery stalks
10 black peppercorns
10g gelatine (about 4 leaves)
2 tablespoons chopped parsley

For the piccalilli
You need to make the piccalilli at least one week ahead of the rest of the dish. Begin by cutting the cucumber in ½ lengthwise again, then cut it one final time into 1cm pieces. Put the pieces in a dish with the cauliflower florets and onion, then sprinkle the salt over everything, leave for 1 hour then rinse the cucumber and vegetables well in cold water and drain them in a colander.

Put the sugar, mustard, turmeric, chilli and the 2 vinegars in a saucepan, give them a mix and then bring them to the boil over a medium heat and simmer for 2-3 minutes. Meanwhile, mix the cornflour with 150ml water, then whisk it into the vinegar mixture and continue to simmer gently for another 5 minutes. Mix the hot liquid with the vegetables and leave the mixture to cool. Once cold, decant it into sterilised Kilner jars. It will keep up to 6 months.

For the ham
Put the ham into a large saucepan together with the rest of the ingredients – but minus the gelatine and parsley – cover with water and bring to the boil and simmer for about 2 hours, until the ham is tender (the cooking time may vary according to the cut and size of the ham). Next, remove the ham from its stock and put it on a plate to cool. Skim off any fat from the stock, then measure out 350ml of it into a clean saucepan and return to a very low heat to keep warm.

If you are using ham hock soak 3 leaves of gelatine in a bowl of cold water for 1-2 minutes until soft – if you are using another cut of ham, then you will need the extra gelatine leaf. Once it has softened, remove the gelatine and squeeze out the excess water before adding it to the hot cooking liquor, together with the parsley. Stir until the gelatine has dissolved then leave the mixture somewhere to cool, but do not let it set.

Meanwhile, cut the ham into rough 1cm cubes, removing any fat, and put it into a bowl. Mix in a little of the cooled stock and pack the mixture into either a suitable-sized terrine mould or a similarly shaped rectangular container. Top up with the remaining stock (you may have some extra left which you can discard). Cover with clingfilm and leave to set in the fridge overnight.

Serving
Dip the terrine into a bowl of boiling water briefly (about 15 seconds) and then turn it upside down on to a chopping board to turn out. Cut it into 2cm thick slices – or scoop it straight from the mould with a large spoon – then pop it on some plates with a little of the piccalilli and serve with some crusty bread.

ELDERFLOWER JELLY WITH RASPBERRIES

Jellies are great fun to make and aren't just for kids' tea parties. We make all sorts of jellies throughout the year in the restaurants, from simple elderflower based ones to ones using perry and even absinth. You can use single fruits or a mixture to set in the jelly and if you are feeling really extravagant try a champagne and wild strawberry jelly. Some thick Jersey cream or a scoop of vanilla ice cream are the only 'right' things to serve the jelly with.

SERVES 4

500ml water
½ lemon, juiced
150g caster sugar
15g gelatine (about 5 leaves)
100ml elderflower cordial
100-120g raspberries

Put the water and lemon juice into a saucepan and bring to the boil over a medium heat. Add the sugar, stirring until it has dissolved, and then remove from the heat. Meanwhile, soak the gelatine leaves in a shallow bowl of cold water for 1-2 minutes until they soften, then remove them and squeeze the excess water from the leaves and add them to the lemon syrup. Stir until the gelatine has dissolved. Add the elderflower cordial, then put the liquid jelly somewhere cool but do not let it set.

Fill some individual jelly moulds or one large one with half of the raspberries, then pour in half of the cooled, but not set, jelly. Put the mould(s) in the fridge for 1 hour to set, then top up the moulds with the rest of the raspberries and unset jelly. This allows the raspberries to stay suspended in the jelly and not float to the top. Return the mould(s) to the fridge to set the jelly again.

Serving
Take the mould(s) out of the fridge and turn out the jellies on to your serving plates – or plate if you've made a large jelly – and serve it with thick Jersey or organic vanilla ice cream.

WILL HOLLAND

There are places in Britain that seem to just conjure up good restaurants. Bray in Berkshire is one and Ludlow in the Welsh Marches is another. Sheltered beneath the Clee Hills in Shropshire in a curve of the River Teme, Ludlow has been a gastronomic hot spot for 15 years, at one time playing host to three highly acclaimed and accoladed restaurants. Quite what magic lurks in the town to make it such a foodie haven is a mystery. Maybe it's in the water that flows in the Teme. Maybe it's just the fact that Ludlow's a damn good market town surrounded by farmland that gives up some wondrous produce.

Whatever the reason, Ludlow is a gourmand's town. The days when Shaun Hill turned out superlatively simple

plates of food at the Merchant House, Claude Bosi challenged the taste buds at Hibiscus and Chris Bradley served consistently brilliant menus at Mr Underhill's at Dinham Weir may be past (the two former chefs moved on a few years ago, Chris has just announced his retirement), but a new culinary era is dawning. And it's happening on the site of what was once Hibiscus. Only it's not called Hibiscus now, it's called La Bécasse: and the new magician in town is a certain Will Holland.

Will opened the restaurant in July 2007 for chef-restaurateur Alan Murchison, who already owned the renowned L'Ortolan restaurant in Shinfield, Berkshire, where Will had been Alan's second-in-command for three years. Alan had been anxious to expand his empire for a while and understood the need for a talented chef like Will to flex his wings on his own, so when Claude Bosi put the site of his Ludlow restaurant on the market he jumped at the chance to buy it. And that's how La Bécasse was born.

La Bécasse is the French name for woodcock, the small game bird with the highly prized liver. The bird's a special treat and so is the restaurant that bears its name. It lies at the bottom of a steep hill and its small, simple frontage hides an Aladdin's cave of culinary treasure within. On arrival (if it's warm enough), guests are led to a wisteria-covered courtyard for a glass of fizz and a simple appetizer – and it's at this stage that you begin to suspect that there is, in the kitchen, a chef who is above the ordinary. No run-of-the-mill cook is going to send out something like a simple trio of curried popcorn, guacamole and sugar coated cashews. The nibbles awaken your taste buds and set the tone for Will's style of cooking. His rule is salty, sweet and sour on every plate.

That rule makes for some imaginative flavour and texture pairings, which in less skilled hands than Will's could be disastrous. But at 29-years-old, he's both experienced enough to achieve his culinary ideas and young enough to be blissfully unaccustomed to the notion of failing. Judging by the reaction he gets from his diners, failure is something he won't ever get close to, though. The fact is, Will's food is immaculate.

You can't get more perfect than a beautifully pan-fried piece of dense and juicy halibut served with smoked sausage, a scattering of fresh honeycomb (sweet and crunchy), delicate curried lime emulsion and three versions of cauliflower (puréed, battered and deep-fried and shaved thinly carpaccio-style). The craft in the dish is amazing; it sounds complicated but its elements are in balance with each other and it eats delicately. Another dish of fresh crab with tomato and coconut consommé with shavings of coconut could easily become rich and out of kilter, but Will's culinary precision and unerring palate mean that its bold flavours almost lift you off your seat with pleasure when you taste it.

Will is obviously a talented chef, but he wasn't born with the craft skills he now has. They have been honed and perfected over the years in some top-notch kitchens under the eyes of some classy mentors. Before he got to a professional kitchen, though, his culinary baptism, at the age of 14, was through a Saturday job at a local butcher's in his home city of Bristol. He kept the job going while studying catering at the City of Bristol College, at the same time getting experience in some of Bristol's best restaurants. All of which stood him in good stead when he graduated and landed a plum job with Gary Jones (now Raymond Blanc's executive chef at Le Manoir aux Quat'Saisons in Oxfordshire) at the well-regarded Homewood Park hotel in Bath. From there he moved on to West Sussex's hugely respected Gravetye Manor hotel to train under Roux-alumni Mark Raffan before, finally, hooking up with Alan Murchison at L'Ortolan in 2004.

Alan was immediately impressed with Will's dedication and skill and knew he had a chef whom he could trust when he was ready to grow his restaurant empire. So, when he found the Ludlow site, there was only one name in the frame. His faith in Will wasn't misplaced. La Bécasse has already picked up the accolade that all chefs dream about, a Michelin star. Restaurant critics who have eaten Will's food have raved about it – the *Daily Telegraph's* Jasper Gerard called his meal, 'one of the most technically accomplished yet sensual lunches I've enjoyed in ages.'

Of course, Will's wonderful food isn't the only story at La Bécasse. Before the restaurant opened, the whole building underwent a refurbishment. Being a listed building meant that certain things, like the wood-panelled walls and the basic structure of small, individual spaces in the dining room, had to be retained. But plush new carpets, new crockery and extra tables were installed; what was once a bar at the entrance to the building was transformed into a

cosy eating space and the courtyard was given a facelift and opened up for guests. It all makes for a quirky and unique layout, one which means you get a thoroughly different experience each time you dine at La Bécasse.

At the centre of any experience, though, is Will's food which constantly surprises and challenges you. He's expert at pinpointing the tastiest part of an animal in his hot dishes and skilled at making the end to any meal memorable with intricate, fun desserts like liquorice panna

cotta and yoghurt sabayon served with a little fresh carrot sorbet. Don't miss, either, a very special spice poached pineapple with homemade ginger bread cake and a saffron risotto. And whatever you do, don't ever tell Will his dishes are nice. 'I hate that word. As a kid my mother would tell us off for using it. What does it mean? Nothing.'

That makes him sound a little arrogant, but Will is not a conceited man. He knows that it is dangerous to rest on your laurels if you want to make your mark on the world – and

the only way to do that, is to get consistency in his cooking; and the only way to achieve that is by hard work. There is a saying that goes, 'never trust a thin chef' – but that should change to, 'never trust a tanned, rested chef'. Will has the pallor of a hard-working chef. If you haven't eaten in Ludlow since the big guns left, you're missing a trick.

La Bécasse
17 Corve Street, Ludlow, Shropshire SY8 1DA
Phone 01584 872 325 **www.labecasse.co.uk**

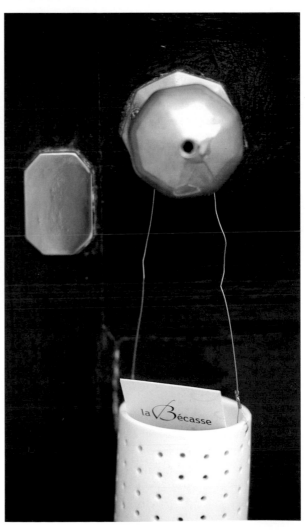

GOAT'S CHEESE MOUSSE, BEETROOT AND RASPBERRY PUREE, PAIN D'EPICE, BALSAMIC JELLY, RASPBERRY AND HAZELNUT DRESSING

It is important to use a well-flavoured goat's cheese when you make the mousse in this dish. I like to use Ragstone – it's made by Neal's Yard Creamery in Herefordshire. Beetroot and raspberry may sound an odd pairing for the purée but they are surprisingly similar in taste and work well together. And the dish has a kick of acidity from the balsamic vinegar jelly which also helps to bring all the flavours together on the plate. I like to use Vege-Gel instead of gelatine for the jelly – you can buy it in large supermarkets and health food shops, or on-line.

SERVES 4

For the pain d'epice
120g rye flour
120g plain flour
20g baking powder
1 teaspoon ground ginger
1 teaspoon ground cinnamon
1 teaspoon ground star anise
250g honey
140ml milk
3 medium eggs
50g caster sugar

For the goat's cheese mousse
250g Ragstone goat's cheese
1 teaspoon white truffle oil
50ml double cream

For the beetroot and raspberry purée
700g beetroot, peeled and finely
  chopped
1 litre water
150ml red wine vinegar
75g sugar
20g salt
500g raspberries, puréed

For the baby beetroot carpaccio
4 baby beetroots, peeled and tops left
  on
500ml beetroot cooking liquor (see
  above)
35g sugar

For the raspberry and hazelnut dressing
10g Dijon mustard
50ml raspberry vinegar
50ml hazelnut oil

For the balsamic vinegar jelly
125g balsamic vinegar
1 heaped teaspoon Vege-Gel

For the garnish
4 teaspoons hazelnuts, toasted and
  crushed
20 raspberries
28 pea shoots

Pain d'epice
Preheat the oven to 165C/gas mark 3. Line an 18cm square cake tin with greaseproof paper.

Sift the flours, baking powder and spices into a large bowl. Warm the honey and milk in a large saucepan over a medium heat until the honey is fully dissolved. Remove from heat. In another bowl, whisk the eggs and sugar until they are pale and fluffy. Add the honey and milk mixture to the dry ingredients and mix until smooth and then fold in the egg and sugar mixture. Do not over mix. Pour into the prepared cake tin, place in the oven and bake for 1 hour. When cooked, remove the tin from the oven and allow the cake to cool in it. Once it is cool, take the cake out of the tin and leave overnight, uncovered, to dry out: this will aid slicing. Using a serrated bread knife, slice the cake –

or pain d'epice – as thinly as possible. Then, using a small round pastry cutter, cut out 40 discs of the pain d'epice. Gather up all the pain d'epice trimmings and blitz them in a food processor to produce fine crumbs. Place the discs and crumbs on a baking tray and dry in the oven on the lowest setting overnight or until crisp. Store in a cool, dry place.

Goat's cheese mousse
Blend the goat's cheese and oil in a food processor until smooth. Add the cream and blend until fully incorporated, but be careful not to over whip the mixture. Divide the mixture into 15g balls, place on a plate, cover with clingfilm and put in the fridge.

For the beetroot and raspberry purée
Put the beetroot, water, vinegar, sugar and salt in a saucepan over a high heat, bring to the boil, and cook rapidly for 15-20 minutes until the beetroot is soft. Remove from the heat and drain the cooked beetroot over a bowl to catch the cooking liquor. Place the puréed raspberries in a clean saucepan over a medium heat. Bring them to a gentle simmer and reduce their volume by half. Put the raspberry purée reduction into a liquidiser with 300g of the cooked beetroot. Blend together until smooth.

Baby beetroot carpaccio
Using a mandolin or sharp knife, slice the baby beetroot lengthways very thinly. Next, place them in a saucepan with the beetroot liquor and sugar and cook over a high heat for 1-2 minutes. Remove and allow to cool in the liquor.

(Continued on page 96)

(Continued from page 94)

Raspberry and hazelnut dressing
Whisk the mustard and vinegar together in a small bowl. Slowly add the oil, whisking continuously until you get an emulsified dressing.

Balsamic vinegar jelly
Put the vinegar and Vege-Gel in a small saucepan over a high heat and bring to the boil rapidly, whisking continuously, then pour the liquid into a small shallow tray and put in the fridge to set. Once it is set, cut the jelly into 5mm cubes.

Serving
Place 3 lines of beetroot and raspberry purée on each plate, then sprinkle over the hazelnuts. Roll the goat's cheese balls in the pain d'epice crumbs and sandwich each ball between 2 pain d'epice discs. Place 5 sandwiches on each plate, along with 5 raspberries, 7 pea shoots, 7 balsamic vinegar jelly cubes and 5 baby beetroot carpaccio slices. Finally, finish the dish with a drizzle of the raspberry and hazelnut dressing.

BONED AND ROLLED RABBIT SADDLE, SMOKED BACON, CARAMELISED CELERY, PRUNE, CAPER AND LEMON CONFIT SALSA

This dish has some classic ingredient matches for the rabbit, but the more unusual inclusion of capers and lemon confit seems to really boost all their flavours to a new level. Get your butcher to bone and roll the rabbit saddles for you, but if this is not an option, then create the dish using a different cut of rabbit – maybe braise some rabbit leg or loin instead.

SERVES 4

For the caramelised celery
1 head of celery
100ml olive oil
10g salt
10g sugar

For the prune purée
100g pitted prunes
Water, enough to cover the prunes

For the lemon confit
1 lemon, zested with a vegetable peeler
   to obtain strips
Water, enough to cover the lemon zest
100g sugar
100g white wine vinegar

For the celery, prune and caper salsa
100g celery
25g pitted prunes
25g small capers
½ lemon, juiced (use the lemon from
   the confit)
½ teaspoon salt

For the rabbit
4 rabbit saddles, boned and rolled
20 thin slices pancetta
25g unsalted butter

Caramelised celery
Preheat the oven to 100C/gas mark 1. Trim the head of the celery and lightly trim its root, so that the heart end remains intact and the head measures 15cm in length. Cut the celery lengthways so that you have four slices that resemble the shape of flames, then place these on a roasting tray and cover with the olive oil, salt and sugar. Cover with kitchen foil and roast in the oven for 6 hours or until the celery is tender, but still holds its shape, then remove it from the oven. Put the celery to one side, reserving the oil to fry it in later.

Prune purée
Place the prunes in a small saucepan and just cover with water. Bring to the boil over a medium heat and gently poach the prunes until they are soft. Drain the prunes over a bowl to catch their cooking liquor, then place them in a liquidiser and blend until the prunes are smooth, using as much or as little of the cooking liquor as required to obtain a purée.

Lemon confit
Cut the strips of lemon zest into fine matchsticks, then place them in a saucepan and cover with cold water. Bring to the boil over a medium heat, then refresh the zest, immediately, in iced water. Repeat the process a further two times. Next, take the blanched lemon zest and place it in a saucepan with the sugar and vinegar. Bring to the boil over a medium heat, then turn the heat down and gently simmer for 1 hour or until the lemon peel is soft, but still holds its shape. Remove from the heat and strain through a fine sieve.

Celery, prune and caper salsa
Peel the celery using a vegetable peeler and discard the 'strings'. Finely chop the celery and prunes and then mix with the remaining ingredients.

Rabbit
Preheat the oven to 175C/gas mark 4. Wrap each boned and rolled rabbit saddle with five slices of pancetta. The pancetta needs to run around the saddle evenly, with the slices parallel to each other – this will help to keep the saddle together once it is cooked. Finally, tie the saddle and pancetta together with thin butcher's twine. Heat a heavy-based metal-handled pan on the stove and add in the butter. When the butter starts to froth, carefully add the pancetta-wrapped rabbit and fry on all sides until the pancetta turns a light brown colour, then place the saucepan in the oven and roast the rabbit for 10-12 minutes. Remove the rabbit from the oven and take off the string from each saddle, then leave the rabbit in a warm place to rest for 6 minutes.

Meanwhile, put the oil left over from caramelising the celery into a frying pan over a medium heat and when it is hot add the celery and fry until it is deep brown in colour.

Serving
Put 2 lines of prune purée on each of your serving plates, followed by a piece of caramelised celery. Carve each rabbit saddle into 5 slices and arrange on top of the celery. Spoon the salsa over and around the rabbit and finish with a sprinkling of lemon confit.

POACHED MALLARD BREAST, CONFIT LEG CANNELLONI, ROOT VEGETABLE CASSOULET, TRUFFLE AND TARRAGON CONSOMME

Wild ducks are very different from their farmed counterparts and have a much tougher meat structure and skin. This means that they need to be prepared and cooked in a different way. I'm not a fan of roasting wild duck or using any form of cooking involving high temperatures. I prefer to gently slow cook them, either by poaching or confiting them. This dish uses a number of different cuts of the duck for my take on a classic French cassoulet. We butcher our own birds, but you can get your butcher to do it for you if you prefer.

SERVES 4

For the duck
2 wild mallard ducks

For the mallard confit
4 mallard duck legs
65g coarse sea salt
1 tablespoon cracked black
  peppercorns
4 sprigs of thyme
4 garlic cloves, roughly chopped
4 bay leaves
4 tarragon stalks
Duck skin
Duck fat

For the truffle and tarragon consommé
1 onion, roughly chopped
1 carrot, roughly chopped
1 leek, roughly chopped
1 stick of celery, roughly chopped
1 bulb of garlic, peeled and roughly
  chopped
2 mallard duck carcasses
1 sprig of fresh thyme
1 bay leaf
6 black peppercorns
6 juniper berries
45g mallard breast trimmings

4 egg whites
½ bunch of fresh tarragon
30g Périgord truffle, finely chopped

For the mallard mousse
90g mallard duck breast trimmings
½ egg white
250ml whipping cream
1½ teaspoons salt
130g mallard duck confit (see above)

For the tarragon pasta
125g pasta flour
28g tarragon leaves
13ml olive oil
4 egg yolks

For the garnish
60 white haricot beans, cooked
8 cubes of swede, blanched and
  measuring 1.5cm x 1.5cm
8 cubes of turnip, blanched and
  measuring 1.5cm x 1.5cm
8 cubes of carrot, blanched and
  measuring 1.5cm x 1.5cm
8 cubes of celeriac, blanched and
  measuring 1.5cm x 1.5cm
4 thin slices of Morteau sausage
20 thin slices of Toulouse sausage
Truffle (reserved from the consommé)
¼ bunch of tarragon, finely chopped
Salt

Duck preparation
Remove the legs, skin and fat from each duck and reserve for the confit. Next, remove the breasts and take out any shot. Cut each breast into a 60g portion. Reserve the breast trimmings for the consommé and mousse. Clean and scrape the cavity of the ducks. Chop the carcasses into small pieces and rinse well under running cold water to remove any excess blood then put to one side to use later in the consommé.

Mallard confit
Put the mallard legs on to a tray and season generously with the coarse sea salt and cracked black peppercorns. Add the thyme, garlic, bay leaves and tarragon. Cover with clingfilm and put in the fridge for 24 hours. The next day, preheat the oven to 80C/gas mark ¼. Remove any excess marinade from the duck legs and place them in a small ovenproof dish with the skin and enough fat to cover the legs. Cover the dish with a lid or some kitchen foil and place in the oven to cook for 12-15 hours, or until the leg meat is tender and comes away from the bone with no resistance. Remove the legs from the fat, remove the skin from each leg and flake the meat off the bone. Discard the leg bones and skin. Strain the duck fat through a fine sieve and keep to use in another dish.

Truffle and tarragon consommé
Put the onion, carrot, leek, celery and garlic in a large saucepan together with the mallard carcasses, thyme, bay leaf, black peppercorns and juniper berries. Cover with cold water, place over a medium heat and bring to the boil. Using a ladle, remove any

(Continued on page 100)

(Continued from page 98)

impurities that may have risen to the surface, then turn the heat down and simmer gently for 6 hours. Remove from the heat and strain the mallard stock through a fine sieve into a clean saucepan. Discard all the bones and vegetables. Blend the breast trimmings (reserved from when you butchered the ducks) and egg white together in a food processor, and whisk this mixture into the hot mallard stock. (Don't forget you need to make sure you have 90g of breast trimmings for the mousse – so don't use all of them at this stage).

Put the stock back over a low heat and simmer gently for 15-20 minutes. As the meat and egg white mixture cooks, they will attract any impurities floating to the top, and leave a crystal clear consommé underneath. Gently pour the consommé through a fine sieve, lined with a muslin cloth, into a clean saucepan. Discard the impurities and season the consommé with salt, then add the tarragon sprigs and truffle and leave them to infuse until the consommé is cold before removing and discarding the tarragon. Remove the truffle and keep the truffle to dress the dish with when you serve it.

Mallard mousse
Place the mallard breast trimmings in a covered container and freeze for 45 minutes to firm the meat, then place the trimmings in a food processor with the egg white and blend until smooth. Gradually add the cream while the food processor is running, but do not over mix. Finally add the salt, then remove the mousse from the food processor and place it in a bowl together with the flaked mallard confit. Mix well and transfer the

finished mousse to a piping bag fitted with a 2cm diameter nozzle.

Lay out a piece of clingfilm flat and pipe a 9cm sausage of the mousse onto the middle. Using the clingfilm to support the sausage, roll it up and tie both ends. Repeat the process until you have 4 sausages in total. Place the sausage in a saucepan, cover with water and bring the water up to 80C using a digital temperature probe to monitor the temperature. Poach the sausages for 10 minutes. Drain off the hot water and refresh the sausages, immediately, in iced water. Once cold, remove the sausages from their clingfilm skins.

Tarragon pasta
Place all the ingredients in a food processor and blend using the pulse button, until a ball of dough forms. Remove the dough and knead it by hand until smooth, then wrap it in clingfilm and put it in the fridge for 1 hour. Once it has rested, roll the dough using a pasta machine, until you have achieved sheets of pasta which are thin, but not transparent. Put a large saucepan of salted water over a medium high heat and bring to the boil, then blanch the pasta sheets in it for 10 seconds. When you take them out, refresh them immediately in iced water. Cut the pasta sheets into 4 rectangles, measuring 9cm x 17cm.

Mallard breasts and garnish
Place half the consommé in a saucepan and bring up to a temperature of 60C. Add the 4 mallard breast portions, ensuring they are totally submerged in the liquid, and poach for 25 minutes. Monitor the temperature of the consommé as it needs to stay as close to 60C as possible. Remove the poached breasts and put them to one

side to keep warm. Turn up the heat and bring the consommé to a gentle simmer. Add the white haricot beans, root vegetables, pasta sheets and all the sausage slices and warm through for 2 minutes, but do not cook. When you are ready to serve the dish, remove the ingredients with a slotted spoon and discard the consommé.

Serving
Warm the remaining half of the consommé. Meanwhile, lay the 4 pasta rectangles on a flat service. Place a mallard sausage along the long edge of one of the rectangles and roll the pasta around the sausage until it is completely wrapped. You will have some of the sheet spare in a 'tail', so to speak, but do not cut this off. Repeat the process with the remaining 3 sausages. Put the pasta-wrapped sausages into your serving bowls (large soup dishes are best) so that the 'tail' of the pasta juts out and gives you a flat base on which to put the rest of the dish on. On each flat piece of pasta place 1 slice of Morteau sausage and 5 slices of Toulouse sausage, followed by a chequerboard of the root vegetable dice, allowing 2 pieces of each vegetable per portion. Carve each mallard breast portion into 5 slices and season with salt. Position the breasts on top of the root vegetables. Mix the warmed white haricot beans with the chopped truffle reserved from making the consommé and the tarragon, then spoon this over and around the mallard breast. Pour some of the warmed consommé around the duck, or serve in a small sauce jug on the side.

PARMESAN CRUSTED SCALLOPS, CURRIED PARSNIP AND SPINACH, LIME EMULSION

Light spicing works really well against the subtle sweetness of scallops and parsnips in this dish. I've introduced it to the crispy Parmesan coating for the scallops and it's also present in my version of the classic Indian dish *saag aloo*, in which I've replaced the traditional potato element with parsnip. The sweet and sour lime emulsion just gives a little bit of acidity to the scallops, cuts the richness of the parsnip and brings a real zing to the dish. Make sure you use diver-caught scallops – they're better and it's a sustainable way of fishing them.

SERVES 4

For the curried parsnip and spinach
700g parsnips, finely chopped
35ml vegetable oil
100g shallots, finely chopped
1 garlic clove
1 teaspoon garam masala
1 teaspoon Madras curry powder
¼ teaspoon turmeric
50g baby spinach, washed
Salt

For the lime emulsion
50ml olive oil
6 limes, juiced and 2 of them zested
50g sugar

For the scallops and curried Parmesan crust
50g 24-month aged Parmesan, finely grated
½ teaspoon mild Madras curry powder
¼ teaspoon garam masala
¼ teaspoon turmeric
½ teaspoon salt
12 large diver-caught scallops, cleaned, roe removed and placed on absorbent kitchen paper
Salt for seasoning

Curried parsnip and spinach
Put a saucepan of lightly salted water over a medium heat and bring to the boil. Add the parsnips and cook for about 5 minutes, until tender but still slightly firm. Remove the parsnips from the heat, drain and put to one side. Heat the vegetable oil in a large saucepan, again over a medium heat, and fry the shallots and garlic in it for 4-5 minutes until soft. Add the spices and continue to cook for 1 minute. Next add the parboiled parsnip and continue to cook for another few minutes. Remove the saucepan from the heat, add the spinach and use the residual heat to wilt the spinach. Season with salt and keep warm.

Lime emulsion
Combine the oil and lime zest in a bowl and leave to infuse for about 15 minutes then strain the oil through a fine sieve. Meanwhile place the lime juice and sugar in a small saucepan over a medium heat and bring to the boil, then simmer gently and reduce until 100g syrup remains. Remove from the heat and, using a hand blender, blitz the lime syrup, then slowly add in the lime oil until the mixture is fully emulsified. Put the lime emulsion into a squeezy bottle and refrigerate until required.

Scallops and curried Parmesan crust
Combine the Parmesan, curry powder, garam masala, turmeric and ½ teaspoon of salt in a bowl. Dab one side of each scallop into the mixture, ensuring a good and even coating. Put a heavy-based non-stick frying pan over a low heat and once warm (but not too hot) place the scallops, cheese crust-side down, into the dry pan. Lightly season the scallops with salt and continue to cook over a medium heat for 2-3 minutes, until the Parmesan is golden brown and crispy. Turn the scallops on to their plain sides, remove the pan from the heat and leave to rest for 1-2 minutes. The residual heat should be enough to finish cooking the scallops.

Serving
Divide the curried parsnip and spinach between your serving plates. Place three scallops per portion on top of this, with the crust side facing upwards. Drizzle a little lime emulsion over and around the scallops.

DARK CHOCOLATE TART, CARAMEL SAUCE, BANANA BREAD, SALTED PARSNIP ICE CREAM

Chocolate and caramel is a well-known flavour match, but banana and parsnip? It works, though. I stumbled upon the idea one morning in the kitchen when I was eating a banana for breakfast while preparing parsnips. The smell coming from the raw parsnips while I had the banana in my mouth sent my brain crazy, so I tried them out together and that was the beginning of this dish. The banana bread recipe comes from the chef Mark Raffan, a former boss of mine. He's served it for many years as part of an amazing afternoon tea at Gravetye Manor, near East Grinstead, West Sussex.

SERVES 4

For the parsnip ice cream
325g parsnip, roughly chopped
500ml milk
75ml whipping cream
5 egg yolks
100g caster sugar

For the banana jelly
125ml Crème de Bananes liqueur
1 heaped teaspoon Vege-Gel
1 leaf of edible gold leaf (optional)

For the tart base
50g icing sugar
75g unsalted butter, softened
125g plain flour
1 egg yolk

For the tart filling
100g dark chocolate (72% cocoa solids)
100ml double cream
40ml milk
25g egg (about ½ an egg), lightly beaten

For the banana bread
200g peeled over-ripe bananas
200g caster sugar
1½ eggs, beaten
1 teaspoon black treacle
200g plain flour
20g desiccated coconut
1 tablespoon baking powder
A pinch of salt
40ml milk
20ml vegetable oil
80g dark chocolate (72% cocoa solids), roughly chopped

For the caramel and banana sauce
75g sugar
15g Crème de Bananes liqueur
1 dessertspoon lemon juice
160g double cream

For the garnish
Cornish sea salt crystals

Parsnip ice cream
Put the parsnips, milk and cream in a saucepan, put on its lid then bring to the boil over a medium heat and gently cook the parsnips until they are tender. Drain through a fine sieve over a bowl and keep the milk and cream. Place the parsnips in a liquidiser and blend until smooth. Reserve 25g of the parsnip purée for dressing the plates. Next, combine the egg yolks and sugar together in a large bowl. Gradually add in the reserved milk and cream, whisking continuously. Once the mixture is well incorporated, return it to the saucepan and cook gently over a low heat, stirring continuously, until the mixture resembles the consistency of a pouring cream. Remove from the heat, add the rest of the parsnip purée and mix thoroughly. Place the mixture into an ice-cream machine and churn according to the manufacturer's instructions. If you don't have an ice-cream machine, place the mixture in the freezer, taking it out every 30 minutes to stir. The ice cream is ready when it holds its shape after scooping. Once ready, store it in a covered container in the freezer until needed.

Banana jelly
Put all the ingredients for the jelly in a small saucepan and bring to the boil rapidly, over a high heat, while whisking continuously. Remove from heat and pour into a shallow 8cm x 5cm tray and put in the fridge to set. When the jelly is firm, cut it into 5mm cubes.

(Continued on page 104)

(Continued from page 102)

Chocolate tart

Preheat the oven to 165C/gas mark 3. Put the icing sugar and butter together in a large bowl and beat until they're light and creamy. Add the flour and mix until fully incorporated. Finally, add the egg yolk. Bring the ingredients together to form a pastry dough. Wrap the dough in clingfilm and allow to rest for 1 hour in the fridge. Remove from fridge and roll out the dough pastry to a thickness of 3mm. Cut into rectangles, measuring 4cm x 8cm. Place on a baking tray, and bake in the oven for 8-10 minutes or until light golden in colour.

Put the chocolate in a bowl, then place the bowl over a pan of gently simmering water (making sure the water doesn't touch the bowl) and melt the chocolate over a medium heat, whisking continuously. Remove from the heat. Put the egg into another large bowl and meanwhile put the cream and milk in a saucepan over a medium heat and bring to the boil, then pour the hot cream and milk onto the egg, whisking as you do so. Finally, whisk the melted chocolate into the custard mixture. Place a cooked sable biscuit rectangle into the bottom of four 4cm x 8cm rectangular moulds, then fill them with the chocolate mixture and put in the fridge to set for 1-2 hours.

Banana bread

Preheat oven to 165C/gas mark 3. Line an 18cm square cake tin with greaseproof paper. Place the bananas, sugar, eggs and treacle into a large mixing bowl and whisk them together using an electric whisk until pale and fluffy. Fold in the flour, desiccated coconut, baking powder and salt. Add the milk, vegetable oil and chocolate and mix everything together, making sure all the ingredients are evenly incorporated. Pour the mixture into the prepared tin, place it in the oven and bake for 1 hour until the cake is golden. Remove from the oven, take it out of the tin and allow it to cool, then remove the crusts and cut the cake into 2cm dice.

Caramel and banana sauce

Place the sugar in a heavy-based saucepan over a medium-high heat to make a caramel. When the sugar turns into a dark caramel and bubbles, remove the saucepan from the heat and add in the remaining ingredients very carefully, otherwise the mixture may spit. Return the saucepan to the heat and slowly bring the sauce to the boil. Remove from the heat and cool down.

Serving

Drizzle the caramel and banana sauce over your serving plates. Remove the chocolate tarts from the moulds by gently warming them with a blow torch or by using a small knife after warming its blade in hot water. Place 1 tart on each plate, followed by 5 cubes of banana bread, 5 cubes of banana jelly and a few dots of parsnip purée. Finally, add a scoop of parsnip ice cream and a scattering of sea salt crystals to each plate.

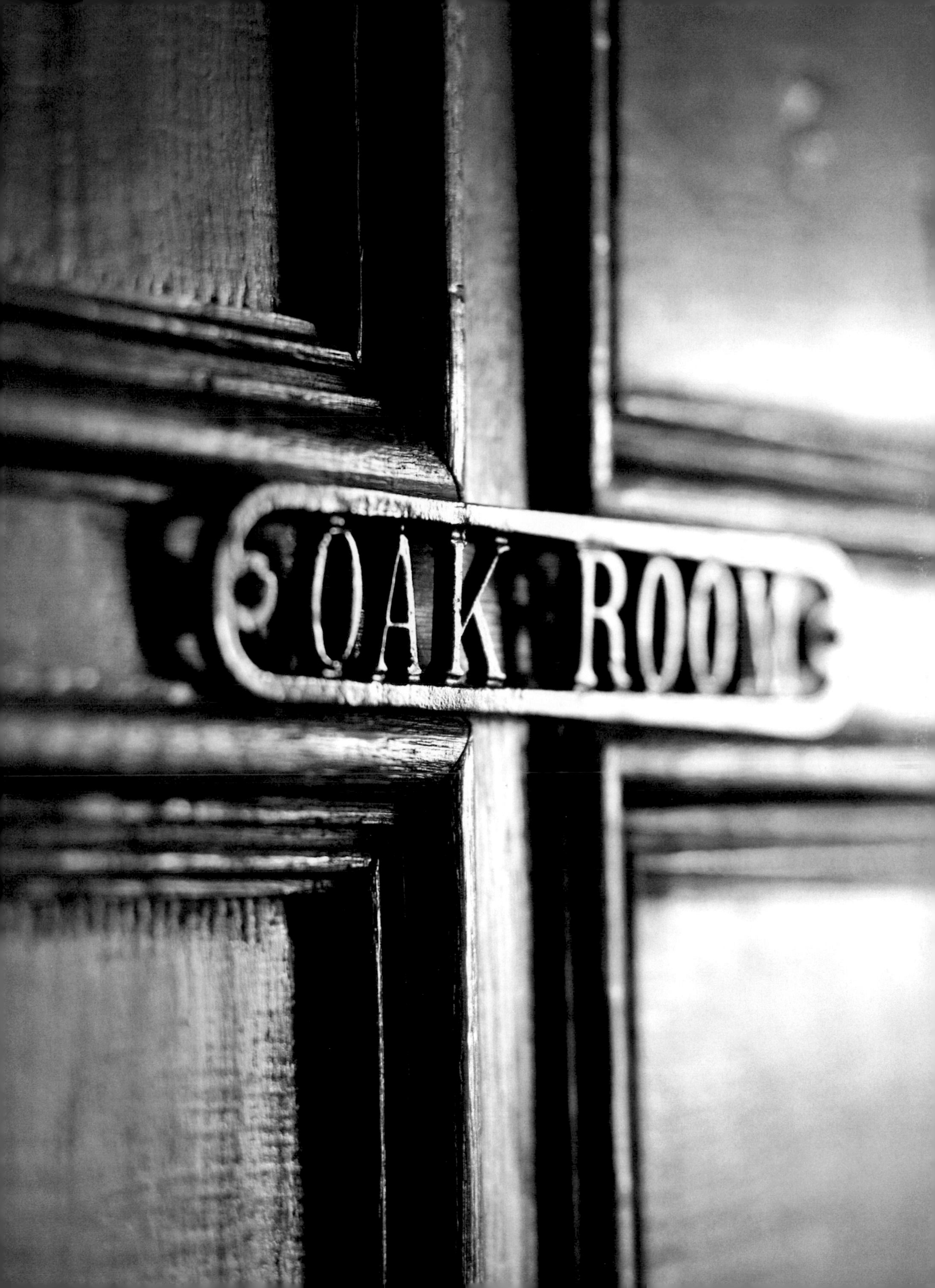
OAK ROO

NIGEL HAWORTH

At 6'1" tall and marathon-runner fit, Nigel Haworth looks like he should be chucking a ball around a cold rugby pitch rather than running a hot sweaty kitchen. But he's not a rugby player, he's a chef – and an extraordinary one at that: one, moreover, who's remained true to his roots. A chef who has, for 25 years, been cementing his position as a Lancastrian culinary ambassador by drawing on regional food traditions and raising them to sublime heights, like the great *terroir* chefs of France. A chef-proprietor who, with business partner and great friend Craig Bancroft, has quietly created one of the finest country house hotels and restaurants in the UK at Northcote in Langho.

To understand the roots of Nigel's fierce pride in his home county you have to look back to his childhood. Born in a the small town of Clayton-le-Moors in Lancashire in 1958, the son of a father who owned his own haulage business and a part-time teacher mother who loved to cook for her family, he has vivid memories of the important part food played in the family's daily life. 'Mum baked a lot. We ate all sorts as kids – from good puddings such as crumbles, rice pudding and Yorkshire puddings with white sauce, to potato hash and lamb neck chops. I saw that cooking could provide real happiness to a person.'

The lesson of food equating with happiness is one that Nigel's never forgotten. Although he's a tough, focused individual, when you step inside Northcote Manor you are welcomed with genuine warmth by a Lancashire man with a twinkle in his eye and a firm handshake. He's the kind of man you would want to share stories with over a pint of bitter down at the local and his food, too, although it is highly crafted, is always understandable – it never tips over into being fancy for fancies' sake. Like Nigel, it tells it like it is.

However, though he's salt-of-the-earth Lancastrian, Nigel has never been insular. Early training at Accrington and Rossendale College was followed by jobs in the south – at the Royal Berkshire hotel in Ascot and London's Grosvenor House hotel in Park Lane – then, when he was 20, he headed off to Switzerland to further his skills. Amongst others, he worked with Natalie Viscardie, one of that country's finest chefs, at the Schweizerhof Hotel in Lucerne.

However, the pull of home was eventually too strong to be ignored and Nigel returned to Lancashire in 1982, armed with a greater understanding of technical cooking learned from the precise nature of the Swiss. He soon realised that, despite an abundance of fantastic raw produce, the standards in restaurants in his home region were seriously grim. Depressed by the lack of opportunity to show off his new craft skills, he decided to take up a lecturing post at his old college.

Then in 1984, fate took a hand in his career. In December 1983, a young restaurant manager, Craig Bancroft, had been given the challenge of turning a newly purchased Ribble Valley property with a rundown restaurant into a first-class country house hotel with an eatery of equal repute. Nigel was invited to get involved and, aged 24, he found himself heading up his own kitchen. Thus was forged Nigel and Craig's business partnership and their love affair with Northcote.

Nigel and Craig were soon given shares in the business and over the next few years the pair found their feet. They were so successful in turning Northcote around that local and national fame wasn't long coming their way – and both the hotel and restaurant began netting awards. In 1989, the pair were able to buy out their business partner and take full control of the hotel – but what they didn't realise was that an economic slump was just around the corner. 'It was a frightening experience. We had borrowed £540,000 to extend and improve Northcote and were faced with losing it all,' recalls Nigel.

Thankfully, they rode the storm and Nigel even picked up the award for Egon Ronay Chef of the Year in 1995. More importantly, Nigel – with a little nudge from a journalist friend Bob Gledhill, the northern editor of hospitality industry magazine *Caterer and Hotelkeeper* – realised he had the perfect opportunity to use his new-found local fame and pioneer the overall promotion not only of Northcote, but also of Lancashire and its wonderful larder of raw ingredients. He had always drawn culinary inspiration from the superb producers on his doorstep: cheesemakers, meat farmers, vegetable growers. Now, he had a chance to put them, as well as his beloved Northcote, on the national stage.

He succeeded in realising that aim spectacularly. His menus are littered with local whinberries, game, rare-breed beef and pork breeds, black pudding and, more recently, foraged berries and leaves. The dishes these are put into are what Nigel would call, 'honest' – but they're always modern, even the interpretations of traditional dishes likes Lancashire hotpot. Nigel has always had a hotpot on his menus. It's Northcote's signature. And his current version of it brought him huge fame, and acclaim, when he cooked it on BBC2's 2009 *Great British Menu*.

The attention that television appearance brought has been the cherry on the icing of the cake that is Northcote. But long before the celebrity of today, Nigel's food had achieved the recognition that all chefs strive for: a Michelin star in the gourmet's guide of choice back in 1996. Gratifying though that was, Nigel sees its benefit as being beyond a personal achievement – more a pat on the back for his whole team and a way of attracting young talent through his doors to train up for the future.

One such young talent is Nigel's own son. Kirk James Haworth has followed his father into the kitchen. After starting off at Northcote, Kirk is now plying his trade in London at some of the country's top restaurants and his father is, not unnaturally, proud of him. 'It would be nice to think that he will go on to be a very successful chef one day. Maybe he'll even return to Northcote to continue what I started 25 years ago.'

Another talent to emerge from within the ranks of Northcote's kitchen team is Nigel's head chef, Lisa Allen, whose shock of blonde hair and bright blue eyes contrast with her softly spoken manner and sometimes bashful attitude. Nigel still oversees the kitchen, but trusts fully in Lisa's abilities to manage a male-dominated team and maintain the high standards that he has set.

It's important that Nigel has a deputy at Northcote in whom he has faith, because these days he and Craig have a culinary empire which demands his attention, too. This encompasses

NIGEL HAWORTH

an outside catering company (which has a contract with Nigel's beloved Blackburn Rovers Football Club) and four pubs under the Ribble Valley Inn branding which the duo launched in 2004. They, too, are becoming justly famous for their use of local produce and tasty, rustic menus. And, as if that wasn't enough, for the past decade Nigel and Craig have staged an international food and wine festival at Northcote, attracting some of the biggest national and international chefs to cook in their little corner of Lancashire.

It's a testament to Nigel and Craig's hard work and vision that the food festival has been copied by other chefs around the country. And Nigel's own crusading zeal for the culinary inheritance of his home county, and dedication to inspiring the next generation of chefs, has continued to win personal accolades, including a trip to Buckingham Palace in 2004 to receive The Prince Philip Medal, the

highest award given out by training and skills body, City & Guilds.

Without Lancashire and Northcote Nigel would certainly still have been a chef to reckon with. With them, he's become one of this country's greatest regional chef-proprietors and living proof that if you have the vision and the raw tools on your doorstep, you don't need to seek the city lights of London to forge a unique culinary identity. Just book yourself into a weekend at Northcote and you'll see what we mean.

Northcote
Northcote Road, Langho, Blackburn, Lancashire BB6 8BE
Phone 01254 240555 **www.northcote.com**
www.thethreefishes.com, www.highwaymaninn.co.uk,
www.theclogandbillycock.com, www.thebullatbroughton.com

LONK LAMB LANCASHIRE HOT POT, ROAST LOIN, PICKLED RED CABBAGE, ORGANIC GARDEN CARROTS AND LEEKS

Over the years Lancashire hot pot has become synonymous with Northcote. This version is the one that I cooked for the homecoming troops on BBC's 2009 Great British Menu. I like to cook with local, preferably organic, produce in my dishes – in the hot pot I always use Lonk lamb (an indigenous Lancashire breed), onions grown locally in Tartleton and Peter Ahscroft's red cabbages which he grows for me in Hesketh Bank. But, obviously, hunt down your own region's native lamb and vegetables.

SERVES 4

For the pickled red cabbage
300g red cabbage, halved and
    quartered
80g coarse sea salt
275ml malt vinegar
140ml white wine vinegar
140ml balsamic vinegar
400ml red wine
250g sugar
5 bay leaves
1 star anise
10 cloves
1 teaspoon black peppercorns
1 teaspoon pink peppercorns
1 stick cinnamon, halved
5 dried chillies

For the hot pot
1 boneless best end of lamb (loin)
1 rack of under shoulder lamb chops
    skinned (back plate removed) and
    cut into 4 chops
440g shoulder, neck and shin of Lonk
    lamb (equal quantities of each), cut
    into 3cm cubes
2½ teaspoons fine sea salt
25g golden granulated sugar
10g plain flour
600g onions, thinly sliced

50g salted butter, melted
500g medium-sized Maris Piper
    potatoes
2 tablespoons of vegetable oil
Two good pinches of white pepper

For the carrots
120g baby carrots
1 tablespoon unrefined sugar
100g butter
500ml mineral water
A pinch of salt

For the leeks
500ml mineral water
2 bundles extra-fine garden leeks
1 tablespoon unrefined sugar
100g butter
A pinch of salt

Pickled red cabbage

Separate out the cabbage leaves and cut away the large stem, then finely slice them. Next put the cabbage in a bowl or on a tray, sprinkle with the coarse sea salt and mix well. Leave to one side for 2-3 hours until it has turned a deep, rich purple-red, then rinse under running water to wash all the salt away and pat dry with some kitchen paper.

Put all the vinegars, wine and sugar in a stainless-steel pan over a medium heat, bring to the boil, then simmer until the volume is reduced by half. In the meantime, put the bay leaves and all the spices into a mortar and pound with a pestle until coarsely ground, then, just before the vinegar reduction is completed, add them to it and allow them to infuse the vinegar for 5 minutes to create an aromatic pickling liquor. Take the pickling liquor off the heat, strain it through a fine sieve and, while still warm, pour it on to the red cabbage and allow the mixture to cool.

Finally, decant the pickled cabbage into a sterilised Kilner jar and seal. (The liquor should just cover the cabbage.)

Hot pot

Preheat the oven to 140C/gas mark 1. Season all the lamb with ½ teaspoon of salt, sugar and a good pinch of white pepper. Dust the lamb cubes with flour and then put them into the base of a heavy hot pot or casserole dish and place the 4 chops evenly around the perimeter of the dish.

Put the onions in a saucepan, together with 15g of the butter and ½ teaspoon of salt, and cook for 2-3 minutes with the lid on over a medium-hot heat until they are translucent but not coloured. Then remove from the heat and spread the onions evenly on top of the lamb in the hot pot or casserole dish. Make sure the top of the chop meat is fully covered with the onions and any juices. The clean bones should be sticking prominently out of the hot pot dish.

Slice the potatoes vertically 2mm thick, place in a medium-sized bowl and add 25g of melted butter, season with 1 teaspoon of salt and a good pinch of white pepper, and mix well. Next, put the sliced potatoes evenly on top of the onions, reserving the best-shaped potatoes for the final layer, and leaving a hole in the centre for the roast loin of lamb to sit in when you serve the hot pot.

Place the hot pot or casserole dish in the oven and cook for 2½ hours, then remove from the oven and brush the potatoes with the remaining melted

(Continued on page 112)

(Continued from page 110)

butter, return to the oven and cook
for a further 15-20 minutes until the
potatoes are golden. In the meantime,
heat the oil in a heavy-based metal-
handled saucepan over a medium-high
heat and sear the best end – or loin
– on all sides until coloured. Then
transfer this to the oven and roast for
8-10 minutes until pink. Remove the
loin and allow it to rest for 2 minutes
on a cooling rack.

Tangled carrots
Put the carrots, sugar, butter and a
pinch of salt in a heavy-based saucepan,
add the mineral water – enough to
barely cover the carrots- and bring to
the boil over a medium heat and cook
for about 4-5 minutes or until the
carrots are tender. Remove the carrots
from the cooking liquor, refresh in iced
water, drain and put to one side while
you reduce the liquor down to a
syrupy texture. Once this is achieved,
pop the carrots back in.

Tangled leeks
Put the mineral water into a saucepan
and bring to the boil over a medium-
high heat, add a pinch of salt and drop
in the leeks, sugar and butter and
rapid boil for I minute. Remove from
the heat and mix the leeks with the
carrots.

Serving
If necessary, place the hot pot back in
the oven for 5 minutes to warm
through before serving. Carve the
lamb loin and then place in the centre
of the hot pot. Serve at the table with
two side dishes containing the pickled
red cabbage, and a mixture of the
tangled carrots and leeks.

LINE-CAUGHT COD ON PIG'S TROTTERS, TRIPE, BROAD BEANS AND PEAS

Tripe and pig's trotters were once staples of regional cooking in the UK but they're often neglected ingredients in the modern kitchen. This is my attempt to showcase them in a sophisticated contemporary way. Essentially, it's a surf 'n' turf dish, with the delicacy of the cod acting as great balance to the taste and textures of the pork and tripe.

SERVINGS 4

For the trotters
2 x 275g suckling pig trotters, singed
    before cooking with a culinary blow
    torch to get rid of any hairs
140g streaky bacon
1 large carrot
2 sticks of celery
½ a medium onion
3-4 parsley stalks
A sprig of thyme
2 litres chicken stock

For the cod
4 x 60g pieces of cod loin, skinned,
    pin bones removed and skin
    reserved
40g new season broad beans
40g new seasons peas
60g pig's tripe, cut into 3cm strips
10g English parsley, finely chopped
Sunflower oil, for deep frying
A pinch of salt

Pig's trotters
Put the trotters and bacon into a heavy-based saucepan, cover with cold water and bring to the boil for 2 minutes over a medium heat, then remove and refresh under cold running water to remove all the scum. Clean the saucepan and put the trotters and bacon back in, then add all the other ingredients, cover them with the chicken stock, bring to the boil and simmer for 2 hours. Remove from the heat and allow the stock to cool.

Remove the trotters and discard the rest of the ingredients, then pass the stock through a muslin cloth or fine sieve into a bowl and put it into the fridge to set – it will form a jelly. Once the jelly has formed, remove any excess fat from the stock.

Carefully pick the meat and skin off the trotters and discard all the bones and cartilage. Shred the meat and skin into small pieces.

Cod
Roll the cod pieces in clingfilm then put them in a Vac Pac bag and cook in a water bath at 47C for 20 minutes. If you haven't got a water bath and Vac Pac machine, poach the fish in a little bit of white wine and fish stock over a medium heat for 4-5 minutes.

Shell the beans and peas. Put a saucepan of salted water over a medium heat and bring to the boil, then blanch the beans and peas in it for 1 minute. Remove from the heat and drain. Take off the inner skin from the broad beans.

Put 80g of the trotter meat together with the tripe, peas and broad beans in a small heavy-based pan, add 200ml of stock and carefully bring to the boil over a medium heat. Add the chopped parsley and continue to simmer until cooked.

Descale the cod skin and cut it into 4 equal pieces. Heat up the sunflower oil in a deep fat fryer to 170C and fry the skin in it for 2-3 minutes until crisp. Remove and drain on kitchen paper.

Serving
Remove the trotter meat, tripe and vegetables from the stock and distribute evenly between four bowls, then remove the cod from the bags and place on top. Finally spoon over the remaining stock.

SEARED LANGOUSTINE TAILS, TEMPURA OF LANGOUSTINE CLAW, TOMATO SALSA, SWEETCORN

This is one of our popular autumnal dishes, inspired by our local shellfish brought in by the boats that fish the Lancashire and Cumbrian coast and the seasonal harvest of sweetcorn and wild trompette mushrooms. You do need a soda siphon to do the dish justice, though (you can buy them from specialist shops or on-line).

SERVES 4

For the tomato salsa
2 plum tomatoes, peeled, deseeded and
    cut into 1cm cubes
½ teaspoon finely chopped red chilli
I dessertspoon finely chopped red
    onion
A pinch of salt
A pinch of sugar
1 teaspoon lime juice
A pinch of chopped coriander

For the leeks
2 x 1.5cm diameter leeks, cut
    lengthways into 20cm batons
1 dessertspoon salt
1 dessertspoon sugar
60ml rapeseed oil
50ml water

For the seared sweetcorn
40g fresh sweetcorn kernels
1 tablespoon clarified butter
1 tablespoon vegetable stock
A pinch of salt

For the trompette mushrooms
15g trompette des morts *mushrooms*
1 teaspoon butter

For the langoustines
8 large langoustines
1.2 litres water
10g celery
10g onion
2 black peppercorns, crushed
1 bay leaf
Splash of olive oil
A pinch of salt

For the tempura langoustine claws
50g self-raising flour
50g fecule (potato flour)
50g cornflour
250g sparkling mineral water
4 langoustine claws
Flour for dusting
Vegetable oil for frying
A pinch of salt

For the sweetcorn foam
140g tinned sweetcorn
20g unsalted butter
150ml full fat milk
150ml double cream
A pinch of sea salt

For garnishing
Coriander leaves

Tomato salsa
Sprinkle the tomatoes with the salt and sugar and gently mix them in. Add all the remaining ingredients, again carefully mixing together.

Leeks
Place the leeks into a Vac Pac bag. Add the salt, sugar, rapeseed oil and water into the bag and seal tightly, then steam for 12 minutes, and then put them in the freezer to chill rapidly, still in their bags. If you haven't got a Vac Pac machine, put the ingredients in a saucepan over a medium-low heat and gently poach the leeks for 45 minutes until they are just cooked. Once cooked, put the leeks and their juices in a plastic bag and pop in the freezer to chill. Once chilled but not frozen solid, take them out of the freezer, remove from the bag, saving the cooking juices, then cut them into 3cm batons – you need to end up with 8 pieces.

Seared sweetcorn
Melt the butter in a non-stick frying pan over a medium heat, add the sweetcorn and gently fry until it is golden brown. Add the vegetable stock and reduce it down, then take the sweetcorn off the heat, put to one side and keep warm.

Mushrooms
Trim the ends of the mushroom stalks, break them in half lengthways, then clean them thoroughly in water and dry them with kitchen paper. Melt the butter in a non-stick frying pan over a medium heat, add the mushrooms and gently sweat for a few seconds. Once cooked, remove them from the pan,

(Continued on page 116)

(Continued from page 114)

put on some kitchen paper to drain, then keep warm.

Langoustines

Prepare the langoustines by removing the entrails. Put the water, celery, onion, peppercorns and bay leaf into a saucepan over a medium heat and bring to the boil, then drop 4 langoustines into the water and blanch them for 2 minutes. Remove and put them into a bowl of iced water. Repeat the process with the remaining 4 langoustines.

Once all of the langoustines are cold, peel them and crack the claws. Put the claws to one side. Heat a little olive oil in a non-stick frying pan over a medium heat and sear the langoustine tails until golden. Remove and place on to kitchen paper, lightly season with salt and keep warm.

Tempura langoustine claws

Heat up some oil in a deep-fat fryer. Meanwhile, put the flour, *fecule*, cornflour and sparkling mineral water together into a bowl and whisk lightly to make a batter. Place into the soda siphon and charge it with three canisters, then release the batter into a stainless-steel bowl. Dust the langoustine claws with flour, then dip them quickly in the batter – the aim is only to lightly cover them – and fry until golden. Remove from the fryer and place on some kitchen paper and lightly season with salt.

Sweetcorn foam

Melt the butter in a saucepan over a medium heat, add the sweetcorn and a pinch of salt and cook gently for 3-4 minutes, making sure the sweetcorn doesn't colour. Add the milk and cream, bring to the boil and simmer for 2-3 minutes. Place into a blender and blend until smooth, then pass through a fine sieve and, if necessary, season with sea salt.

Serving

Reheat the leeks in their cooking juices in a saucepan over a low heat and, once warmed through, lightly season with salt. Remove from the pan, pat dry on absorbent paper, then place two leek batons on the bottom of each serving plate. At the top of each plate place a small spoon of the tomato salsa. Place two seared langoustines on top of the leeks and a tempura langoustine claw on top of the tomato salsa. Finally, sprinkle around the trompette mushrooms, seared sweetcorn and carefully spoon the sweetcorn foam around the plate. Finish with a few coriander leaves.

'CORNED' GOOSNARGH DUCK, DUCK HAM AND SCRATCHINGS

This dish is about two things: showing off and respecting a great ingredient (our local Goosnargh duck) by using every little bit of it; and memories. Childhood memories of corned beef streaked with fat – which I've translated into 'corned duck'; recollections of my years in Switzerland and its wonderful tradition of cured meat; and nostalgia for everybody's favourite bar snack of the 1980s, pork scratchings! Don't forget, though, you need to cure the duck breasts for 9 days before you serve the dish!

SERVES 4

For the duck
1 x 2.5kg cornfed duck
A pinch of chopped rosemary
1 orange, zested
100g coarse sea salt

For the duck ham
2 x 300g breasts of Goosnargh duck
2 x 20g salt
2 x 2g pepper
2 x 4g pink salt

For the duck scratchings
Duck skin reserved from carcase
Oil for frying
A few pinches of sea salt

For the duck jelly
3 x duck carcases, fat removed and chopped into small pieces

For the pea and broad bean mousse
100ml milk
150ml whipping cream
½ small garlic clove
75g frozen peas
50g shelled broad beans, plus 16 extra beans for garnish
25g spinach
1 leaf of gelatine, softened in cold water
1 egg white
A pinch of salt

Chicken and duck liver parfait
75g chicken livers
75g duck livers
2 shallots, finely sliced
½ garlic clove, finely chopped
100ml port
50ml Madeira wine
50ml brandy
A pinch of tarragon
100g unsalted butter, melted
A pinch of freshly ground black pepper
A pinch of salt
A pinch of pink salt
A pinch of sugar

For the onion fondue
40g butter
200g onions, finely sliced
1 teaspoon of salt
1 teaspoon of black treacle
A pinch of salt

For the port sauce
100ml port

Duck
Remove the breasts and legs from the duck, keeping all the excess skin from the neck and around the parson's nose to make the scratchings with later. Put the breasts to one side and place the duck legs and duck skin on a stainless-steel tray, sprinkle them with rosemary and orange zest, then the salt, making sure you cover the duck legs well. Cover with clingfilm and put into the fridge to marinate for 8 hours, then wash off the marinade under cold, running, water and dry the duck legs and skin with some kitchen paper.

Place the legs in a Vac Pac bag, then poach them in a water bath at 80C for 12 hours. (If you haven't got a Vac Pac machine or water bath, cook the legs very slowly in some duck fat for 4 hours in the oven at 100C/gas mark ½.). Once cooked, put the duck legs in the freezer to chill quickly, then carefully remove them from the bag and drain off the cooking juices through a fine sieve into a bowl. Put the juices in the fridge to chill and once the fat has solidified skim this off, leaving the jellified juices behind. Keep the juice jelly to add to the duck – and keep the fat to use later, too.

Remove the skin from around the duck legs and store them with the other duck skin already reserved for the scratchings. Flake the duck meat from the bones, then carefully cut it into 5mm cubes and put to one side.

(Continued on page 118)

(Continued from page 117)

Duck ham

Put the duck breasts on a stainless-steel tray. Make two separate cures with equal quantities of the salts and pepper, then rub one cure on one breast. Repeat the process with the second cure and remaining breast. Cover both with clingfilm and put in the fridge to marinate for 12 hours. Remove from the fridge and wash off the marinade under cold running water, then dry the duck breasts with some kitchen paper. Wrap each breast in muslin cloth, tie them well then hang them up with string in a well ventilated area for 9 days to cure.

After the breasts have cured, remove the muslin cloth and place them on a tray in the freezer, laying them as flat as possible. When frozen, remove and slice thinly on a slicing machine, you will only need 12 slices – 3 slices per person.

Duck scratchings

Cut the duck skin into 4cm x 1cm strips. Heat the oil to 170C then fry the skin in it for 4-5 minutes until crisp, draining it on kitchen paper once it is cooked. Sprinkle with sea salt while still hot and allow to cool, then place the scratchings into some small cellophane bags for serving.

Duck jelly

Preheat the oven to 180C/gas mark 4. Put the duck bones in a roasting pan and roast in the oven for 10 minutes. Remove and place the bones in a muslin lined colander, or a large fine sieve, over a bowl so that you catch the juices.

Place the juices in a small freezer-proof container and quickly chill them in the freezer. When the fat has set, skim it off from the juices and keep to one side to use later – you should be left with 100ml of duck stock underneath the fat. Freeze the stock and then allow it to thaw out through a fine muslin cloth, or a fine sieve, over a bowl. Do the same with the jelly reserved from the duck legs and then mix the two sets of juices together and put the mixture in the fridge to set.

Pea and broad bean mousse

Put the milk, cream and garlic into a saucepan over a medium heat and bring to the boil. Simmer for 2-3 minutes until you have reduced the liquid's volume to 150ml (roughly half its volume). Add the peas and 50g of broad beans and bring back to the boil. Remove the mixture from the heat and blend it in a liquidiser or food processor with the spinach until smooth. Meanwhile, soak the gelatine leaf in cold water for 1-2 minutes. Once softened, take out and squeeze to get rid of excess water, then add it to the still-warm vegetable purée, stirring until it dissolves. Next pass the purée through a fine sieve into a clean bowl and allow to cool.

Whisk the egg white to a soft peak, then carefully fold-in the purée and season with a little salt, if necessary. Set to one side – but don't put it in the fridge or the mousse will set

Chicken and duck liver parfait

Trim the duck and chicken livers of sinew and wash thoroughly under cold running water, then drain them and pat them dry with some kitchen paper. Melt a little of the butter in a frying pan over a low heat, add the shallots

and garlic and cook gently until they are translucent but not coloured. Add the alcohol and gradually reduce the mixture down, continuously stirring, until you get a jam-like consistency. Remove from the heat and cool.

Place the livers in a Vac Pac bag, add the jam and all the other ingredients, excluding the butter, and poach the livers in a water bath for 10 minutes at 65C. Once cooked, remove the livers from the water bath and chill them quickly in the freezer. Once they're firm, place them in a Pacojet machine with the rest of the butter and freeze. Blitz twice in the Pacojet and reserve.

If you haven't got a Vac Pac, water bath or Pacojet machine, make a liver parfait in the following manner. Melt half the butter in a frying pan. Add the shallots and garlic and cook gently until they are translucent and soft but not coloured. Add the alcohol and gradually reduce the mixture down to a jam-like texture, stirring as you do so, then add in the remaining butter and once it has melted remove the mixture from the heat. Transfer the onions into a sealable freezer bag, add the livers, the tarragon and all the salts, pepper and sugar, seal and put it into a saucepan of gently simmering water for 10 minutes. Remove, transfer everything to a food processor or liquidiser and blend until you have a smooth pâté. Push through a fine sieve, then place in a terrine dish and set in the fridge.

Onion fondue

Melt the butter in a saucepan over a low heat, add the onions together with a teaspoon of water, put on the lid and gently sweat the onions over a low heat for 10 minutes until they are soft but not coloured. Remove the lid and continue to cook the onions slowly until they begin to break down and caramelise, stirring continuously. Add the treacle and, if necessary, a pinch of salt and remove from the heat.

Port sauce

Put the port into a saucepan over a medium heat and bring to the boil, then simmer until you have reduced it down to a syrup consistency.

Serving

Place a small teaspoon of onion fondue in the base of a Kilner jar. Put 1 teaspoon of liver parfait into the jar, then drizzle ½ teaspoon of port syrup over that. Put some cubed duck meat in a small bowl and add 150ml of jelly and a pinch of salt if necessary, then fold in 1 level teaspoon of duck fat and check the seasoning again, adding a little salt and pepper if necessary. Next divide this up equally between the jars.

Cut 4 of the slices of duck ham into long thin strips and sprinkle these on top of the duck jelly. Spoon 1½ tablespoons of pea and broad bean mousse over the strips, then cut the reserved broad beans in half and put four beans in the mousse. Put the jar lids on and put in the fridge to chill.

When you are ready to serve, place the jars on your serving plates or small wooden boards. Skewer the remaining slices of duck ham on 4 bamboo skewers (2 slices per person), pop them alongside the jars and add a packet of duck scratchings.

TINY CHOCOLATE AND CHERRY DESSERTS, LIQUID CHOCOLATE, CHOCOLATE CUSTARD, JELLY, CHERRY SORBET

Every menu needs an indulgent chocolate dessert and this is one that we run in the spring and summer at Northcote when the cherry season's in full swing. It's an intricate recipe, but worth the trouble. You'll find that you have extra quantities of certain elements of the dish but just keep these and use them up later. Using a paint sprayer is a must to get an even coating of chocolate on the liquid squares — you can buy them at DIY and hardware stores. And the crackling candy — or space dust — can be ordered on-line through specialist suppliers like MSK Ingredients (www.msk-ingredients.com)

For the chocolate custard
100ml full fat milk
190ml double cream
2 dessertspoons caster sugar
25g chocolate (55% cocoa solids),
  roughly chopped
3 egg yolks
1 vanilla pod
20g demerara sugar
20g crackling candy

For the liquid chocolate
60g chocolate (70% cocoa solids),
  roughly chopped
40g milk chocolate (33% cocoa
  solids), roughly chopped
175g double cream
75ml milk
25g clear honey
½ vanilla pod, split and seeds removed
A pinch of salt

For the chocolate spray
250g chocolate (70% cocoa solids)
  roughly chopped
25g cocoa butter

For the cherry sorbet
150ml fresh cherry juice
200g cherry purée

100ml stock syrup
12ml sour cherry purée
1 large lemon, juiced

For the pulled sugar
1 dessertspoon sugar
30g liquid glucose
200ml water
½ teaspoon lemon juice

For the cherry jelly
150ml cherry juice
50g cherry purée
1 teaspoon sour cherry purée
1 teaspoon lemon juice
30ml stock syrup
2g agar agar gel

For the dipped cherries
10 cherries, stalks retained
100g chocolate (55% cocoa solids)

For the chocolate 'paint'
62g sugar
62ml water
20g cocoa powder
62ml double cream

For the kirsch foam
2½ gelatine leaves (about 4g)
150ml milk
40ml UHT whipping cream (55% fat)
30g caster sugar
1 tablespoon kirsch liqueur

Chocolate custard
Put the milk, cream and 1 dessertspoon of caster sugar into a saucepan over a medium heat and bring to the boil. Meanwhile, whisk the egg yolks and 1 heaped dessertspoon of caster sugar in a bowl until light and fluffy. Once the milk and cream has come to the boil, take it off the heat and gradually add the chocolate, stirring continuously until it has melted and is thoroughly incorporated. Next, slowly add the

chocolate milk to the egg yolks and gently whisk until everything is fully incorporated. Fill a bowl with ice and place the chocolate mixture on top to cool.

Preheat the oven to 94C/gas mark ¼. Line a large baking tray with a sheet of acetate. Clingfilm the bottom of 10 moulds (4cm deep x 3⅓cm diameter) and place them on the tray, then fill each mould with the chocolate custard until they are three quarters full. Put into the oven and cook for 28 minutes until they are set. Remove and allow to cool then put in the fridge to chill overnight.

Liquid chocolate
Put all the chocolate into a bowl and place it over a pan of gently simmering water (making sure the water doesn't touch the bowl) until the chocolate has melted, stirring occasionally. Once melted, remove from the heat.

Meanwhile put the cream, milk, honey, vanilla seeds and salt into another saucepan over a medium-low heat and bring to the boil. Give it a stir to make sure the honey is incorporated properly, then remove from the heat and pour over the chocolate. Leave the mixture to stand for 1 minute then mix with a hand blender until all the ingredients are fully incorporated. Skim off the foam from the top of the chocolate then strain the liquid through a fine muslin cloth or sieve.

Line a small baking tray with a sheet of silicone paper — it needs to be 22cm x 13cm with a depth of 2cm: if you have some non-stick cooking spray, coat the tray before lining it with paper

(Continued on page 122)

(Continued from page 120)

as this will hold it in place firmly. Pour the liquid chocolate into the tray, then place it in the freezer until it has set solid. Once set, remove the chocolate from the tray and cut into 4cm x 4cm squares, then place the chocolate squares carefully on to a tray lined with parchment paper and return to the freezer. You will probably have some surplus squares – these will keep for up to 1 month.

Chocolate spray
Put the chocolate and cocoa butter in a bowl and place the bowl over a pan of gently simmering water (making sure the water doesn't touch the bowl) stirring occasionally until the chocolate has melted. Once melted, remove from the heat and transfer to a small paint sprayer.

Break up a large cardboard box and remove one side. Remove the chocolate squares from the freezer and place on a silpat mat or large sheet of silicone paper within the cardboard box, then spray them with the chocolate, taking care to coat them evenly. Return the squares to the freezer for 10 minutes, or until the chocolate spray has solidified, then take them out, turn the squares over and spray the other side. Again, put in the freezer to solidify.

Cherry sorbet
Put all the ingredients together in a bowl and mix thoroughly. Pass the mixture through a muslin cloth or a fine sieve, then place it in an ice-cream machine and churn as directed in its instructions. After churning, decant the sorbet into a container and put in the freezer to set completely. If you haven't got an ice-cream machine place the mixture in a shallow dish in the freezer, taking it out every few minutes to stir. When the sorbet

is slushy put it into a freezer-proof bowl and put it in the freezer to set completely.

Pulled sugar
Make a caramel by heating the sugar and glucose to 170C-175C over a medium heat in a pan. When the sugar starts to turn golden, whisk in the water and lemon juice, then pour the mixture in to a baking tray lined with silicone paper and leave to set. Warm in the oven on a low heat until the sugar is pliable, then pull the sugar into small, loose spheres and allow to set again.

Cherry jelly
Put all the ingredients, except the agar agar, into a saucepan and bring to the boil over a medium heat. Once the boil is reached, whisk in the agar agar and bring back to the boil whisking continuously. Remove from the heat and pass through a fine sieve. Next, pour the mix into a deep tray lined on the bottom with a sheet of acetate – the tray needs to be 19cm x 32cm and 2cm deep – then put into the fridge to set. Once the jelly has formed, take out of the fridge and carefully cut it into 2.5cm squares. Put back in the fridge.

Dipped cherries
Put the chocolate into a bowl and place the bowl over a pan of gently simmering water (making sure the water doesn't touch the bowl) until the chocolate has melted, stirring occasionally. Once melted, remove from the heat and dip the cherries in the chocolate, making sure they are coated evenly, then place the dipped cherries on to a sheet of silicone paper and leave to set.

Chocolate 'paint'
Put the sugar and water in a saucepan and bring to the boil over a medium heat. Add the cocoa powder and whisk-

in well then take the mixture off the heat, pour it into a small bowl and chill over a bowl filled with ice. Once it has cooled, whisk in the double cream, transfer the mixture into a squeezy bottle and put in the fridge.

Kirsch foam
Soak the gelatine leaves in cold water until soft. Meanwhile, put the milk, cream and sugar into a saucepan and bring to the boil over a medium heat. Take off the heat. Remove the gelatine from the water, give it a squeeze to get rid of excess water and add it to the milk, stirring until it dissolves. Then pass the mixture through a fine sieve into a bowl, cover with clingfilm and leave to cool. When cool, decant it into a soda siphon, load the gun with two cartridges and put in the fridge to chill.

Serving
Pipe a small round of chocolate 'paint' at the top of your serving plates, then pull this with the nozzle to create a vertical swipe. Put a chocolate square in the middle of each plate and a square of jelly below this. Remove the chocolate custards from the fridge and briefly warm the exterior of the moulds with a culinary blow torch to loosen them (or run a warmed flat-bladed knife around the rim of the moulds). Pop the custards out onto the plate above the chocolate square, sprinkle them with demerara sugar and caramelise the sugar with a culinary blow torch. While still warm, sprinkle on the crackling candy. Place the pulled sugar on top of the custard, a dipped cherry to the right of the jelly, and pop a scoop of sorbet onto the chocolate square. Spoon over the kirsch foam, place the chocolate swirl on top.

TOM KITCHIN

About a mile away from the picture postcard centre of Edinburgh, with its medieval cobbled streets and imposing castle, lies Commercial Quay. It's in Leith, once a less than salubrious docklands area of Edinburgh, but these days better known for its open-fronted bars and funky night spots; and, even more recently, as a foodie destination. The gastronomic credentials are due in no small part to an aptly named restaurant called The Kitchin. Cross over a little road bridge that spans the Water of Leith and you'll find it, housed in a row of identical green business units along the quay. Its frontage is unremarkable but step inside and you'll enter a little bit of earthly paradise – one of the great restaurants of Britain. And inside The Kitchin's kitchen stands Tom Kitchin: a chef uniquely named for the job.

With a name like his, you'd have thought Tom's destiny would have been sealed at birth, but it took the influence of

some great French chefs to turn this unassuming, fresh faced 31-year-old man into a culinary genius himself. Long before he trained with them, though, the first sparks of culinary curiosity had been sown in Tom almost by accident.

Tom grew up in Kinross, about 20 miles north of Edinburgh. At 13 he was washing pots and pans in the local pub to earn some extra pocket money. In the winter the local poachers would come in with their day's hoard and Tom often found himself plucking grouse and pheasant (he still buys game in its plumage for the restaurant and de-feathers on site). It wasn't long before he had graduated to helping prepare food for the pub's menu; soon he was spending most of his time in the kitchen and school was relegated to being nothing more than a hobby.

The owner of the pub could see Tom's potential and arranged for him to go and work at Perthshire's famous Gleneagles hotel one summer. His summer job was an eye-opener for Tom into the world of professional catering. At Gleneagles, 70 chefs slaved away in the kitchen: before, at the pub, it had been him and just a handful of chefs. The difference was daunting, but it didn't scare Tom. He'd got the cooking bug. He left school for good, aged 16, and signed up for catering college, eventually joining Gleneagles full-time.

Two years later he crossed the border into England and wound up in kitchen of the great Pierre Koffmann at the latter's iconic London restaurant La Tante Claire. The restaurant was one of only a handful of restaurants in the UK that had been awarded three Michelin stars and Pierre's Gascon-based food was revered by chefs and diners alike. To have a place in his brigade was a coup for a greenhorn Scottish chef.

Tom soon found out his new boss was a hard taskmaster. His kitchen was run in French and for the 'young laddie' from Kinross it was a culture shock. Tom struggled at first but soon regained his confidence and was able to take his first three months, stuck in a corner chopping herbs, in his stride. And despite telling his mother after two days that he wanted to go home to Scotland, he mentally gave himself a year to see if he could make the grade at La Tante Claire.

Make the grade, he did, staying at La Tante Claire for five years in total, although his time with the Gascon master was sandwiched around a year in Paris. But from Pierre, Tom learned his craft and imbibed his boss' passion for direct, robust flavours and as well as his absolute respect for produce. From Pierre he learned how to think on his feet and how to cook from the heart rather than by numbers. To respond to produce rather than just follow a set-in-stone recipe.

The relationship forged between Tom and the Frenchman is still strong. The two of them often talk several times a week and Tom turns to Pierre for advice on all aspects of his business. And such is the older man's respect for his protégé that when Tom and his wife Michaela opened The Kitchin in 2006 he gifted them all the old crockery from La Tante Clare – still pristine though it had been languishing in storage since he'd closed La Tante Claire in 2002. Pierre even helped out in the kitchen during the Leith restaurant's early weeks of life.

However, Pierre Koffmann is not the only great French chef to have moulded Tom. The latter also spent crucial years in France with two revered godfathers of modern French cuisine, Guy Savoy (in Paris) and Alain Ducasse (in Monte Carlo). From them, particularly Ducasse, he acquired a little more culinary pizzazz and presentational polish. But though he learned some fancy modern skills and can make contemporary jellies and sassy sorbets if he so chooses, Tom has never forgotten those early La Tante Claire lessons which placed flavour above everything.

His food is unfussy, gutsy with a gloss – or as Tom himself puts it, 'honest and simple.' And its roots are totally in his local larder. He cooks with Scottish seafood, Scottish beef, Scottish game, Scottish fruit – the dishes on his menus always give a nod to his suppliers – and he cooks within seasons. He calls his philosophy 'from nature to plate' but it is what the French would call *terroir* cooking.

Tom's absolute devotion to flavour comes out in dishes like his razor fish – or 'spoots' – cooked with chorizo, lemon and finely sliced vegetables; they're served back in their shells with a delicately balanced mixture of herbs. Tom's love of local Scottish seafood also shines through in his roasted langoustine tails served with an intricate slice of rolled pig's head – the pork underlining the meaty texture of the large, juicy Scottish prawns.

There is a strong sense of theatre in all of his dishes, many of which are served at the table in the stylish, high-ceilinged dining room – all part of Tom's desire to put a big smile on each and every one of his diners' faces. The ultimate star of the show is a roast rib of Scottish beef carved at the table and served with its bone marrow and a red wine sauce, so thick and unctuous it could have been pumped straight from the North Sea. Don't indulge too much on the beef, though, because you'll miss some exquisite desserts. A beautifully light crowdie cheesecake mousse for one thing; or a refreshing green apple sorbet with champagne soup.

Tom's food rarely misses a beat, so it's no surprise that The Kitchin has been showered with awards ever since it

opened, including a Michelin star a mere six months after it launched and the AA Scottish Restaurant of the Year award in 2007. And in the same year Tom himself won two 'chef of the year' accolades – at the Catering in Scotland Awards and the Scottish Chef Awards. Of course, he doesn't run the restaurant on his own: Michaela is in charge front-of-house and sets the tone for the breezy feel of the waiting service in the cool, slate grey dining room.

It's a busy, busy, busy place, The Kitchin. There's a large viewing window looking into the kitchen from the dining room and chefs fly by it like dazzling tropical fish at the height of an evening's service. The dining room buzzes with animated talk as people sit shoulder-to-shoulder discussing plate after plate of mouth-watering food. These days, such is The Kitchin's fame, film stars sit next to young aspiring chefs.

Everyone's drawn to The Kitchin, though, by the man with the cherubic face and wild, curly hair who's so totally immersed in his passion for food; who cooks like an old fashioned chef – without gizmos or fancy bits of kit – yet still manages to retain an air of modernity about his menus. Tom Kitchin's food isn't just good, it's out of this world. If ever there was a man who lived up to his name, this is he.

The Kitchin
78 Commercial Quay, Leith, Edinburgh EH6 6LX
Phone 0131 555 1755 **www.thekitchin.com**

ARISAIG RAZOR CLAMS WITH DICED VEGETABLES, CHORIZO, SAUTEED SQUID AND WILD HERBS

Razor clams are known as 'spoots' in Scotland because they 'spoot' water as they dive in and out of the sand. They are found widely along the Scottish coastline and we get ours from Arisaig on the west coast. I ate them at a local pub served with chorizo and loved the combination of the two ingredients. I've taken that idea and produced a more refined version for the restaurant. Before you use them, don't to forget to wash the clams well under running water to remove any sand and grit.

SERVES 4

2 tablespoons olive oil
1 carrot, cut into 5mm cubes
1 courgette, peeled and cut into 5mm cubes
1 fennel bulb, cut into 5mm cubes
100g podded broad beans
8 razor clams, washed
2 shallots, finely chopped
100ml white wine
100g cooking chorizo, chopped into 5mm cubes
100ml whipping cream
50g chives or parsley, chopped
3 anchovies, chopped
1 lemon, zested and juiced
20g unsalted butter
100g squid, trimmed, cleaned and cut into triangles
Salt and freshly ground black pepper

For the garnish
3 sprigs of dill, chopped
1 bunch of chives, chopped
1 bunch of amaranth leaves, chopped
2 sprigs of chervil, chopped
10g wild edible flowers (optional)

Heat 1 tablespoon of the olive oil in a saucepan and gently cook the carrots, courgettes and fennel for 3-4 minutes until they are soft. Remove from the heat. Bring a saucepan of water to the boil over a medium heat, add the broad beans and simmer for 3-4 minutes. Drain, and when cool enough to handle slip the beans out of their inner pods.

Take a saucepan large enough to hold all the razor clams and place it over a high heat. Add the clams, shallots and white wine and immediately cover the pan with a tight-fitting lid to allow the clams to steam. After 30 seconds, all the razor clams should spring open. Strain the cooking liquor from the steamed clams and discard any clams that are unopened. Keep the cooking liquor aside to make the sauce. When cool enough to handle, remove the clams from their shells and keep the shells for serving. Slice the razor clam meat thinly at an angle and discard the brown intestine.

Pour the reserved cooking liquor into a saucepan, bring to the boil over a medium heat then simmer and reduce its volume by half. Add the reserved carrots, courgettes, fennel and broad beans, together with the chorizo, cream, chives or parsley, and anchovies, stirring constantly. Once the cream thickens slightly, add the razor clams, lemon juice and zest, and finish with the butter to create a glossy sauce.

Season the squid with some salt and pepper. Heat the rest of the olive oil in a frying pan over a high heat, add the squid and cook quickly for 30-40 seconds.

Serving
Place two clean razor clam shells on each plate, then fill them with the razor clams, vegetables and creamy juices. Add the squid and finish with the fresh herbs and flowers.

BONED AND ROLLED PIG'S HEAD, WITH ROASTED LANGOUSTINE TAILS AND CRISPY PIG'S EAR SALAD

After five years of working alongside Pierre Koffmann, I became heavily influenced by his use of different cuts of pig. He is particularly famous for his dish of pig's trotters, but I like to cook and serve a whole pig's head. I sometimes serve this as one of the dishes on our surprise tasting menu and the customers are definitely surprised to receive it, but the majority love to eat it.

SERVES 4

1 pig's head, boned and rolled
2 pig's ears, wrapped in muslin
2 carrots, roughly chopped
1 stick celery, roughly chopped
1 white onion, roughly chopped
2 bay leaves
4 sprigs of fresh thyme
1 teaspoon of dried Herbes de
    Provence
½ teaspoon ground cumin
1 teaspoon fennel seeds
3 tablespoons olive oil
12 langoustine tails
Mixed salad leaves, dressed with a
    little extra virgin olive oil
Salt and freshly ground black pepper

Place the pig's head, pig's ears, carrots, celery, onion, bay leaves and thyme into a very large stock pot. Cover with water, put over a medium-low heat and bring to the boil, then simmer for 4 hours. Remove the stock pot from the heat and set aside to cool.

Take the pig's head out of the cooled cooking liquor. Remove the cheeks and put to one side. Separate the fat from the skin of the whole head and discard the fat. Lay out a piece of clingfilm on a chopping board and place the skin, hair-side down, onto it. Shred the pig's cheek and mix together with the Herbes de Provence, cumin and fennel seeds. Season well with a pinch of salt and freshly ground black pepper. Lay a line of the pig's cheek mixture along the middle of the skin and roll up into a sausage. Wrap tightly in the clingfilm and place in the fridge to set for 12 hours. Remove from the fridge and slice the sausage into pieces, 5cm thick. Put 1 tablespoon of olive oil into a frying pan over a medium heat, add the pieces of sausage and cook for 1-2 minutes, then set them to one side, and keep warm.

To make the crispy pigs' ears, trim and discard the muscles from the ears. Wrap the ears in clingfilm and place in the fridge for 6-8 hours with a heavy object on top of them to press them flat. Remove from fridge and shred the ears very finely with a sharp knife. Heat 1 tablespoon of the olive oil in a frying pan over a medium heat, then add in the shredded ears. Fry for 1-2 minutes and then flip over and fry the other side until crisp. Remove from the heat, drain on kitchen paper and keep warm until needed.

Peel the langoustines and remove the intestinal tracks. Heat the rest of the olive oil in a heavy-based pan, season the langoustines and fry them for 1-2 minutes, depending on size, until pink.

Serving
Place a few salad leaves on your serving plates. Top with a slice of the pig's head sausage, crispy pig's ears and, finally, the langoustine tails.

OX TRIPE WITH RED PEPPERS AND CRISPY OX TONGUE

I like to cook with underrated cuts of meat, like ox tripe and ox tongue, and serve it to customers who have never tried it before. It often takes them out of their comfort zone, but nine out of ten of them are pleasantly surprised and love the results. You need to buy your tripe ready blanched from a good butcher or market. If you can't get fresh tripe, then use frozen. Traditionally tripe is served with piquant flavours, such as parsley and capers, but here I've introduced a southern European influence by using garlic, smoked paprika and red peppers as the dominant flavours.

SERVES 4

For the ox tongue
500ml water
2 carrots, peeled and roughly chopped
1 onion, peeled and roughly chopped
½ head of garlic
Bouquet garni
1 ox tongue
Salt

For the tripe
10ml olive oil
1 onion, roughly chopped
2 carrots, roughly chopped
1 tablespoon tomato purée
½ head of garlic
1 teaspoon cumin powder
1 teaspoon smoked paprika
1 bouquet garni
100ml white wine
300ml chicken stock
1kg ox tripe, blanched and cut into
*   2cm strips*
6 red peppers, skinned and cut into
*   1 cm strips (see note)*
Salt and freshly ground black pepper

Note: place the peppers in a hot oven for 2-3 minutes before peeling.

For the garnish
2 tablespoons mini croûtons
1 tablespoon pickled garlic, sliced
1 tablespoon of pitted black olives,
*   finely chopped*
2 tablespoons olive oil
1 tablespoon of chopped chives, finely
*   chopped*

For the ox tongue
Put the water in a large saucepan and bring to the boil. Add all the ingredients and cook the tongue for 4-5 hours until it is tender. Remove from the heat and leave it to cool in the cooking liquor. Once cool, take the tongue out of the cooking liquor and put to one side. Discard the vegetables and stock.

Tripe
Preheat the oven to 150C/gas mark 2. Heat the oil in a metal-handled heavy-based saucepan over a medium heat, add the onions and carrots and cook gently for 4-5 minutes. Add the tomato purée, ½ garlic head, cumin, smoked paprika and bouquet garni and cook for a further 2-3 minutes. Next, add the white wine, chicken stock and tripe and season with salt and black pepper. Place the saucepan in the oven and cook the tripe for 2½-3 hours until it is tender. Remove the carrots and onions, add the red pepper and cook for another hour. Remove the bouquet garni.

For the garnish
Mix the croûtons, garlic and black olives together in a bowl. Add the olive oil and the chives and mix well.

Serving
Reheat the tripe if necessary. Cut 4 x 2cm slices of ox tongue. Melt a little oil and a knob of butter in a frying pan over a medium-high heat, add in the ox tongue and cook for 1 minute on each side until crisp. Place the tripe, some red pepper and a bit of the tripe stock in the bottom of four individual bowls. Slice the ox tongue and place on top of tripe. Finish with the garnish of croûtons, garlic and black olives.

RUMP OF DORNOCH LAMB WITH RED ONION AND SZECHUAN PEPPER COMPOTE

Dornoch lamb is raised in very harsh conditions in Sutherland on the north coast of Scotland. The lambs feed on sea vegetables and seaweed, close to the shoreline. As a result, they have a great fat covering on the rump and the meat is packed full of flavour. It's not so good as a spring lamb, but is excellent later at its peak around August time. In this recipe I've married the lamb with Moroccan flavours I picked up from my time working in the south of France – szechuan peppers, red peppers and dried apricots.

SERVES 4

For the lime
50g sugar
50g water
1 lime, thinly sliced

For the compote
2 tablespoons olive oil
3 red onions, thinly sliced
1 lemon, zested and cut into thin strips
15g szechuan peppercorns, lightly crushed and tied in a muslin cloth
50g dried apricots, chopped
150ml lamb jus
Salt

For the chickpea garnish
10ml chicken stock
10g unsalted butter
100g chickpeas, cooked
50g cooked broad beans
50g red pepper triangles, made by cutting a red pepper into small triangles
20g pickled garlic, sliced
Salt

For the lamb
2 tablespoons olive oil
4 x 150g lamb rumps
Salt and freshly ground black pepper

Lime
Preheat the oven to 50C/gas mark ¼. Put the sugar and water into a saucepan and bring to the boil over a medium heat to create a sugar syrup. Once all the sugar is dissolved, remove from the heat and leave to cool. Dip the lime slices into the sugar syrup and place them on to a baking tray, lined with greaseproof paper, and dry for 3-4 hours in the cool oven until crisp. Set aside.

For the compote
Warm the olive oil in a heavy-based pan over a medium heat. Add the onions and a pinch of salt and cook gently for 4-5 minutes. Add the strips of lemon zest and szechuan peppercorns in the muslin cloth and cook for a further 2 -3 minutes. Then add the apricots and lamb jus and cook slowly over a low heat for 1½ hours until the onions are very soft.

For the chickpea garnish
Put the chicken stock, butter and a pinch of salt in a saucepan over a medium heat and bring to a gentle simmer. Add the chick peas and broad beans and warm through gently for 1-1½ minutes. Just before serving, add the red peppers and pickled garlic and heat through thoroughly.

For the lamb
Preheat the oven to 180C/gas mark 4. Heat the oil in a metal-handled heavy-based pan until hot. Season the lamb with salt and pepper and seal it in the oil for 3-4 minutes until well-coloured on all sides. Next place the pan in the oven for 3-4 minutes, before turning the lamb over and cooking it for a further 3 minutes. Remove from the oven and keeping warm.

Serivng
If necessary, reheat the compote and chickpea garnish. Divide the compote between your serving plates and add some of the chickpea garnish on top of this. Carve the rumps of lamb, add a few slices to each plate and finish off the dish with the slices of lime.

EARL GREY JELLY WITH CITRUS SALAD

I think tea is totally under used in puddings and I like to use Earl Grey in this recipe to create a simple and fresh dessert. It's a favourite in the restaurant, especially in the summer. The citrus salad works well with the bergamot flavours of the Earl Grey jelly. Although I haven't included it here, I often serve either an Earl Grey or crème fraîche sorbet with the dish as well.

SERVES 4

For the citrus salad
2 oranges
2 blood oranges
2 pink grapefruits
2 white grapefruits
2 limes

For the Earl Grey jelly
2½ gelatine leaves
8 oranges, juiced
5 Earl Grey tea bags
50g sugar
10g fresh mint, cut into fine strips

Citrus salad
Peel and segment all the citrus fruits. Arrange them neatly in individual serving bowls, cover and place in the fridge whilst making the jelly.

Earl Grey jelly
Soak the gelatine leaves in cold water for 3-4 minutes until soft. Meanwhile, pour the orange juice into a saucepan and bring it to a simmer over a medium heat. Add the tea bags and sugar to the saucepan. Remove the gelatine from the water and squeeze out any excess water and add to the warm orange juice, whisking until it is dissolved. Remove the saucepan from the heat and leave the tea to infuse for a further 15-20 minutes. Next, pass the liquid through a fine sieve into a bowl and place in the fridge to cool for 10-15 minutes, being careful not to set the jelly. Remove the jelly and bowls of citrus salad from the fridge. Pour the still liquid jelly over the citrus segments, ensuring all the fruit is completely covered. Sprinkle the mint over the jelly and replace the bowls in the fridge for 1½-2 hours, to set completely.

Serving
Remove the bowls from the fridge. Wipe around the rim to remove any condensation and if you have it, place a scoop of sorbet in the middle of each dish.

ATUL KOCHHAR

Fifteen years ago if you'd suggested going out for a posh Indian meal to your friends, they'd probably have thought you were pulling their leg. Back in the 1990s, most people still equated Indian restaurants with their local curry house. Good for a cheap, convivial night out, but hardly haute cuisine or chic. That's all changed now, thanks to the efforts of a handful of top Indian chef-restaurateurs – and to one in particular. Atul Kochhar.

Atul's London restaurant, Benares, is one of the city's culinary hotspots. A chic, moody restaurant – all black granite and gleaming minimalist design, with antique chests and soothing pools of water festooned with floating flowers – it is, perhaps, our capital's most seductively glamorous fine-dining restaurant. And at its centre sits Atul's equally alluring food.

Rooted in the traditional cuisine of his homeland, the Indian sub-continent, that food is unique because it also envelops classical French cooking techniques, amazing British produce and a stylish, contemporary presentation. Walk in through Benares' discreet entrance on Berkeley Square, sit yourself down at its bar with a 'passionate lassi', scan the menu and you might find yourself ordering batter-fried black bream with crushed garden peas and Gorkha tomato chutney; or fennel-infused Kentish lamb chops with goat's cheese and wild rocket salad; or even curry leaf and tarragon-infused lobster rillets. In short, you'll be asking for something that is inspirationally Anglo-Indian; something that is expertly and subtly spiced; something that is beautifully and precisely presented.

Atul's meticulousness and mastery of spicing can be traced back to his childhood. He grew up in Jamshedpur, north-east India, and as a boy excelled in sciences at school. His father, who owned a catering company, noted his son's fastidious nature and urged him to study engineering or medicine. But Atul had other ideas. Being one of six children growing up in a religious family meant that, his father's job aside, food played a central role in the Kochhar household; and Atul loved helping his mother in the kitchen. 'We would have big family meals once a week and the dining room was always the hub of the house,' he remembers. 'I can still recall the excitement and satisfaction I would feel getting to experiment with lots of unknown ingredients.'

However, despite his growing obsession with food, Atul knuckled down and signed up for medical school. He managed to stick it for two weeks before walking out. 'My parents were naturally unimpressed, but I had a burning desire to become a chef,' he says. Cooking, he also realised, was his ticket to see the world and he soon packed his bags and headed off for New Dehli to train at the Oberoi School of Hotel Management.

The Oberoi group is India's most revered breeding ground for aspiring chefs and gives its young cooks a grounding in French classical cuisine as well as in its own and other Asian food cultures. Atul lapped up every scrap of culinary knowledge flung at him – during his training and, once he had graduated, from the kitchens of the group's luxury five-star hotel in New Delhi. After only a year at the hotel, he was promoted to the position of sous chef (second-in-command to you and me). He was on his way.

Working in the kitchens of one of the world's leading hotels was exciting, but Atul soon felt he had learnt all he could in his native land. So when, at the end of 1994, he was offered the chance to become the head chef at a soon-to-be launched restaurant called Tamarind in London's exclusive Mayfair district he didn't hesitate – he was on the plane to England before you could say garam masala. And he's never looked back.

At Tamarind he began to develop and perfect the cooking for which he is famed today. London loved his food and so did the critics and guidebooks. So much so, that in 2001 at the age of 31, Atul became one of the first Indian chefs to be awarded a Michelin star – an accolade many of his British-born colleagues could only dream of.

The kudos that went with the award gave him the springboard from which to launch his own restaurant, Benares, in 2003. Being his own boss meant Atul was free to give full rein to his culinary creativity but with his own restaurant came other, business responsibilities. They began right from the word go because refurbishment of the restaurant site took much longer than expected and Benares launched four months later than planned. 'The first few months were so tough, I remember not sleeping at all!'

Always a quick learner, Atul soon found out he was a restaurateur with flair. Once it found its groove, the chic sophistication and superlative cooking of Benares began to pull in the crowds and net newspaper inches – and Atul himself began to get offers to make television appearances. One of these really spread his fame beyond his adopted city of London and made him a household name in the UK. Beating the British housewives' darling, Gary Rhodes, on the first series of the massively successful *Great British Menu* in 2006 sealed Atul's reputation. From then on he was recognised nationally as a chef who'd reinvigorated a cuisine locked in tradition.

Further series of *Great British Menu* followed – as did a Michelin star for Benares, in 2007. And on the back of his involvement in the show came opportunities to create 'brand Kochhar' – to write books, do more TV and, importantly, open two more restaurants in 2008. One, Ananda, is in Dublin, the other, Vatika, is set among the beautiful surroundings of an English vineyard in Hampshire.

As at Benares, the food at both Atul's new restaurants continues to breakdown the preconceptions about Indian cuisine. The dishes on their menus use Asian and both classical and contemporary western techniques to push beyond, yet also to experiment within the confines of, traditional Indian cooking – itself a great melting pot of different religions and cuisine cultures.

At Vatika, its location in the heart of the Hampshire countryside also influences Atul's ambitions for the restaurant's food. He and his head chef Jitin Joshi (who initially worked for Atul at Benares) source most of their produce from within a 10 mile radius of Wickham, where the restaurant is located. And they're hoping to grow their own vegetables, too, by leasing some adjoining land. 'We want to champion local ingredients and what Hampshire stands for. Like Charles Darwin's theory of evolution

through natural selection, I believe that my food has to adapt to its surroundings to prosper.'

Resting on his laurels is not something that Atul does. Despite his apparent relaxed demeanour he is always plotting the next chapter of his career – and 2010, will see him open another two restaurants. One on the 57th floor of Abu Dhabi's Marriott Central Market hotel, the other on cruise giant P&O's new superliner the *Azura*.

His life, these days, is plotted with precision, with Benares – 'the place where I truly express myself' – still at the centre of operations. Yet though he and his cooking have travelled a long way since his Indian childhood, at heart this 40-year-old is still very much the little boy who enjoyed nothing more than cooking for his family. These days his family cooking is centred around his wife and two young children, six-year-old Amisha and three-year-old Arjun. When they grow up, should they want to follow in their father's footsteps, they will find he has trailblazed an amazing path for them. A path that changed the perception of Indian cooking at the highest levels of the restaurant industry.

Benares Restaurant & Bar
12a Berkeley Square House, Berkeley Square, London W1J 6BS
Phone 020 7629 8886 **www.benaresrestaurant.com**
Vatika
Wickham Vineyard, Botley Road, Shedfield, Southampton SO32 2HL
Phone 01329 830 405 **www.vatikarestaurant.com**
Ananda
Sandyford Road, Dundrum Town Centre, Dublin 14, Ireland
Phone 00 353 1296 0099 **www.anandarestaurant.ie**

WILD MUSHROOM AND SWEETCORN BIRYANI PARCELS WITH SAUTEED MUSHROOMS AND RAITA

Wild mushrooms are one of the treats of the British autumn. They're great with cumin, as are blackberries – another autumnal delight. So it seems apt to combine both in the same dish. Of course you can get cultivated mushrooms throughout the year, so if you want, just adapt the recipe to what you can get hold of – and if you can't get hold of blackberries, blueberries are a good substitute.

SERVES 4

Raita
300g Greek yoghurt
1 teaspoon toasted cumin seeds, crushed in a pestle and mortar
100g blackberries, puréed
Salt

For the biryani parcels
1 tablespoon vegetable oil
1 tablespoon butter
1 teaspoon cumin seeds
2 green cardamom
1 bay leaf
2 garlic cloves, finely chopped
200g onions, finely chopped
2 large Portobello mushrooms, roughly chopped
100g wild mushrooms, roughly chopped
70g sweetcorn kernels
1 teaspoon ground coriander
½ teaspoon ground cumin
½ teaspoon red chilli powder
½ teaspoon garam masala
½ tablespoon tomato purée
1 tablespoon white truffle paste (optional)
2 tablespoons single cream
400g basmati rice, cooked (with 1 bay leaf, 1 cardamom and 2 cloves)
2 tablespoons finely chopped coriander

8 sheets of large filo pastry
110g butter, melted
Salt and freshly ground black pepper

Wild mushrooms
½ tablespoon butter
½ tablespoon vegetable oil
1 garlic clove, crushed through a garlic press
½ teaspoon coriander seeds, crushed
¼ teaspoon chilli flakes
50g almonds, lightly toasted and halved
100g mixed wild mushrooms, roughly sliced
1 tablespoon lemon juice
Salt

For the garnish
A few large sprigs of coriander
20g coriander cress
20g red amaranth
Black truffle shavings

Raita
Put all the ingredients into a food processor and blend together until well combined, then transfer to a container and put in the fridge to chill.

Biryani parcels
Preheat the oven to 180C/gas mark 4. Heat the oil and butter in a saucepan over a medium-high heat, add the cumin seeds, green cardamom and bay leaf and cook until the spice seeds pop open. Add the chopped garlic and cook until lightly coloured, then add the chopped onion and cook until it, too, is lightly coloured. Add the Portobello and wild mushrooms together with the sweetcorn kernels and cook for 2-4 minutes to sweat the mushrooms. Next, add the ground spices and cook for another 2 minutes, stirring to make sure everything is mixed together, before adding the

tomato purée, white truffle paste and cream. Finally, add the rice and chopped coriander, then taste and add a little salt and freshly ground black pepper if necessary. Remove the mushroom rice from the heat.

Brush one side of each sheet of filo pastry all over with melted butter, then place 4 sheets on top of the other 4 sheets to make a double-layered pastry skin. Spoon ¼ of the mushroom rice into the centre of each pastry sheet, fold the sides over the rice filling, then roll the pastry into a parcel and brush each parcel all over with melted butter and seal them. Put the biryani parcels and the coriander sprigs for garnishing on a baking tray and bake in the oven for 2-3 minutes until the parcels are golden, then remove.

Mushrooms
Heat the oil and butter in a frying pan over a medium heat. Add the crushed garlic, coriander seeds and chilli flakes and cook for 1 minute. Next throw in the almonds, followed by the mushrooms and cook for a further 2 minutes, stirring to make sure everything is well mixed. Add the lemon juice and if necessary season with a little salt.

Serving
Scatter the sautéed mushrooms and almonds around your serving plates. Put a biryani parcel, cut in ½, on each plate. Place a dried coriander sprig on top, and finish with some truffle shavings, coriander, cress and red amaranth leaves. Serve with a side bowl of the chilled blackberry raita.

SOFT SHELL CRAB WITH CRISPY FRIED SQUID AND A TRIO OF CHUTNEYS

In the UK, soft-shell crabs are usually sold frozen, but a good fishmonger should be able to order fresh ones for you. The best ones are from Cromer in Norfolk and the West Country. Squid is actually one fish that is better frozen – because as it thaws the protein in the squid relaxes. Fruit chutneys with a bit of sharpness to work against their sugar element always work well with fish – I just change the fruit according to the seasons. And if you're not familiar with chaat masala, it's an Indian spice mix which you can either make yourself or buy from Asian supermarkets or on-line at www.spicesofindia.co.uk. One final bit of advice – it's best to fry the crab and squid concurrently when you make this dish.

SERVES 4

For the plum chutney
2 tablespoons vegetable oil
½ teaspoon of mustard seeds
1 red chilli, broken into pieces
200g canned plums, stoned and cut in half
2 tablespoons raisins
1 teaspoon salt
8 tablespoons sugar
½ teaspoon ground coriander
100ml water
50ml white vinegar
2 drops of rose essence

For the mint and coriander chutney
200g mint, stalks removed
100g coriander, stalks removed
20g ginger, roughly chopped
2 green chilles
2 tablespoons lemon juice
100g Greek yoghurt
1 teaspoon chaat masala
A pinch of sea salt

For the passion fruit chutney
500ml passion fruit purée
300g granulated or palm sugar
¼ teaspoon chilli flakes
Salt

For the crab
1 tablespoon ginger-garlic paste
½ teaspoon ground turmeric
½ teaspoon ground coriander
¼ teaspoon red chilli powder
1 teaspoon Dijon mustard or mustard oil
2 tablespoons chopped coriander
1 tablespoon finely chopped ginger
1 tablespoon lime juice
2 tablespoon rice flour
1 tablespoon cornflour
4 jumbo soft shell crabs
Vegetable oil, for deep frying
Salt

Note: garlic-ginger paste is made with equal quantities of garlic and fresh ginger. Blend the ingredients together with 10% of their total weight in water.

For the squid
500g squid, cut into rings and frozen briefly to tenderise
2 tablespoons rice flour
2 tablespoons corn flour
1 tablespoon red chilli powder
1 tablespoon ginger-garlic paste
1 tablespoon lime juice
2 teaspoons chaat masala
Vegetable oil
Salt

Note: Chaat masala is made from amchoor – a dried ground mango – cumin, kela namak – often called black Indian salt – ground coriander, ground ginger, salt, black pepper, asafoetida and paprika.

For the garnish
A handful of baby rocket leaves
A handful of cress

Plum chutney
Heat the oil in a saucepan over a medium-high heat, then add the mustard seeds and red chilli. Once the seeds begin to crackle, add plums, raisins, salt, sugar, coriander powder, water and white vinegar. Continue to cook on a low heat until the mixture reduces and becomes thick. Remove from heat and add 2 drops of rose essence and cool. Decant into sterilised jars. You can keep the chutney for up to two months.

Mint and coriander chutney
Put the herbs, ginger, chillies and lemon juice into a blender or food processor and process until smooth. Pour the purée into a bowl, then stir in the yoghurt, chaat masala and, if necessary, a pinch of salt. Cover with clingfilm and store in the fridge.

Passion fruit chutney
Mix the passion fruit purée, palm sugar and chilli flakes together in a saucepan over a medium heat and bring to the boil, then gently simmer slowly until a thick consistency is achieved. Remove from the heat and cool.

Crab
Mix all the spices and dried ingredients together in a bowl, then add the crabs, making sure you coat them well with the marinade. Put to one side and marinate for 30 minutes. Heat the oil in a wok or deep-fat fryer over a high heat to 180C then drop in the crabs and fry them for about 2-3 minutes until they are crisp. Drain them on kitchen paper.

Squid

Defrost the squid. Mix the rice and corn flours, red chilli powder, ginger-garlic paste and lime juice together in a bowl, then add the squid rings and coat them thoroughly. Sprinkle the rings with a pinch of salt and chaat masala. Heat the oil in a wok or deep-fat fryer over a high heat and when very hot drop in the squid rings and fry them in batches for about 1-1½ minutes until they are a light golden colour and crispy. Drain them on kitchen paper towel.

Serving

You need to serve this dish quickly while the crab and squid are both still hot and crispy. Pop both on to your plates, add a swipe each of the plum chutney and the mint and coriander chutney. Add a few baby rocket and cress leaves and finish by drizzling a little passion fruit chutney over the crab micro leaves.

ROASTED VENISON WITH PUMPKIN PULAO

You may not associate venison with Indian cooking, but its robust flavour means it can handle a bit of spice and the meat used to be very popular in some regions. The trick of marrying it with spices is in the preparation of a good balanced marinade that will not overpower the character of venison meat. Follow this recipe and I promise you'll end up with a dish for a special occasion.

SERVES 4

For the pear and lemon chutney
100g cooking apples, sliced and then finely cubed
4 lemons, pips removed then sliced and blanched in boiling water
100g red onions, finely chopped
50g raisins
2 tablespoons lemon zest, roughly chopped
15g jaggery or brown sugar
¼ teaspoon ground cinnamon
¼ teaspoon ground nutmeg
¼ teaspoon red chilli powder
2 tablespoons of chopped ginger
150ml white wine vinegar
A pinch of saffron
400g pears, cored and roughly chopped

For the sauce
1kg venison bones and trimmings
½ large onion, roughly chopped
1 carrot, roughly chopped
2 garlic cloves, roughly chopped
2 tablespoons chopped ginger
1 tablespoon tomato purée
½ teaspoon ground cumin
½ teaspoon ground coriander
¼ teaspoon garam masala
300ml red wine
1 litre chicken stock
50g butter

½ tablespoon lemon juice
Splash of vegetable oil
Pinch of sugar (optional)
Salt and freshly ground black pepper

For the pumpkin pulao
1 tablespoon vegetable oil
¼ teaspoon cumin seeds
¼ teaspoon nigella seeds
4 tablespoons chopped onions
300g yellow pumpkin, skinned and finely cubed
½ teaspoon ground turmeric
¼ teaspoon red chilli powder
¼ teaspoon garam masala
½ tablespoon tomato paste
1 tablespoon mango pickle, finely chopped
200g basmati rice, cooked
1 tablespoon finely chopped coriander
Salt

For the venison
1½ tablespoons Dijon mustard
1 tablespoon toasted sesame seeds
1 tablespoon clear honey
½ teaspoon red chilli flakes
¼ teaspoon turmeric powder
600g venison fillet, cut into four
A few violet petals
A splash of vegetable oil

Pear and lemon chutney
Put all the ingredients, excluding the pears, in a heavy-based saucepan over a medium heat and bring to boil, then simmer for 45-50 minutes – or until the mixture thickens. Add the pears and cook for a further 30-40 minutes then spoon the chutney into a sterilised Kilner jar. The chutney will keep for 3-4 weeks.

Sauce
Heat a little vegetable oil in a saucepan over a high heat, add the venison bones and trimmings and quickly sear them until they brown, then turn the heat down a little, add the vegetables and cook for 5-7 minutes until they just begin to soften and the onions are translucent. Add the tomato paste, spices, red wine and chicken stock, bring to a simmer and cook gently for 1 hour. Remove from the heat and strain the sauce through a fine sieve, then return it to the heat and reduced down until it reaches the consistency of a thick sauce. Add the butter and lemon juice, season with a little salt and pepper and remove from the heat. If necessary, add a pinch of sugar to balance the flavours.

Pumpkin pulao
Heat the oil in a saucepan over a medium heat, then add the cumin and nigella seeds and cook them until they pop. Add the chopped onions and cook until they are translucent – it shouldn't take more than 1-2 minutes. Turn the heat down, add in the pumpkin and cook it for 5-7 minutes. Next, add all the ground spices, cook for 1 minute, then add the tomato paste and mango pickle. Check the seasoning and add if necessary a little salt, then continue to cook until the pumpkin is mushy. Once it is, mix in the rice and chopped coriander.

Venison
Preheat the oven to 200C/gas mark 6. Mix the mustard, sesame seeds, honey, chilli flakes and turmeric together in a bowl to make a marinade. Heat the oil in a saucepan over a high heat and sear the venison fillet. Once the meat

(Continued on page 146)

(Continued from page 144)

is sealed, take it off the heat and apply
the marinade liberally then roast the
venison in the oven for 5-9 minutes –
if you like your meat rare, cook it for
a little less time. Remove and rest the
meat in a warm place for 2-4 minutes
before cutting and serving.

Serving
If necessary, warm the pulao rice through
over a low heat. Put a spoonful of rice
on your serving plates, slice the venison
pieces in half and place the slices next to
the rice. Pop a little pear chutney on the
plate and drizzle some of the sauce
around the meat. Finally, finish with
few violet petals.

PEAR PARCEL AND STAR ANISE ICE CREAM

Serving desserts for lunch is always tricky – you have to keep things light and to the point. This dish does just that and has a lovely autumnal flavour match in pears and star anise. Just make sure you don't get heavy-handed with the ghee, though. It's rich and used lightly adds a lovely flavour to the pastry, but it can take the edge of the dish's lightness if you're not careful.

SERVES 4

For the star anise ice cream
250ml milk
250ml double cream
4 star anise
4 yolks
100g castor sugar

For the pears
4 pears
15ml lemon juice
1 vanilla pod, split and seeds removed
85g unsalted butter
120ml Poire William liqueur
50ml ghee
8 sheets of filo pastry
A pinch of salt
250g caster sugar

Star anise ice cream
Put the milk and cream into a saucepan over a medium heat and bring to the boil. Remove from the heat and add the star anise, then leave them to infuse for 3 hours. Next, strain the mixture through a fine sieve into a clean saucepan, return to the heat and bring to the boil again. Meanwhile, mix the egg yolks and sugar together in a bowl. Once the milk and cream have come to the boil, remove it from the heat and gradually pour it over the egg mixture and whisk thoroughly to form a custard. Return the custard to the heat and cook, stirring continuously, until it begins to thicken. When it is thick enough to coat the back of a wooden spoon, remove from the heat and chill over a bowl of ice or in the fridge. When the custard is cool, strain it into an ice-cream machine and churn until firm. If you don't have an ice-cream machine, place the mixture in the freezer, taking it out every 30 minutes to stir. The ice cream is ready when it holds its shape after scooping.

Pears
Peel and core the pears and slice each one into 6 pieces. Put the pears, lemon juice, vanilla seeds, salt and butter in a saucepan over a very low heat and gently cook the fruit. It should take between 2½-3 hours Once the pears are soft, remove from the heat and add the Poire William liqueur. Cool down overnight in the fridge.

Preheat the oven to 180C/gas mark 4. Strain the pears. Completely brush one side of each filo pastry sheet with ghee and then layer 2 sheets on top of each other for each parcel. To make the parcels, place 6 pear slices in the centre of each double-skinned pastry sheet and fold the sides over the pears, then roll up the pastry into a parcel, brush the outside of the parcel with ghee and make sure the parcel is sealed. Place the parcels on a baking tray in the oven and cook for 30 minutes until the pastry is golden.

Serving
Remove the parcels from the oven and put one on each serving plate. Finish with a scoop of star anise ice-cream.

WHITE CHOCOLATE AND PISTACHIO PARFAIT WITH CHERRY COMPOTE, CHERRY SORBET AND AMARETTO SAUCE

Chocolate, pistachio and cherry, for me, is a flavour-match made in heaven – and the way they're combined in this recipe is bold, straightforward and always works. Kuldeep – my pastry chef – is the man that deserves the credit, though. If you're skilled, like him, you can make your own chocolate moulds, but as this involves tempering chocolate I'd always advise taking the easy way out and buying some good-quality, ready-made moulds.

SERVES 4

For the cherry sorbet
30ml stock syrup
100ml cherry purée

For the white chocolate pistachio parfait
60g sugar
1 teaspoon pectin
2 egg whites
87g white chocolate
1 leaf of gelatine
30g pistachio nuts, blanched
180g double cream, whipped
4 chocolate moulds

For the cherry compote
24ml water
1 tablespoon lemon juice
6 peppercorns
40ml port
200g cherries, stoned and then halved
35g sugar
¼ teaspoon pectin

For the amaretto chocolate sauce
40ml condensed milk
25ml milk
40g dark chocolate (70% cocoa solids)
5ml amaretto syrup

NB: *make the amaretto syrup by heating 3ml amaretto liqueur and 2 tablespoons of sugar in a saucepan over a low heat, stirring as it warms to dissolve the sugar.*

Cherry sorbet
Put the stock syrup and cherry purée in a saucepan over a medium-low heat and bring to the boil. Transfer to an ice-cream machine and churn according to its instructions and once churned put in a freezer-proof container and put in the freezer. If you haven't got an ice-cream machine, then place the pear mixture in a shallow dish in the freezer, taking it out every few minutes to stir. When the sorbet is slushy put it into a freezer-proof bowl and put it in the freezer to set completely.

White chocolate and pistachio parfait
Put the sugar, pectin and egg whites in a bowl. Put the bowl over a saucepan of gently simmering water, making sure that the water does not touch the bowl. Whisk the sugar and egg whites together over the heat until it reaches 60C then remove from the heat and continue whisking until the meringue has cooled down.

Meanwhile, melt the chocolate in a bowl over another saucepan of gently simmering water, stirring occasionally and making sure the bowl does not touch the water. Once melted remove from the heat. Put the gelatine into a bowl of cold water for 1-2 minutes until it is softened. Remove and squeeze out the excess water, then add it to the chocolate and stir to dissolve.

Add the melted chocolate and whole pistachios to the meringue, folding-in gently. Next, fold-in the whipped double cream and once it is thoroughly incorporated pour the mixture into chocolate moulds and put in the fridge for 1-2 hours to set.

Cherry compote
Put the water, lemon juice, crushed peppercorns, port and cherries into a saucepan and bring to the boil over a medium heatl. Add the sugar and pectin and stir until the sugar is dissolved, then bring the mixture back to the boil and simmer for 30 minutes. Remove from heat and cool, then strain the mixture through a fine sieve.

Amaretto chocolate sauce
Put the condensed milk and milk into a saucepan and gently warm over a low heat. Meanwhile, melt the chocolate in a bowl over a saucepan of gently simmering water, making sure the bowl does not touch the water. Once it has melted, remove it from the heat and add the milk to the chocolate. Mix well, then add the amaretto syrup.

Serving
First of all, drizzle some amaretto chocolate sauce on your serving plates. Take the white chocolate and pistachio parfait out of the freezer. Loosen the parfaits by briefly heating the outside of the moulds with a culinary blow torch or gently running a warm flat-bladed knife around the edges of the moulds. Pop the parfaits out on to the plates, over the sauce. Add a scoop each of cherry compote and cherry sorbet. If you want, you can also garnish with a couple of preserved morello cherries.

DANNY MILLAR

Situated at a crossroads on the A22 just 5 miles from Comber on the way to Downpatrick in Country Down, Balloo House is as close to an oasis as Northern Ireland can muster. Its plain, white-washed façade may not hint at the enchanted firelit, refuge within but step over the threshold into its cosy, wood-panelled bar, experience a wonderful, warm welcome and you'll suddenly find a place full of pure joy. A place where time just stops. Very much like the pint of Irish stout that is obligatory as you walk in, a meal at Balloo House can never – should never – be rushed.

Originally a coaching inn dating back to the 1600s, Balloo House is these days a combination of a stone-flagged brasserie on the ground floor and fine dining elegance upstairs. But how did a drinking hole for horse-backed messengers and tradesmen (as the local Bridgestone restaurant guide puts it) metamorphose into one of

Ireland's finest foodie destinations? The answer is simple – with the help of its 37-year-old chef-proprietor Danny Millar and some great local raw produce.

Balloo House is a just a mile from Strangford Lough, the largest sea inlet in the British Isles. Its 150 square kilometres of water contains some of the best seafood in Ireland. Lobster, langoustine and crab that are so sweet and succulent it makes you wonder why, until recently, they were almost totally exported to Spain and Europe. The local landscape is green and fertile, too, with cattle, poultry and arable crops in abundance. Top-quality vegetables almost throw themselves out of the ground at you around here. In short, Danny has a great set of tools with which to create his menu.

Many chefs are blessed with great produce, few cook with Danny's passionate and intelligent simplicity. He really cares about his ingredients and resists the temptation to muck about with them, changing his menu regularly to reflect the very distinct Irish seasons. Seafood, game, hearty stews and pies all segue seamlessly into each other throughout the year. Not-to-be-missed delights range from poached local sea trout with homemade salad cream, to a venison salad with crispy sweetbreads. Each dish is served without a fanfare but as you eat them they each feel like a loving embrace from an old friend.

Danny's love affair with food came out of, on the face of it, a challenging upbringing in the middle of strife-torn Belfast at the height of the Troubles. His family was large (four boys and four girls) and his father was unemployed for a while. Life was tough to say the least. Belfast in the 1970s was on fire, bombings were normal and death was a very real part of everyday life. In fact, Danny's parents moved house twice before they settled; their first home was burnt down during a particularly violent sectarian exchange and the second one was next door to a pub, the bombing of which blew the living room wall down.

Despite the dangers and hardship, food was always given due attention in the Millar household. Danny remembers very simple meals with the emphasis on sustenance and volume – large pots of soup, or beef shin stews with potatoes and cabbage. The seeds of his own culinary career, however, were sown when he was 12-years-old and was given the option of taking a simple home economics class at school. A schoolboy crush on his attractive female teacher sealed the deal – he signed up and was soon bringing home goodies like shortbread and cakes. He quickly became the 'bees knees' amongst appreciative friends and family as he delivered his weekly food parcels – and the connection between giving food and giving people pleasure is something he's clearly never forgotten.

Bitten by the culinary bug, at the age of 16 Danny headed off to catering college securing, when he left a couple of years later, his first proper job at the Portaferry Hotel on the banks of Strangford Lough. This was a top-class kitchen and Danny was blown away by seeing whole turbot, langoustine and lobster fresh from the lough's waters come through its doors. When Portaferry's chef, his first mentor, left to go and work in England, Danny followed him to a hotel in rural West Sussex, eventually spreading his wings to work in Europe at a large spa resort in Germany's Black Forest.

When he took the job, he didn't speak German. But Danny loved it and his spell in Germany really made him understand the importance of cooking seasonally. It introduced him, as well, to the very particular style of German cuisine, to traditional dishes such as fillets of venison served, pork-pie like, in pork fat. Danny found the food inspirational and stayed five years, soaking up knowledge like a sponge. 'I think German food is incredibly underrated and everything I know about cooking I learned in Germany,' he maintains.

Home ties were strong, though, and in 1995 he eventually returned to Northern Ireland to work at Shanks restaurant in Bangor, at the time one of the most prestigious restaurants in the country. Its chef-proprietor was the late, much missed, Robbie Millar, one of the pioneers of modern Irish food, and Danny spent two years with him before taking up his first head chef job at The Narrows restaurant back in his old stomping ground of Portaferry. Here he once again revelled in having the lough's fine seafood landed right outside his kitchen door. It's no wonder, when the opportunity at Balloo House came along in 2006, that he jumped at the chance of returning to the area.

Before that happened, though, he had one more culinary port-of-call: working for one of Northern Ireland's most famous and influential restaurateurs, Paul Rankin, at his Belfast restaurant, Cayenne. Paul was about as famous as any Irish chef had ever been: he'd put Northern Ireland on the

culinary map by winning a clutch of accolades for his former restaurant, Roscoff, and become well-known through his many appearances on television. When Danny joined Cayenne as its head chef, Paul had a restaurant empire of several restaurants and cafés. At first, the relationship between the two chefs flourished, but after four years, the strains and size of the Rankin empire took its toll on both men. When Danny heard on the grapevine that the new owner of Balloo House, Ronan Sweeney, needed an inspirational chef, he couldn't wait to get back to the countryside surrounding Strangford Lough.

Going into business with Ronan, and returning within spitting distance of the lough, proved to be a perfect decision. The area just seems to suit Danny's cooking down to the ground, allowing him to make real connections between his produce

DANNY MILLAR

larder outside the kitchen door and what he puts on the plate in front of his customers. The local environment is the engine house for his menu. Strangford lobster served with polenta and Parmesan gnocchi; Portavogie turbot with white bean purée with celeriac and truffle mash and wild mushrooms; Dexter rump steak from down the road with slow-cooked shin and red wine pie and duck-fat chips. All these are typical of the type of dishes that bestride the Balloo House menu.

Like Danny's bespectacled face, these dishes have an engaging honesty about them; and that openness carries through to the whole restaurant because he has an innate understanding of hospitality that cannot be taught or learned. It's in his marrow. That's why the thing that really fires his enthusiasm is seeing the smiles of joy on his diners' faces as they tuck into a meal in his dining room. 'I tell my staff, if you don't love what you are doing you might as well give it up!' he says.

But if you're thinking of paying Balloo House a visit, here's a bit of free advice. Don't wear a belt – if you do, you'll have to loosen it. The food's that good. And once you've had your first sweet bite of Strangford seafood you may never want to leave your table at all.

Balloo House
1 Comber Road, Killinchy, Newtownards BT23 6PA
Phone 028 9754 1210 **www.balloohouse.com**

CHICKEN AND VEGETABLE BROTH WITH BUTTERED SODA FARLS AND CHICKEN LIVERS

A twist on a broth my Mum used to make with left-over chicken. Occasionally she would use a shin of beef as the base for the broth. It's a very homely, comforting dish and I serve it with soda farls – or soda bread – which is a typical Ulster accompaniment. At Balloo House I spread some crushed chicken livers onto the soda farls, which makes the dish a little more sophisticated for the restaurant.

SERVES 4-6

For the soup
3 medium organic free-range chickens
3 free-range chicken carcasses, roughly chopped
4 litres of cold water
1 onion, finely chopped
1 carrot, finely chopped
2 sticks celery, finely chopped
A small handful of fresh parsley stalks

For the chicken livers
100g chicken livers, trimmed and veins removed
100ml buttermilk
50g butter
Salt and freshly ground black pepper

For the soup garnish
4 baby courgettes, sliced
1 bunch baby carrots, sliced
4 spring onions, cut into batons
100g barley, cooked
100g peas, shelled and cooked
100g broad beans, podded and blanched

For the soda farls
250g plain flour
½ teaspoon bicarbonate of soda
1 teaspoon salt
1 teaspoon sugar
200ml buttermilk
1 egg yolk, beaten

Drizzle of vegetable oil
100g unsalted butter
2-3 tablespoons of chopped parsley

Soup

Remove the breasts and leg meat from the chicken and place in the fridge. You only need the leg meat for this dish – save the breasts to use in something else.

Place the rest of the chicken along with the chicken carcasses into a large saucepan. Cover with water and bring to the boil over a medium heat. Drain, then return the chicken to the saucepan and add the vegetables and parsley stalks and cover with the 4 litres of cold water. Bring to the boil again, reduce the heat and simmer for 1½ hours. Add the reserved chicken legs to the saucepan and cook for a further 20 minutes, or until cooked through. Remove the legs from the stock and shred the meat off the bones with a fork. Place the meat into a dish, cover with clingfilm and chill in the fridge until needed.

Allow the stock to cool down to room temperature, cover with clingfilm and chill in the fridge. When chilled, strain the stock through a fine sieve into a container and then freeze it overnight. Next day, dip the sides of the container in hot water for a few seconds to loosen the frozen stock from the sides and tip it into a sieve, lined with a muslin cloth, placed over a clean bowl. Allow the stock to defrost through into the bowl, leaving behind any impurities in the cloth.

Chicken livers

Place the chicken livers into a bowl and add the buttermilk, making sure the livers are covered. Now cover the bowl with clingfilm and put the livers in the fridge for 2 hours. Drain, pat dry and put to one side until needed.

Soup garnish

Put the chicken stock into a clean saucepan and bring to the boil over a medium heat. Drop in and blanch the courgettes, carrots and spring onions for 2-3 minutes. Add the shredded chicken leg meat, the barley, peas and broad beans. Warm through thoroughly for 4-5 minutes. Remove from heat and keep warm.

Soda farls

Put the flour, bicarbonate of soda, salt and sugar into a bowl and mix together. Make a well in the centre and add the buttermilk and egg. Mix lightly until everything comes together to form a dough. Roll out the dough on a floured work surface to 1cm thickness and cut it into rounds with a 4cm pastry cutter. Lightly flour on both sides. Brush a frying pan with a little vegetable oil and warm over a low heat, then drop in the soda farls and cook for 4-5 minutes on both sides, or until golden and cooked through. In a separate pan, melt the butter and fry the cooked soda farls for 2-3 minutes on both sides to crisp them up.

Serving

Season the chicken livers with salt and freshly ground black pepper. Melt the 50g of butter in a frying pan until foaming, then pop in the livers and fry them for 2-3 minutes on both sides, or until golden-brown but still slightly pink in the middle. Transfer the livers to a bowl, crush them with a fork, then spread them onto the toasted soda farls and sprinkle over a little of the chopped parsley. Meanwhile, put the chicken soup into a saucepan and bring to the boil over a medium heat. Check the seasoning and add salt and black pepper if necessary. Ladle the soup into 4 serving bowls and serve the soda farls topped with chicken livers on the side.

LOIN OF SPRING LAMB WITH HISPI CABBAGE, PEAS, BACON AND SHEPHERD'S PIE

Everyone loves a shepherd's pie and this is my version, well one of my versions. We often substitute venison for the lamb, top the pie with a butternut squash purée and serve it with some loin of venison on the side. However we do it, it's always very tasty. Shepherd's pie is a homely dish, but in the restaurant we serve it with a little bit of finesse and the different cuts of lamb provide an extra dimension of luxury. If you can't get hold of hispi cabbage, Savoy cabbage is fine.

SERVES 6

For the shepherd's pie
1 tablespoon vegetable oil
500g neck of spring lamb
2 large carrots
1 onion, finely chopped
2 tablespoons tomato purée
5 sprigs of thyme
4 garlic cloves, finely chopped
2 litres of chicken stock
300g desirée or other floury potatoes
150g butter
150ml double cream
Salt and freshly ground black pepper

For the rack of lamb
4 x racks of spring lamb
1 tablespoon light olive oil
4 sprigs of thyme

For the mushy peas
150g shelled fresh peas
1 shallot, sliced
1 clove of garlic, finely sliced
1 sprig of mint, finely chopped
100ml double cream

For the cabbage and bacon
50g butter
400g hispi cabbage, finely sliced
100g smoked streaky bacon, finely chopped
8 spring onions
100g shelled fresh peas

Shepherd's pie
Preheat the oven to 140C/gas mark 1. Put the vegetable oil into a deep roasting tray and place over a medium heat until hot, then seal the neck of lamb in it until the meat is golden brown. Add the carrots, onion, tomato purée, thyme, garlic and chicken stock. Place in the oven and braise for 2-3 hours until tender. Take out and allow to cool. Remove the lamb and carrots. Flake the meat and chop up the carrots into small cubes. Strain the stock through a fine sieve into a clean saucepan, replace on the heat and reduce it until it reaches a sauce consistency. Taste to check the seasoning and if necessary add a little salt and pepper. Return the flaked lamb and cubed carrot to the sauce and keep warm.

Boil the potatoes in salted water until cooked. Put the butter and cream into a saucepan over a medium heat and bring to the boil. Push the potatoes through a drum sieve or potato ricer into a clean saucepan and add the butter and cream mixture. Add a little salt and pepper if necessary.

Racks of lamb
Trim all sinew and fat from the racks of lamb. Heat the olive oil in a frying pan over a medium-high heat, then add in and gently cook the racks of lamb with the thyme for about 4-5 minutes on each side or until the meat is pink in the middle (if your pan isn't big enough, do this in two batches). Alternatively, cook the racks in a medium-high oven for about 15-20 minutes, or until pink in the middle. Remove the lamb from the heat and put it to one side to rest.

Mushy peas
Place a saucepan of salted water over a medium heat, bring to the boil and blanch the peas in it for 2-3 minutes, until they are just tender. Remove one third of the peas and set aside. Add the shallot, garlic, mint and cream to the remainder of the peas and bring them back to the boil. Drain, season the vegetables with a little salt if necessary, then put into a blender or food processor and blitz to a purée. Add in the whole peas to the purée and mix well.

Cabbage and bacon
Melt the butter in a large saucepan over a medium heat. Add the cabbage and bacon and cook them for 2 minutes. Add the spring onions and peas and cook for a further 2 to 3 minutes, remove from the heat and keep to one side.

Serving
Reheat all the elements where necessary. Place a spoonful of mushy peas into a Kilner jar. Add in a layer of shepherd's pie filling and top it with mashed potato. Put some cabbage on your serving plates, carve the racks of lamb and place four cutlets per portion on top of the cabbage.

ROAST RIB OF DEXTER BEEF WITH POTATO BOXTY AND ROAST AUTUMN VEGETABLES, GRAVY AND HORSERADISH SAUCE

Few dishes can beat a great roast beef on a Sunday. I like to use Dexter beef which is a rare Irish breed that at one point was in danger of dying out, but as a result of campaigning is now growing in numbers again. Our beef is raised by our butcher on a farm just 10 minutes from the restaurant. The animal is smaller than the average beef cattle with a good depth of fat which is like butter, helping to produce the most wonderful flavour in the meat. The potato boxty is a classic Irish garnish – the potato cake.

SERVES 5

For the horseradish sauce
20g horseradish, finely grated
2 tablespoons cider vinegar
1 teaspoon English mustard
1 teaspoon caster sugar
150ml crème fraîche, drained
Salt and freshly ground black pepper

For the beef and vegetables
200g carrots
200g beetroot
200g parsnips
2 large onions
2.25kg rib of Dexter beef (minimum
    of 5 rib bones)
2 tablespoons olive oil
Salt and freshly ground black pepper

For the potato boxty
100g butter
100g spring cabbage, finely shredded
1 bunch spring onions, finely sliced
100g bacon, finely chopped
200g potatoes, cooked and roughly
    mashed
Salt and freshly ground black pepper

For the gravy
2 shallots, sliced
2 cloves of garlic, crushed
2 sprigs of thyme
1 tablespoon flour
1 litre chicken stock

Horseradish sauce
Put the horseradish and vinegar in a saucepan over a medium heat and bring to the boil. Remove from the heat and leave the horseradish to infuse for 1 hour, then add the remaining ingredients and season with salt and pepper.

Beef and vegetables
Preheat the oven to 180C/gas mark 4. Cut the carrots, beetroot, parsnips and onions into similar-sized chunky pieces and place in a roasting tray. Generously season the outside of the beef with salt and black pepper. Heat the oil in a frying pan over a medium-high heat until smoking, then sear the beef on all sides for 3-4 minutes until golden-brown all over. Place the beef on the roasting tray with the vegetables and roast in the oven for 35-40 minutes. Remove the beef from the tray and leave to rest on a warm platter for 15 minutes, reserving the cooking juices in the tray. Keep the vegetables warm on a separate plate.

For the potato boxty
Melt half of the butter in a frying pan, add the cabbage, spring onions and bacon and gently cook for about 5 minutes until the vegetables are soft. Add the mashed potato to the pan, mix well with the vegetables and season again with a little salt and pepper if necessary. Remove from the heat and allow everything to cool slightly, then shape the mixture into 5 equal-sized patties. Melt the

remaining butter in a clean frying pan over a medium high heat and fry the patties for 2-3 minutes on both sides or until golden brown all over. Remove and place on some kitchen paper.

Gravy
Place the tray used to cook the beef over a high heat and add the shallots, garlic and thyme. Cook for 4-5 minutes, until the shallots are starting to colour. Then add the flour and the chicken stock and continue to cook over a high heat, stirring frequently to scrape up any browned bits from the bottom, until the gravy is reduced in by one third in volume. Taste and add a little salt and pepper if necessary, then remove from the heat and strain through a fine sieve.

Serving
Carve the beef, allowing 1 rib per portion. Place the ribs on each serving plate accompanied by the vegetables and a potato boxty. Serve with the gravy in a boat and the horseradish sauce in a dish on the side.

POACHED WILD SEA TROUT WITH CRAB AND POTATO SALAD, PICKLES AND SALAD CREAM

Growing up, the only fish my Mum served the family was salmon out of a tin, together with some potato salad and different jars of pickles. So here I have recreated that combination of ingredients, but using wild sea trout in place of the tinned salmon. I just love the sweetness of the salad cream alongside the sour flavours of the pickles, while the crab lifts the potato salad out of the ordinary.

SERVES 4

For the pickled beetroot
8 baby beetroots
1-2 handfuls of sea salt
300ml red wine vinegar
100g brown sugar
1 teaspoon caraway seeds

For the pickled cauliflower
*1 small cauliflower, outer leaves
    removed and cut into small florets*
300ml cider vinegar
100g caster sugar
2 sprigs of fresh tarragon
½ teaspoon of black peppercorns
½ teaspoon of mustard seeds

For the pickled baby onions
8 baby onions
300ml cider vinegar
100g caster sugar
1 teaspoon mustard seeds

For the pickled cucumber
*1 small cucumber, peeled and halved,
    deseeded and cut into batons*
1-2 tablespoons sea salt
50ml white wine vinegar
2 tablespoons English mustard
20g sugar
½ bunch of dill

For the sea trout
1 x 1kg wild sea trout
200ml fish stock
50ml white wine
2 teaspoons of chopped parsley stalks
*2 teaspoons of chopped tarragon
    stalks*
Salt and freshly ground black pepper

For the salad cream
2 free-range hard-boiled egg yolks
2 tablespoons English mustard
½ lemon, juiced
1 tablespoon caster sugar
2 tablespoons white wine vinegar
150ml evaporated milk
150ml olive oil
Salt and ground white pepper

For the crab and potato salad
6 new potatoes
*1 small bunch of chives, finely
    chopped*
*1 small bunch of flat leaf parsley,
    finely chopped*
150g white crab meat

Pickled beetroot
Preheat the oven to 200C/gas mark 6. Scrub the beetroot, then place it on a bed of sea salt in a roasting tray and bake in the oven for 20 minutes, or until tender. Remove the beetroot from the oven, peel off the skin and slice and place into a bowl. Put the vinegar, sugar and caraway seeds in a stainless-steel saucepan over a medium heat and bring to the boil. Once the sugar has dissolved, pour the pickling liquor over the warm beetroot. Leave to marinate for 15-20 minutes, drain and put to one side.

Pickled cauliflower
Put a saucepan of water over a medium heat and bring to the boil. Blanch the cauliflower florets for 30 seconds in it, then drain and put them in a bowl. Put the vinegar, sugar, tarragon, peppercorns and mustard in a stainless-steel saucepan over a medium heat and bring to the boil. Once the sugar has dissolved, pour the pickling liquor over the warm cauliflower. Leave to marinate for 15-20 minutes, drain and put to one side.

Pickled baby onions
Put a saucepan of water over a medium heat and bring to the boil. Drop in the baby onions, skin on, and cook for 1 minute. Drain, peel and slice the onions in half, keeping the root intact, and place into a bowl. Put the vinegar, sugar, and mustard seeds in a stainless-steel saucepan over a medium heat and bring to the to the to the boil. Once the sugar has dissolved, pour the pickling liquor over the warm onions. Leave to marinate for 15-20 minutes, drain and put to one side.

Pickled cucumber
Place the cucumber in a colander and sprinkle it with the sea salt. Leave for 2 hours, then rinse in cold water, pat dry with a clean tea towel and put it into a bowl. Mix together all the remaining cucumber pickle ingredients in a bowl to make a dressing, then pour this over the cucumber. Leave to marinate for 15-20 minutes. Drain and put to one side.

Sea trout

Gut, clean and fillet the sea trout.
Remove any pin bones and skin.
Lightly season the fillet with salt and
freshly ground black pepper, then cut
it into four equal portions. Put the fish
stock, white wine, parsley and
tarragon into a large saucepan over a
medium heat, bring to the boil then
reduce to a simmer, pop in the fish and
gently poach the sea trout for
4 minutes, or until the fish is just
cooked through. Remove the saucepan
from the heat and keep warm.

Salad cream

Place all of the salad cream
ingredients, apart from the oil and
seasoning, into a food processor.
Blend, then slowly pour in the oil, still
blending, until you have a smooth,
emulsified cream. Add a little salt and
freshly ground black pepper to season.

Crab and potato salad

Put a saucepan of water over a
medium heat and bring to the boil,
add in the new potatoes, unpeeled,
and cook for 8-10 minutes, or until
tender. Drain, remove the skins and
keep warm. Divide the salad cream in
half, keeping one half to one side to
use later. Place the second half in a
bowl and add in the chives, parsley
and crabmeat. Put the potatoes in a
bowl and crush with a fork, then
combine them with the salad cream
and crabmeat mixture. Season with a
little salt and freshly ground black
pepper.

Serving

Spoon some crab and potato salad into
the middle of your serving plates. Place
the sea trout fillet on top, add a little of
the beetroot, cauliflower, onion and
cucumber pickles around and drizzle
some of the remaining salad cream
around the edges of the plates.

RHUBARB AND CUSTARD

I love the simplicity of the description of this dish and the fact that it evokes memories of happy times. It basically involves a lovely upside-down vanilla sponge, a rhubarb compote and a rich custard ice cream. It's always a crowd pleaser in the restaurant.

SERVES 4

For the custard ice cream
250ml whole milk
250ml double cream
2 vanilla pods, split and the seeds
   scraped out
5 free-range egg yolks
130g caster sugar

For the rhubarb compote
300g rhubarb, trimmed and cut into
   batons
200g caster sugar
1 vanilla pod, split and the seeds
   scraped out
1 orange, juiced

For the sponge
4 free-range eggs
180g caster sugar
2 vanilla pods, split and seeds scraped
   out
200g unsalted butter, melted
180g flour, sieved

Custard ice cream
Put the milk, cream, vanilla pods and seeds into a saucepan and bring to the boil over a medium heat. Once the boil is reached, turn off the heat and remove the vanilla pods. In a large bowl, whisk together the egg yolks and sugar until they are pale and fluffy, then slowly add the cream mixture, whisking all the time. You need to end up with a smooth creamy custard. Return the mixture to a clean saucepan and cook over a low heat, stirring continuously, until the custard is thick enough to coat the back of a wooden spoon. Strain the custard through a fine sieve into a clean bowl, cover with clingfilm and place into the fridge until completely cool. Pour two thirds of the chilled custard mixture into an ice-cream maker and churn according to the manufacturer's instructions, then transfer the ice cream to a freezer container and freeze until ready to serve. If you don't have an ice-cream machine, place the custard into the freezer, taking it out every 30 minutes to stir. The ice cream is ready when it holds its shape after scooping. Keep the remaining custard to one side.

Rhubarb compote
Put the rhubarb, sugar, vanilla pod and seeds and orange juice into a saucepan over a low heat and gently simmer for 5-6 minutes, or until the rhubarb is soft. Remove from the heat and discard the vanilla pod. Check for sweetness and add a little more sugar if necessary. Blend one third of the rhubarb compote in a liquidiser until smooth, keeping the rest of the compote to one side.

Sponge
Preheat the oven to 170C/gas mark 3. Place the eggs, sugar and vanilla seeds into a bowl over a saucepan of gently simmering water, making sure the water does not touch the bowl, and mix the ingredients together for 10 minutes with an electric whisk until they are light and fluffy. Gradually add the melted butter to the egg mixture, continuing to whisk until it is fully incorporated. Remove the bowl from the heat and fold in the sieved flour until you have a smooth mixture, taking care not to overwork the mixture. Lightly butter and flour 4 moulds, measuring 7.5cm in diameter. Place a spoonful of the reserved rhubarb compote into the bottom of each mould. Pour the sponge mixture on top of the compote until the moulds are two thirds full. Place the moulds into a deep roasting tray, then pour enough boiling water into the tray to come halfway up the moulds. Cover the tray with kitchen foil and bake in the oven for 8-12 minutes, or until the sponge is risen and cooked through (the sponge should be springy to the touch when it is ready). Remove from the oven.

Serving
Gently warm the puréed rhubarb compote and remaining custard over a low heat. Turn the rhubarb sponge carefully out on to four serving plates and serve with a scoop of custard ice cream, puréed rhubarb compote and custard.

NATHAN OUTLAW

[In February 2010, Nathan Outlaw moved his restaurant from Fowey to the St Enodoc Hotel in Rock, near Padstow.] Restaurant Nathan Outlaw lies in the heart of Daphne du Maurier territory, in the sleepy Cornish harbour town of Fowey. Situated on the town's highly exclusive and desirable Esplanade, it has quickly become one of the true destination restaurants in Britain. Its modern, clean dining room, with a sweeping view over the River Fowey estuary and secret smugglers' coves, is full of life and bonhomie and Nathan's food has become a very big reason to park your yacht right outside the restaurant and pop in for dinner. This is pirate country and Restaurant Nathan Outlaw is a mighty treasure chest indeed.

Nathan entered the food world very early, at the tender age of 14, working alongside his father, who was also a chef. After college in Kent, it was a stint at the InterContinental London, Park Lane hotel under the highly respected chef Peter Kromberg that put him on his way.

He stayed in London, spending a formative time working with French maestro Eric Chavot and, briefly, Gary Rhodes, and you can see echoes of Gary in his clean interpretations of British standards. Dishes like his leek and potato soup with brown shrimp and mustard, or his veal with piccalilli – slivers of pink outdoor-reared rose veal lying on a light streak of cauliflower purée that come with a delicious homemade piccalilli (see recipe, page 168). His menu is packed full of such simple-sounding treats but it takes a chef of great skill and confidence to do so little to ingredients.

Nathan's passion is fish, as some beautifully delicate pieces of lemon sole sitting in a bowl of lovely, lemony sauce with wild garlic dumplings proves (see recipe, page 175). This obsession began when, at an early stage in his career, Nathan turned his back on London and headed west to work in the kitchen of the Cornish culinary king, Rick Stein, at Padstow. It's this experience that has had the greatest effect on his life. Not only did he meet his future wife, Rachel, at Rick's Seafood Restaurant but he also absorbed the way Rick understands the individual needs of each fish species and how to show it off to its best advantage. Nathan's happy just to use simple sauces with fish, often made from mayonnaise bolstered with fish stock; he doesn't have a problem letting a piece of lightly cured salmon sit naked on a little marinated beetroot risotto. It's Rick Stein with bells on!

Apart from Rick, one of Nathan's greatest culinary influences has been the cerebral and meticulous John Campbell. Prior to going it alone in Cornwall in 2003, Nathan was head chef to Campbell's executive chef at the much-acclaimed Vineyard at Stockcross near Newbury where he picked up John's ability to make ambitious dishes consistently possible.

The Vineyard was recognised by the most influential restaurant guidebook of them all (at least for chefs), Michelin, but Nathan soon earned its attention in his own right. In 2003, at the youthful age of 25, he opened his own restaurant in another Cornish fishing village, Rock. It shared its name with that of Captain Pugwash's erstwhile vessel, the Black Pig, and was awarded a Michelin star a mere eight months after opening. It put Nathan's name onto the food map of Britain and into an elite group of chefs. The experience also taught him humility, as it wasn't very long before he was pulling down the shutters for the last time and back on the hunt for work, after closing the Black Pig for good. But despite the bitter lesson of the closure, his Black Pig experiment had shown Nathan the level of culinary and business finesse he needed to gain a coveted place in the red guidebook.

The setback was temporary. It wasn't long before Nathan had the chance to open his eponymous eatery in Fowey. Putting your name above the door of a restaurant is a brave thing to do but shows the confidence of this, now, 31-year-old chef. His confidence was vindicated, too – in 2008 – when Michelin awarded his little gem of a restaurant a 'rising two star' status. That puts him into a truly exclusive club.

The Marina Villa Hotel, which plays host to restaurant Nathan Outlaw, overlooks Fowey's marina harbour at its back and sits directly on the street at its front. It's one of those places that gets you a little excited as you walk in, even though it probably needs a lick of paint in places and a new roof. Who cares, when it's so beautifully personal?

The restaurant is free from the sometimes clinical, homogenous feel so often found in similar establishments. You won't find tablecloths here and the staff chat freely about their love of the dishes. It's wonderfully Cornish, as is the food. Nathan's tasting menu, in particular, is a meandering journey through West Country produce culminating in some spectacular desserts.

A chef that loves desserts is a chef that leaves his customers happy and Nathan's are an alluring co-production with his pastry chef, Gordon Gray, another graduate of Stockcross. Peanut mousse with espresso 'soil' (included here) is all Gordon's and extremely impressive, showing, like Nathan's creations, a lightness of touch coupled with a real desire to experiment.

For the record, Nathan is an easy-going man with an inviting smile. His laugh is genuine and he has some immensely impressive, fiery-red sideburns, though, luckily, these don't seem to indicate a temper to match. Entering his restaurant kingdom down a windy staircase, you pass the kitchen, its energy held back by a simple swing door, its boiler-house atmosphere of culinary activity much in evidence through a small window.

The kitchen has a wall of fame, above the work surface, where notable diners are invited to write a note. The scrawlers are a motley crew of comedians, television stars and rock legends. Nathan only lets those who 'are worthy' sign and one or two have been denied!

The kitchen is open each evening and for weekend lunches and it maintains a leisurely ebb and flow throughout the day. Activity starts early, with chefs slowly checking over deliveries and preparing the fish and vegetables, while any meat gets trimmed up and popped into slow-cooking water baths. As the sun slowly moves over the estuary outside the pace quickens, until the first orders are taken at seven o'clock for the dinner service.

Each night that the restaurant is open, people come out of the inky Cornish night to sit in Nathan's low-ceilinged dining room and discover what magic he can conjure up in the

kitchen. In the summer, regulars opt for the corner table with a 180-degree view of the river and sit watching the boats in the estuary rise and fall on the tide as the sunset comes in – just before they tuck into their veal or wreckfish, or whatever joyous main dish they've chosen. It makes for the perfect mid-course *amuse-bouche* and shouldn't be missed.

If you can't make it to Fowey for the sunset, Nathan has another ace up his sleeve. A sweeping estuary view of the River Camel from the terrace of his newly opened grill, back in his old stomping ground of Rock. The view is more panoramic than at Fowey because the mouth of the Camel is less dramatic – but it's still beautiful enough to lift the heart as a sunset pre-dessert. Nathan opened the restaurant in May 2008 at the St Enodoc Hotel and it allows him to showcase Cornwall's wonderful seafood and unique meat, like oysters from nearby Porthilly and pork from the rare breed Cornish black pig, in a much more robust but equally delicious way.

But whether you're in Fowey or Rock, don't let the sunsets and striking geography blind you to the reason you're there – to eat Nathan's wonderful food. There's just one thing, whatever you do don't mention to any well-heeled local clientele that their chef is a bit of a Kentish pirate, who has evaded all Cornish coastal patrols and smuggled himself right into their Cornish heartland. **[In February 2010, Nathan Outlaw moved his restaurant from Fowey to the St Enodoc Hotel in Rock, near Padstow.]**

Restaurant Nathan Outlaw
and **Outlaw Seafood & Grill**
The St. Enodoc Hotel, Rock, Cornwall PL27 6LA
Phone 01208 863394 **www.enodoc-hotel.co.uk**

ROSE VEAL, RED ONION COMPOTE AND CAULIFLOWER CHEESE WITH PICCALILLI SAUCE

With its pickles, cauliflower and veal this dish is, for me, a celebration of an important part of our British culinary heritage. I only use veal reared to welfare-friendly standards by the Real Veal Company. Their calves are reared in the open air at Bocaddon Farm near Looe and slaughtered much later than they would be in Europe. The pressed chuck veal element needs to be made overnight.

SERVES 4

For the braised veal
500g veal chuck, trimmed of fat and sinew
1 medium onion, finely diced
2 cloves of garlic, finely chopped
2 carrots, peeled and finely chopped
1 tablespoon chopped thyme
Sunflower oil
500ml beer
200ml reduced veal stock
Sea salt

For piccalilli glaze
2 garlic cloves, chopped
1 tablespoon ground turmeric
2 tablespoons English mustard
½ tablespoon ground ginger
½ tablespoon cayenne pepper
2 tablespoons mustard seeds
200ml water
200ml white wine vinegar
100g caster sugar

For the red onion compote
4 red onions, finely sliced
1 star anise
1 orange, zest removed and juiced
100ml port
100ml red wine
50ml red wine vinegar
50ml honey
Sea salt

For the cauliflower cheese
1 cauliflower, trimmed, cored and chopped into equal-sized pieces
20g unsalted butter
1 tablespoon of water
100g goat's cheese

For the piccalilli sauce
50g caster sugar
2 garlic cloves, roughly chopped
1 teaspoon turmeric
50g fresh ginger, peeled and sliced
1 bay leaf
50ml red wine vinegar
200ml beer
200ml veal stock
1 teaspoon of English mustard
2 courgettes, cut into thin matchsticks
100g green beans, top and tailed, then blanched
Sea salt and pepper

For the veal loin
4 x 140g veal sirloin pieces, trimmed of sinew and fat
Sea salt
Olive oil

Braised veal
Heat a heavy-based pan on the stove. Add some oil and then brown off the meat. This should take no longer than 2 minutes, as the aim is to colour the veal without cooking it through. Once the meat is sealed, remove it from the pan, drain off any juices and keep it to one side. Add a little more oil to the pan and then soften the onions, garlic, carrots and thyme in it for 2 minutes. Return the veal back to the pan, then add the beer and the veal stock. Cook over a low heat for 2 hours, topping up with water if required. When the veal begins to fall apart, take the pan off the heat. Pick out the fat and sinew from the meat while it is still hot, then season it and mix it together with some of the cooking liquor. Line a terrine mould with clingfilm and push the meat into the terrine. Put it in the fridge overnight to cool and set.

Piccalilli glaze
Place all the ingredients into a saucepan over a medium heat and reduce down to a syrup consistency.

Red onion compote
Place all the ingredients into a saucepan, except the honey. Cook down the onions until all the liquid is reduced to a sticky sauce. Once this is done, add the honey and season.

Cauliflower cheese
Place the cauliflower, butter and water into a pan and cover with a lid. Cook the cauliflower over a medium heat until it is soft. Remove the lid and continue cooking until the liquid has reduced down and able to coat the back of a spoon. Transfer the cauliflower into a food processor and

(Continued on page 170)

(Continued from page 168)

blend until smooth. Add the goat's cheese – you can vary the amount depending on your personal taste and the strength of the cheese.

Piccalilli sauce
Place the sugar into a saucepan over a medium heat until the sugar begins to form a caramel. Add the garlic, turmeric, ginger and bay leaf. Let them sizzle for 30 seconds and then add the vinegar. Reduce to a thin syrup and then add the beer and reduce the sauce by half before adding the veal stock. Reduce back down to a purée consistency, then add the mustard, making sure it's well-blended into the sauce. Sauté the courgettes for 30 seconds in some sunflower oil, then add in the blanched green beans for a further 2 minutes. Season with salt and keep hot until you serve.

Veal loin
Season the veal with the sea salt and the oil. Seal it in a Vac Pac bag and cook at 65C for about 18 minutes. When the veal is pink in the centre, take the bag out of the water. If you haven't got a Vac Pac machine, seal off the veal in a frying pan, then transfer it to an oven at 200C/gas mark 6 and cook for 8 or 10 minutes until it is pink in the centre, then remove from the oven.

Serving
Cut the pressed chuck veal into small cubes and heat it through in the oven. Reheat the piccalilli purée and put some in a piping bag. Take the veal loin out of the Vac Pac bag, pat it dry and place a frying pan on the stove over a high heat. When the pan is hot place the loin in and colour it on all sides for about 1 minute. Do not overcook it. Remove from the heat and slice. Meanwhile, take a medium-sized pastry brush, dip it into the glaze and make a diagonal swipe of the glaze on the plates. Add the red onion compote on top of the glaze, then a little courgette and beans and a couple of blobs of cauliflower purée. Add some of the veal cubes and then the sliced sirloin. Finally, put a little piccalilli sauce over the veal cubes and sirloin.

WRECKFISH, MUSSELS AND SAFFRON WITH RED PEPPERS AND BLACK OLIVES

Wreckfish is very local to the Cornish coast and is often called stone bass. Taste and texture-wise, it's a bit of a cross between sea bass and sea bream, so you could substitute either of these in the recipe if you need to. Grey mullet works well, too. If you can't get Roseval potatoes, pink fir or any other waxy potato will do.

SERVES 4

For the mussels
400g live mussels
200ml water

For the shellfish stock
1kg frozen prawns, with shells on
1 onion, chopped
2 carrots, peeled and chopped
4 ripe tomatoes, roughly chopped
6 garlic cloves, halved
Zest and juice of an orange
Water to cover

For the saffron sauce
750ml fish stock
250ml shellfish stock (see above)
2 ripe tomatoes, roughly chopped
1 sprig of tarragon
Pinch of saffron
50ml unsalted butter

For the potatoes and pepper
16 medium Roseval potatoes
100ml olive oil
1 large red pepper
Pinch of salt

For the wreckfish
4 x 200g wreckfish fillets
Oil
Sea salt

For the garnish
600g baby spinach

40g pitted black olives, roughly chopped
Extra virgin olive oil to finish the dish

Mussels
Heat a pan with a tight-fitting lid until it is very hot. Add the mussels and then add the water carefully, watching out for the steam. Place the lid on and steam the mussels for 2 minutes until they open. Drain the mussels, reserving the cooking juices. Pick the mussel meat out of the shells and wash off any sand and grit. Cool the mussels and chill in the fridge.

For the shellfish stock
Place the prawns onto a tray and roast for 45 minutes in a medium-hot oven. After about 40 minutes cook the vegetables and orange zest in a saucepan until they are just beginning to soften, making sure you retain their colour. Remove the prawns from the oven and add them to the zest and vegetables. Cover with water and orange juice and simmer for 1 hour, then pass the stock through a sieve, place it in a fresh pan and reduce it by half over a medium heat. Cool down and put into the fridge.

Saffron sauce
Place all the ingredients into a saucepan over a medium heat and reduce to a sauce that coats the back of a spoon. Pass through a sieve and keep warm.

Potatoes and pepper
Place the potatoes in a Vac Pac bag with the oil and salt. Seal the bag and cook in a water bath or saucepan at 95C for 30-40 minutes. The potatoes should be cooked but still retain their shape. If you haven't got a Vac Pac machine, boil the potatoes for about 20 minutes in the normal way, then

sauté them in a frying pan in a bit of olive oil.

Place a wire rack or trellis over a naked flame, put the pepper on it and blacken it all over until the skin starts to blister. Alternatively, blister it under a hot grill. Transfer the pepper to a bowl and cover with clingfilm. Leave it for 20 minutes, then peel the black skin away and deseed the pepper. Finish by cutting it into 1cm squares.

Wreckfish
Preheat the oven to 180C/gas mark 4. Heat a non-stick pan on the stove and add some oil. Place the fish skin-side down into the pan and season with salt. Cook the fish on the skin until it starts to go golden, and then place it in the oven and cook for a further 4 or 5 minutes. Remove from the oven and flip the fish over to the flesh side and remove from the heat.

Serving
Heat a frying pan over a medium heat and colour off the potatoes for 3 minutes. Season them if necessary. Mix together the spinach and olives of the garnish, along with the red pepper and transfer them to a saucepan over a medium heat to warm through. Once the spinach has wilted, add the mussels and continue warming everything for a further 1 minute. At the same time warm the saffron sauce. Remove vegetables from the stove and adjust the seasoning if necessary. Place the potatoes in the centre of your plates, surround them with the vegetables and spoon some saffron sauce over them. Finally, drizzle a little extra virgin olive oil over everything and place the wreckfish on top.

DUCK WITH SMOKED DUCK PANCAKE, PLUMS AND BUTTERNUT SQUASH

This recipe was inspired by those great duck pancakes you get at Chinese restaurants. I like to use local ducks from the Cornish Duck Company, but you can use any variety, just make sure the quality's good. And, of course, I use Cornish Sea Salt, but any good sea salt is fine. If you want to, you can use two whole ducks butchered down rather than buying the breasts and legs separately – if you do this you can also make your own duck stock from the bones. I'd also advise curing the duck legs for the pancake stuffing overnight.

SERVES 4

For the pancake stuffing
3 tablespoons salt
3 tablespoons caster sugar
½ tablespoon duck spice – see below
1 orange, zested
4 duck legs
2 stem ginger balls, chopped
50ml stem ginger syrup – extracted from the jar that contains the stem ginger
1 medium bunch of spring onions, sliced on the angle
100ml duck stock
Sea salt

Note: make the duck spice with 50g each of peppercorns, cloves and cinnamon, plus a star anise. Dry roast the spices in a pan, then blitz them in a blender or crush them with a pestle and mortar.

For the pancakes
300g flour
3 eggs
50g melted butter
500ml milk
250ml water
5g table salt
10g chopped coriander
Sunflower oil

For the duck sauce
100g sugar
1 star anise
½ mild chilli
1 garlic clove
25g fresh ginger
¼ cinnamon stick
1 teaspoon pink peppercorns
1 teaspoon coriander seeds
150ml white wine
150ml white wine vinegar
350g duck stock
125ml veal stock

For the white cabbage
150ml white wine vinegar
150ml white wine
75g sugar
1 clove of garlic, chopped
1 star anise
2 cardamoms
¼ teaspoon white peppercorns
¼ teaspoon coriander seeds
1 white cabbage, outer leaves removed and finely shredded
1 Savoy cabbage, blanched and shredded
1 red chilli, deseeded and chopped finely

For the pickled plums
50ml white wine vinegar
50ml white wine
50ml water
50g caster sugar
2 plums, cut in half then stoned and quartered

For the squash purée
20g unsalted butter
20ml olive oil
1 large butternut squash, peeled, deseeded and thinly sliced
20g fresh ginger, grated
2 garlic cloves, grated
100ml water
Sea salt, to taste

For the duck breasts
4 good-quality duck breasts, trimmed of sinew and with the skin scored
Sea salt

Pancake stuffing
Make a cure for the duck legs by mixing 3 tablespoons of table salt and caster sugar, the duck spice and the orange zest together. Rub this cure thoroughly over the duck legs and then put them into the fridge for 12 hours. When you remove the duck legs from the fridge, wash off the cure and pat the legs dry. Now, smoke the legs in a smoker for 1 hour. If you haven't got a smoker, take a roasting tray, or wok, put some natural wood chippings (I like oak or apple) at the bottom, light them, place a rack over the chippings, put the duck legs on the rack, cover with tin foil and put on the stove over a very low heat for about 30 minutes. Once the legs are smoked, place them into a Vac Pac bag and cook in a water bath for 3 hours at 95C. If you haven't got a Vac Pac or water bath, cook them in the oven at 110C for about 2½ hours. When the legs are cooked, pick off and shred the meat from the bones.

Add the stem ginger, ginger syrup, spring onions and duck stock to the cured and smoked leg meat and mix well. Divide the mixture into equal portions, ready to fill the pancakes. If you have some mixture left over you can freeze it for up to a month.

Pancakes

Place all the pancake ingredients into a food blender or liquidiser and whisk vigorously until they are well blended. Heat a little sunflower oil in a non-stick pan and begin to cook the pancakes, setting them aside until you are ready to stuff them with the duck leg meat.

Duck sauce

Use a good heavy-based saucepan to make the duck sauce. Place it on the stove, add the sugar and cook over a medium heat until it forms a caramel. Add the spices and cook in the caramel for 30 seconds. Then add the wine and vinegar and reduce to a syrup. Add the stocks and reduce to a sauce consistency thick enough to coat the back of a spoon. Strain the sauce and put it to one side.

White cabbage

Put all the ingredients – except the white cabbage, the Savoy cabbage and chilli – into a saucepan and bring them to the boil to make a pickling liquor. Once brought to the boil, take it off the heat and strain the mixture over the white cabbage and allow it to cool. Make sure the cabbage is submerged or it will discolour. Put on one side until you plate the dish. (The Savoy cabbage and chilli are added at the last minute before serving.)

Pickled plums

Place all the ingredients for the pickled plums, bar the fruit itself, into a saucepan and bring to the boil over a medium heat. Add the plums and cook them for 30 seconds only. Remove the mixture from the heat and allow it to cool.

Squash purée

Place a saucepan with a tight-fitting lid onto a medium heat. When the pan is hot, add the butter and the olive oil to the pan, followed by the remaining ingredients, then cook the squash out for a few minutes, until it begins to soften, making sure it doesn't colour. Add the water and place the lid on the saucepan. Stir every 5 minutes until the squash is pulped. Remove the lid and cook the mixture down to remove any excess liquid (you don't want it to be a wet mixture), then transfer it to a food processor and blend until smooth. Keep the purée hot if you are serving straight away, otherwise place it in the fridge.

Duck breasts

Heat a frying pan large enough to hold the duck breasts comfortably over a medium heat. Season the duck breasts with a little salt and then place them in the pan, skin-side down. You don't need oil – the fat on the duck is sufficient as it renders down. Cook the duck breasts for about 2 minutes until golden – turning each breast on its ends as well as either side – then finish on the skin for another 2 minutes. After 10 minutes, remove the duck from the pan and rest for a further 10 minutes.

Serving

Roll your duck leg meat into your pancakes and warm them through in the oven on a low heat – no more than 160C/gas mark 3 – for 5 minutes. Reheat the squash purée in a microwave and place the duck breast into the oven for 3 minutes to heat through. Warm your white cabbage and add the Savoy cabbage and some chilli. Reheat your plums. Arrange the purée on the plate followed by the pancake and plums, then the cabbage. Slice the duck breast and place it on top of the cabbage. Finally, add a little sauce.

LEMON SOLE, WILD GARLIC AND POTATO DUMPLINGS WITH LEMON AND OLIVE OIL SAUCE

This is one of our most popular dishes. I'm lucky enough to have foraged wild garlic brought to the kitchen, but if you can't get any then you can substitute it with baby spinach and some ordinary young garlic – or change the herb used in the oil and dumplings altogether to rosemary or thyme. You can substitute the Maris potatoes, too, just remember to use a floury type of potato.

SERVES 4

For the pickled garlic
50ml white wine vinegar
50ml white wine
50ml water
50g caster sugar
3 cloves of garlic, peeled, germ removed and sliced as thinly as possible
Pinch of salt

For the lemon mayonnaise
5 egg yolks
1 lemon, zested and juiced
300ml sunflower oil
300ml olive oil
Salt

For the sauce
100g lemon mayonnaise (see above)
20ml double cream
Fish stock, for thinning down (see note below)
100g spinach
Sea salt

Note: make the fish stock with the bones of the sole. Place them into a pan and cover with water. Bring to the simmer and cook for 30 minutes, skimming away the impurities all the time. Remove from the heat and allow for settling and cooling. Strain the stock into a new pan and reduce the liquid by half. Put in the fridge until required.

For the wild garlic oil
500g wild garlic leaves
500ml olive oil

For the dumplings
300g Maris Piper potatoes
1 egg yolk
3 tablespoons grated Parmesan
10g chopped wild garlic stalks
10ml wild garlic oil
63g pasta flour (grade 00)
Sunflower oil
Sea salt

For the lemon sole
2 x 600g whole lemon sole, filleted and skinned
Oil for cooking
Sea salt

For the garnish
1 lemon, peeled and segmented and cut into little triangles
Flat leaf parsley, finely chopped

Pickled garlic
Place the pickling liquids, sugar and salt into a pan. Bring to the boil and pour over the sliced garlic. Allow to cool and then keep in a Kilner jar or airtight container for use. The pickle will keep for up to one month. Before serving, decant into a squeeze bottle if you have one.

Lemon mayonnaise
Put the yolks, lemon juice and zest into a bowl and whisk together until pale and starting to thicken. Then slowly whisk in the oil, being careful not to split the mixture. Season with salt and put in the fridge to cool.

The sauce
Put the mayonnaise and cream into a saucepan. Keep it off the heat and add the fish stock, bit by bit, until you have a velvety sauce with a consistency like double cream. Slowly heat the sauce over a low heat. Make sure you don't allow the sauce to boil. Add the spinach and as soon as it has wilted, remove the saucepan from the heat. Check and adjust the seasoning if you need to.

The garlic oil
Bring a saucepan of water to the boil, and while it is heating get a bowl of iced water ready. Put the garlic leaves into the boiling water, making sure you save the stalks for use later in the dumplings. Cook for 3 minutes and then refresh in cold water. When the leaves are cold, drain them and squeeze out the excess water, then place them in a food processor. Add the olive oil and blend for 5 minutes. Place the oil mixture into a saucepan and bring to the simmer. Pour the liquid into a muslin-lined sieve and place in the fridge over night. Decant into a squeeze bottle ready to use later.

(Continued on page 176)

(Continued from page 175)

The dumplings
Bake the potatoes in a hot oven for
1 hour. When they are cooked, halve
them and scoop out the cooked centre
from the skins. Pass this through a
drum sieve or a potato ricer. Add the
egg yolk, Parmesan, wild garlic stalks
(picked from the garlic leaves
previously), oil and flour, then fold the
mixture together and season with the
salt as to your own taste.

Bring a saucepan of salted water to
simmering point and add a little
sunflower oil. Flour a flat surface
and divide the potato mixture up into
12 and roll it into small balls about
the size of a Malteser (three dumplings
per portion). Gently add the balls to the
simmering water and cook until they
float to the surface; it will take about
one minute. Remove them and plunge
them into ice-cold water. When they
are cold, place them in a container,
sprinkle a little wild garlic oil over
them and put them in the fridge.

The lemon sole
Preheat the grill, then place the lemon
sole fillets on to an oiled tray and
season with the salt. Just before
serving, place the fish under the grill;
the fillets should take no more than
3 minutes to cook.

Serving
Heat a non-stick pan over a medium
heat, add the dumplings and gently
colour them for 1 minute. Place some
spinach and sauce in the centre of each
plate, then arrange three dumplings
around this and place the fish on top.
Finish off by topping the fish with
some pickled garlic, lemon triangles
and parsley.

PEANUT MOUSSE AND BRITTLE, COFFEE 'SOIL', CARAMEL BANANA AND BANANA ICE CREAM

I couldn't possibly take any credit for this dish as it was created by Gordon Gray, my long-standing right-hand man and pastry chef. It's based on classic childhood flavours, peanut butter and bananas, and uses some very cheffy bits of kit. But don't worry if you haven't got an ice cream or Vac Pac machine or a water bath, because I've given you alternative cooking techniques.

SERVES 10

For the peanut mousse
80g peanut butter
70ml semi-skimmed milk
3½ leaves of gelatine, soaked in cold water
150g egg white
100g caster sugar
350ml double cream

For the peanut brittle
85g caster sugar
1 tablespoon glucose
45g unsalted butter
Pinch of bicarbonate of soda
125g unsalted peanuts, finely chopped

For the coffee 'soil'
125g caster sugar
45g ground coffee beans
50g cocoa powder
6g sea salt
90g butter, softened

For the peanut and chocolate purée
60ml double cream
180ml glucose
45ml water
150g milk chocolate
60g peanut butter

For the banana ice cream
250ml double cream
250ml milk
60ml glucose
100g egg yolk
60g caster sugar
60g banana purée

For the espresso syrup
200g glucose
1 shot of espresso coffee
50ml stock syrup

Note: make the stock syrup from equal quantities of sugar and water.

For the caramel banana
5 bananas (firm but not green), cut in half
100ml caramel sauce

Note: if you want to make your own caramel sauce you need 100g caster sugar, 50ml water. Put the sugar in a saucepan over a medium heat, when it starts to caramelise add the water to make a sauce.

Peanut mousse
Wrap 10 moulds or ramekins with clingfilm and place on a tray. Combine the peanut butter and milk together in a saucepan and place it on the stove over a low heat to warm through. Take it off the heat and add the softened gelatine. Put to one side. Whisk the egg white in a bowl and when it has almost peaked, add the sugar. Continue to whisk for 3 minutes. In another bowl, semi-whip the cream. Now add the peanut mixture to the egg white and carefully fold-in. Add and fold in the cream and when thoroughly mixed place the uncooked mousse into a piping bag. Pipe into the moulds and chill in the fridge for 2 hours.

Peanut brittle
Make a direct caramel by heating the sugar and glucose over a medium heat in a pan. When the sugar starts to turn golden, whisk in the butter until it emulsifies and then quickly add the bicarbonate of soda and quickly fold-in the peanuts. Pour onto a non-stick silicone mat or paper and allow the caramel to cool. When it has hardened, break the brittle into 4 pieces and place 1 piece onto a tray lined with silicone paper and heat in the oven until soft. Remove from the oven and lay it on a flat surface. Place another sheet of silicone on top and roll out as thinly as possible. Place the tray with the flattened silicone back into the oven until the brittle is soft again and then take it out. Using your mousse moulds as a template for size and shape, cut out 5 pieces of brittle biscuit with a pastry cutter. Remove these from the tray and allow to cool and harden. Repeat the whole procedure with the other 3 pieces of brittle so that you end up with 20 brittle biscuits.

Coffee 'soil'
Combine the sugar, coffee, cocoa powder and salt in a bowl. Slowly add the butter and then spread out the mixture onto a tray lined with silicone paper. Place in the oven and bake for 1½ hours at 100C. Remove from the oven and cool, then blend the mixture in a food processor until a fine breadcrumb texture is achieved.

(Continued on page 179)

(Continued from page 177)

Peanut and chocolate purée
Combine the cream, glucose, water and milk chocolate in a saucepan over a medium heat. Bring the mixture to the boil and then pour it over the peanut butter. Place and blend the mixture in a food processor and then pass it through a fine sieve.

Banana ice cream
Place the cream, milk and glucose in a pan on the stove over a medium heat and bring to the boil. Meanwhile, whisk the egg yolk and sugar together in a bowl. When the liquid boils, pour it over the egg mixture and whisk thoroughly to form a custard base. Add the banana purée and then chill the mixture in the fridge. When it is cool, strain it into an ice-cream machine and churn until firm. If you don't have an ice-cream machine, place the mixture in the freezer, taking it out every 30 minutes to stir. The ice cream is ready when it holds its shape after scooping.

Espresso syrup
Mix all the ingredients together in a saucepan off the heat, then transfer to the stove and bring to the boil over a medium heat. Remove from the heat and allow the mixture to cool.

Caramel bananas
Heat a pan of water or a water bath to 95C. Place the bananas into Vac Pac bags with 2 tablespoons of caramel sauce per banana and seal, then cook in the water for 10 minutes. Remove the bananas and cool them down. If you haven't got a Vac Pac machine, put the bananas into a container with 300ml of cold caramel sauce, cover it with clingfilm and leave for about 8 hours.

Serving
Demould the mousse. Put a little purée onto each plate then place a brittle biscuit either side of each mousse and put this on top of the purée, but a little to one side. Now place one tablespoon of espresso 'soil' opposite the mousse. Slice the bananas and place some between the mousse and the 'soil' then put a scoop of ice cream on top of 'soil'. Lastly, drizzle some espresso syrup around the plate.

BRUCE POOLE

It's a risky business standing amid the echoes of genius. And the chandeliers were still shaking from the shockwaves caused by Marco Pierre White, the original rock star chef, when Bruce Poole took charge of the kitchens of a small local restaurant just off Wandsworth Common in February 1995. White had famously walked away from cooking at his former south-west London haunt, Harvey's, on Bellevue Road and the restaurant was slowly limping towards extinction.

Its owner, Nigel Platts-Martin, was having success with his other, central London, restaurant, The Square, under the stewardship of chef Phil Howard, and was considering shutting up shop in leafy Wandsworth, but he decided on one last throw of the dice. He put in a call to Bruce, who

had once worked at The Square, asking him to take on the head chef position at Harvey's and see if he could turn things around. Bruce, who was successfully running a kitchen in Fulham a few miles away, declined. He wasn't interested in captaining a sinking ship.

Never one to take no for an answer, Nigel came back with a different offer: why not run the whole shebang? Lock, stock and barrel. Bruce had started out as a hotel manager before defecting to the kitchen, he knew all about leading a team – and this time he accepted Nigel's offer. Chez Bruce was born.

Wisely, Bruce didn't try to emulate Marco. Having spent the previous few years cooking in a neighbourhood eatery he knew what brought people out to their local restaurant and set about, albeit inadvertently, creating the best local restaurant in London: a fact confirmed in 2006, when Chez Bruce was voted London's favourite restaurant in the Hardens Guide.

The same year brought him other accolades, despite the fact that Bruce is not a man who craves the limelight. Rather, he's a hard working chef's chef – an opinion reinforced by his 2006 Catey Chef Award from the hospitality industry bible, *Caterer and Hotelkeeper* magazine. The dining room at Chez Bruce underlines his no-nonsense personality, too. It's free from fancy banquettes and heavy chairs – its wooden seats and casual setting mean people can relax on arrival. The room has one main window overlooking Wandsworth Common, which bathes it in soft, natural light during the day and gives it an inky backdrop by night.

As for Bruce's food, its real beauty is that it is designed with only one intention; to be eaten. It's French in style and British at heart. It doesn't strive to impress with clever techniques or fancy flavour combinations. Not that Bruce doesn't have some interesting things happening on his plates, it's just that he cooks what he fancies eating on any given day. Dishes like cod with olive oil mash, rich as the finest velvet; a damn fine rib-eye steak served simply with perfect béarnaise and some fat, crunchy chips; or pork choucroute with all the other parts of the pig kindly cooked to perfection to go alongside. Anglo-French comfort food at its finest.

Bruce's love affair with French food began as a child, caravanning around the country with his parents during the summer holidays. But he didn't think about cooking professionally for a living until his mid-twenties. Instead, after graduating from Exeter University with a degree in history, he initially embarked on a career in hotel management.

His passion for cooking remained nascent until restaurateur and food writer Simon Hopkinson hired him as one of his team at London's famous Bibendum restaurant in the early 1990s; Bruce's training in the kitchen now really began. Simon was a hard taskmaster but Bruce sucked up knowledge like a sponge and set himself a goal of sticking at it for a year before making a final career decision. It helped that he stood shoulder-to-shoulder in the Bibendum kitchen with some other inspiring young chefs who went on to make their mark in London restaurants: Jeremy Lee (Blue Print Cafe), Henry Harris (Racine) and Phil Howard (The Square).

After a stint with Phil at The Square, Bruce finally found himself in charge of his first kitchen at Chez Max in Fulham early in 1994. His natural air of authority and culinary confidence made his transition to head chefdom easy and helped make the restaurant a Mecca for West London foodies. So when Nigel Platts-Martin asked Phil Howard if he knew of anybody who could take on the Harvey's site, he told Nigel to look up Bruce. The rest, as they say, is history.

The name, Chez Bruce, was not Bruce's idea. It was Nigel who suggested it and the juxtaposition of the French 'chez' with the blokiness of his own moniker appealed to his sense of humour and dispelled his natural aversion to putting his name above the door. By instinct, Bruce is a team player and he takes pleasure in nurturing the young chefs that pass through the Chez Bruce kitchen. These days he oversees three London restaurants, each of which he jointly owns with Nigel. All three — Chez Bruce, La Trompette in Chiswick and The Glasshouse in Kew — have a Michelin star and all are headed up by ex-Chez Bruce chefs. There are similarities in their menus, but each restaurant is unique. 'The way we work is just simply to get on with it, we don't have recipes as such and I encourage the guys to cook their own food,' says Bruce, who also likes to eat in his own restaurants to check they're up to scratch. What better endorsement is there?

From day one at Chez Bruce, one dish has always been on the menu – crème brûlée; and it's a thing of beauty. One of the best in the country, Bruce learnt it from Simon Hopkinson and its genius lies in the refined richness of its custard. Actually, it's sturdier than many crème brûlées but what it loses in lightness it gains in flavour. Served wide and shallow, with the perfect amount of sugar crunch on top, it looks like a golden, frozen lake; one, though, that gives way under excited prodding or a single tap with the spoon-back. Bruce makes it by eye but follow the recipe and you can't fail – it is an absolute winner.

The brûlée is synonymous with Chez Bruce and has contributed to the many accolades that Bruce has won over

the years. But he never set out to win awards, just to run a successful restaurant. Most chefs strive to win a Michelin star, yet being awarded one for Chez Bruce in 1999, though it came as a much appreciated and welcome surprise, hasn't given Bruce nearly as much pleasure as those won subsequently by his protégées at La Trompette and The Glasshouse. He likes to stand behind others, preferring to push their talents rather than his own skills.

He may prefer to stay in the background, but Bruce cuts an imposing figure, standing at over six foot tall with broad rugby player's shoulders and, invariably an overnight shadow on his chin. He doesn't often walk the restaurant floor, preferring to leave that to Chez Bruce's effervescently charming restaurant manager Edward Arthur, but he doesn't need much prompting to talk passionately and uncompromisingly about what he believes food should be – cooked from the heart with big flavours and unfussy presentation. That's why his dining room is full of relaxed people and clean plates and his only problem is the infinitely happy one of fitting-in everyone who wants to eat at Chez Bruce. The word is well and truly out: Chez Bruce is London's best local restaurant!

Chez Bruce
2 Bellevue Rd, London SW17 7EG
Phone 020 8 672 0114 **www.chezbruce.co.uk**

CRAB AND SPINACH SALAD WITH VINAIGRETTE OF ARTICHOKES, GREEN BEANS, COCKLES AND CHIVES

Buying a live crab and cooking and preparing it yourself will always yield better and moister crab meat, but this is not always practical as it is a fiddly job and decent enough crabs are rarely available to the domestic cook. So buying a pre-cooked crab is fine, just make sure it's not dressed. You need to remember, too, to buy a waxy variety of potato; rosevals, rattes or charlottes are all fine.

SERVES 4

1 large cock crab, cooked
1 teaspoon tomato ketchup
A splash of Tabasco sauce
A pinch of saffron, moistened in
    boiling water
1 lemon, juiced
1 dessertspoon mayonnaise
A pinch of cayenne pepper
200g cockles
A splash of white wine
1 large cooked globe artichoke,
    heart, choke and leaves discarded
100g green beans, cooked and
    refreshed in iced water
8 cooked waxy new potatoes, skinned
    and still warm
1 large handful baby spinach leaves
1 large bunch chives, finely chopped
Olive oil
Sea salt and freshly ground pepper

For serving
Hot buttered sourdough toast

Take the brown crabmeat and blend it in a processor, together with a teaspoon of ketchup, a dash of Tabasco, a few threads of saffron moistened in a little boiling water and a small slug of olive oil (about a dessertspoon should do it). Blend the ingredients well, then check the seasoning, add a little lemon juice and pass the mixture through a fine sieve. This dressing should be the consistency of a thin mayonnaise and it's optional, too. It's not central to the success of the dish but it's a shame to waste the brown crabmeat.

Take the white crabmeat and combine it in a bowl with just enough mayonnaise to bind it together. Be careful not to add too much mayonnaise as this will make the mixture rather rich and sickly – you will need much less mayonnaise than you think. Season the mixture with a pinch of cayenne pepper, a squeeze of lemon juice and a little salt if required.

Place the cockles in a saucepan with a splash of white wine and steam over a medium heat until they are opened. Remove them from the pan, reserving the cooking liquor, and pick the cooked meat out of the shells, discarding any that have remained closed.

Finely chop the artichoke and green beans into even dice of approximately 2mm.

Thinly slice the potatoes, which should still be warm, and season them with a little olive oil, sea salt and freshly ground pepper, then dress the spinach leaves in the same way.

Combine the diced artichoke and green beans with the cockles, 1 dessertspoon of the cockle cooking liquor, two dessertspoons of olive oil, seasoning, a dash of lemon juice and the chives. Now check the seasoning; the lemon juice should be discernible but not overpoweringly assertive.

Serving
Place the potatoes in the middle of a plate with the spinach leaves on top. Shape some of the white crab meat between two spoons and place this on top of the spinach. Spoon some of the brown meat dressing over this and, finally, dress the plate generously with the cockle, artichoke and green bean vinaigrette and serve with some hot buttered sourdough toast.

POT ROAST VEAL CHEEK WITH RISOTTO ALLA MILANESE, FENNEL AND GREMOLATA

Any slowly braised meat will work well in this recipe. Oxtail, shin of beef, ham hock or lamb shoulder would all combine successfully with the risotto, but nothing beats the classic northern Italian combination of veal, rice, saffron, butter and Parmesan. You can cook the veal the day before if you want to.

SERVES 4

4 cheeks of veal or osso bucco chops cut from the shin
Half a bottle of dry white wine
2 large onions, one halved the other finely chopped
1 head of celery, roughly chopped
1 large leek, roughly chopped
2 large carrots, roughly chopped
1 tin of tomatoes
Half a split head of garlic
3 cloves of garlic, finely chopped
A bay leaf
A bunch of thyme
Small bunch of rosemary
1.2 litres veal or chicken stock (or a combination of the two)
1 large head of fennel (or two smaller heads)
1 lemon
Vegetable oil for cooking
Salt

For the risotto
I onion, finely chopped
1 garlic clove, crushed
A big pinch of saffron
200g Arborio or Carnaroli rice
600ml light chicken stock or water
100g butter
A big handful of grated Parmesan
Olive oil for cooking
Salt

For the gremolata
1 bunch of flat leaf parsley, finely chopped
I lemon, zested and the zest finely chopped
2 garlic cloves, finely chopped

For serving
Side dish of green leaf salad

Set the oven at 120C/gas mark 1. If the veal is bloody or wet, rinse it with water and dry it off with some paper towel. Once dry, season the veal pieces really well. Heat some vegetable oil in a large, heavy-based pan and sauté the veal in it over a high heat until the meat is golden and crusty. Remove the meat from the pan and deglaze the pan with the white wine until the wine has all but disappeared and has a syrupy consistency. Mix these syrupy pan juices with the veal and set aside.

In a separate saucepan, sauté the chopped onions, carrots, celery and leek until coloured and softened. Add the tomatoes, garlic and herbs and cook for 10 minutes or so over a medium heat. Add the veal and its winey juices, then the meat stock – the veal should be just covered, so if there is not enough stock, top up with a little water. Bring everything to a careful simmer, then skim off any impurities and continue to cook the veal, uncovered, in the oven for about 2 hours, or until the veal is completely soft but not collapsing. As the stock gradually reduces in the oven, baste the meat occasionally. If necessary, top up with water during the cooking process but be careful not to dilute the unctuousness of the stock. Once it is cooked, remove the veal from the oven and leave it to cool. (You can cook the veal a day ahead of the risotto if you

want, but only remove it from its cooking liquor once it has cooled.)

Once the veal has cooled, strain off the stock through a fine sieve and discard the vegetables and herbs. Place it in a saucepan on the stove over a medium heat and bring it to the boil, then skim off any impurities and reduce it until a pleasing sauce flavour and texture is reached. The amount of reduction required, if any, will depend on the strength of the original stock used. If the sauce is a little thin and tastes bland, reduce it further by simmering. If you're in luck and the sauce already tastes delicious, then it is adequately seasoned and will require no further attention.

Trim and quarter or halve the fennel (depending on the size of the bulbs), place it in a saucepan in some vigorously salted water which has been acidulated with a generous squeeze of lemon juice and boil until cooked. The fennel is cooked when it can be easily pierced with a skewer or knife. Once cooked, remove it from the saucepan. If you're cooking well ahead of serving the dish, place the fennel in iced water – this will help it to retain its bright colour. If you are serving straightaway, keep the fennel warm and ready for plating.

Next, place the veal and the skimmed and reduced sauce in a wide, shallow saucepan and gently reheat them over a low heat, basting the meat continuously in order to glaze it. Keep tasting the sauce and if it begins to seem a little strong, top it up with a little water. Do not rush this process as the veal is delicate and likely to turn to

(Continued on page 188)

(Continued from page 187)

an unappetising mush if you try to hurry things – the veal should be reheating in the stock at the barest tremble of a simmer.

Risotto

While the veal is reheating, make the risotto. Sweat the finely chopped onion in some olive oil with the crushed garlic clove and the saffron. Add the rice and enough hot water or light chicken stock gradually until the rice is cooked – it needs to retain a bit of a bite and you may not need the full 600ml, or conversely you may need a little bit more. Finish with the butter and most of the Parmesan. Check the seasoning and add salt if necessary.

Gremolata

Combine the parsley, lemon zest and garlic to make the gremolata – have this ready before the risotto is finished.

Serving

Serve the veal and fennel on top of the risotto and sprinkle generously with the gremolata. Hand round some extra Parmesan separately and. if you want, add a side dish of simple and refreshing green leaf salad.

COPPA SALAD WITH CELERIAC REMOULADE

Coppa is the cured and spiced rolled shoulder of pork from northern Italy. It is quite a fatty type of salami and goes particularly well with the mustardy attack of the remoulade. Freshly sliced, high-quality charcuterie (of which the Italians and Spanish are the undisputed champions) always makes the most elegant first course.

SERVES 4

One small celeriac, peeled
1 tablespoon mayonnaise
Dijon mustard, to taste
Meaux-style grain mustard, to taste
Broad leafed parsley, chopped
Thinly sliced coppa – as much as you
  feel is appropriate for a starter (I
  like lots)
Salt

For serving
Toasted brioche or country bread and
  baby gherkins

Thinly slice the celeriac (2mm thick is about right), then chop these slices into long even strips about two or three times the length-and-breadth of a matchstick. Put them into a colander, season well with salt and mix thoroughly, then leave to one side to disgorge water from the celeriac for at least an hour. After an hour or so, gather up the celeriac and squeeze dry in a clean cloth – put into a mixing bowl.

Add a good tablespoon of mayonnaise and add both mustards to taste. I like quite a lot of mustard but not too much mayonnaise. Add the chopped parsley and check the seasoning; if you have adequately salted the celeriac at the beginning, it should not need any extra.

Serving
Simply arrange the sliced meat on a big white plate and put a generous spoonful of the celeriac remoulade in the middle. I like to serve it with toasted brioche or country bread with French baby gherkins (cornichons).

CREME BRULEE

These delectable custard desserts can be either cooked on the stove, as in this recipe, or baked in a bain marie in a slow oven. I prefer the stove method as it seems to produce a slightly less eggy and more luxuriously velvety texture – don't ask me why – and I like to caramelise the sugar crust with a blow torch. One final tip – the custard seems to work best if you make the crème brûlée a day ahead of serving and refrigerate it in ramekins overnight.

SERVES 4-6

600ml double cream
1 large vanilla pod, split
6 egg yolks
75g caster sugar
Demerara sugar for glazing

Place the cream together with the split vanilla pod and its seeds into a saucepan and bring to the boil on the stove over a medium heat. At the same time, beat together the egg yolks and the sugar in a large bowl. Take the scalded cream off the heat and add it, a little at a time, to the egg yolks, whisking as you go along to make sure the ingredients are incorporated properly until you get a custard. Return the custard to the saucepan and place it back on the stove over a moderate heat, whisking it continuously in a circular motion until it begins to thicken. The precise temperature is important here because if it is not cooked enough, the custard will not set when cool. If it gets too hot, it will curdle and all is lost. I watch the custard like a hawk as it cooks and reckon that if the mixture travels half way around the pan of its own accord after a vigorous flick with the whisk, then it is ready. I have never temperature probed the custard but I've been assured that 84C is the magic number.

When you can't stand the stress any more, and deem your custard adequately cooked, get it off the heat and out of the pan in double-quick time. Dithering here can prolong the cooking process and lead to disaster. Quickly pour the whole lot through a sieve and then into ramekins. If there is a fine airy scum on top of the custard, it has not been cooked enough. The odd air bubble is a good sign but not a raft of very fine airy ones. Set the ramekins aside until the custard has cooled down, then refrigerate them for at least four hours or, even better, overnight.

Serving
There is no substitute for glazing with a blow torch. Ignore recipes which instruct you to put your grill 'on to its highest setting' – you will simply be wasting your time. Sprinkle some demerara sugar onto the top of each custard and smoothe evenly with your finger tip. The sugar should be in a flat, one-granule-depth coating. Fire up the torch and cook the sugar until it caramelises to a pleasing golden burnish – it only takes a few seconds. Return the ramekins to the fridge until the glaze is chilled and hard – it should take about 15 minutes. If you're short of time (or impatient like me) then you can halve the time by putting them into the freezer. Once glazed, they will keep quite happily for a couple of hours but thereafter the crisp sugar coating will begin to soften and weep into the cream.

HOT CROUSTADE OF CHERRIES AND ALMONDS WITH KIRSCH CREME CHANTILLY

I really love hot, crisp desserts, and frangipane and this one ticks all those boxes. There's an added bonus, too, because you get a wonderful waft of cherries when you break the little parcels – or croustades – open. They are made with a fine pastry like feuille de brik or filo – brik is better if you can get hold of it because it is slightly thicker; if you use filo I'd advise using a double skin of pastry for each croustade. And you need perfect equilateral pastry triangles when you're making the croustades – if you get this part right, this dessert is a doddle.

SERVES 4

200g ripe stoned cherries (about 35 in total)
1 dessertspoon caster sugar
A splash of water
100g butter
100g caster sugar (plus a bit extra for cherry compote)
3 large eggs, lightly beaten
100g ground almonds
4 sheets of feuille de brik (or 8 sheets of filo pastry)
1 egg yolk, lightly beaten
100g clarified butter, melted
Icing sugar, to taste (for dusting and for the Chantilly)
Kirsch, to taste
200ml double cream, chilled
1 vanilla pod, split

Reserve 20 cherries for the croustades and place the rest in a saucepan with a dessertspoon of sugar and a little splash of water over a medium heat for about 5 minutes to make the compote. You need very little water as the cherries will exude delicious juices as they cook. Once the compote is done, set it aside and put it in the fridge to chill.

Make a frangipane by creaming the butter and 100g of the caster sugar, either by hand or in a mixer. Add gradually and, alternately, the beaten eggs and ground almonds. This will yield more frangipane than you need for this recipe but it is difficult to make in smaller quantities and it is always useful in other desserts – it should keep for up to one week in the fridge. The frangipane can be made beforehand and refrigerated, but it needs to be at cool room temperature when assembling the croustades.

Preheat the oven to 180C/gas mark 4. Cut each sheet of pastry into a large, neat, even-sided triangle, discarding the trim. Using a pastry brush, carefully paint a 1cm border with beaten egg yolk on the triangles – this will act as glue. Working fairly quickly, place a small spoonful of frangipane in the middle of each one, arrange 5 of the reserved cherries on top of the frangipane and gather up the sides of each triangle to form a slightly crumpled tent shape – not dissimilar to the Hogwarts sorting hat featured in Harry Potter movies. Seal the edges well with your fingers to make the parcels air tight.

Carefully paint these parcels – or croustades – with melted clarified butter (using a water spray filled with the melted butter is best for this, or use a fine pastry brush) and dust with icing sugar. Bake in the preheated oven until pleasingly golden and crisp – about 15 minutes. Once done, take out of the oven and rest for 5 minutes before serving.

While the croustades are cooking, make the kirsch crème Chantilly. Add a generous slug of kirsch to the chilled double cream in a big bowl. Scrape the seeds from the split vanilla pod and add to the cream, together with icing sugar to taste – avoiding over-sweetening the cream. Whisk everything together with a balloon whisk until the cream thickens perceptibly. Try to avoid over-whisking the cream or it will become heavy and unpleasantly buttery. It should be visibly thickened but still retain a slight loose floppiness.

Serving
Place the croustades on the plate with a little cherry compote and serve the kirsch crème Chantilly on the side in a sauce boat.

GLYNN PURNELL

The moment you walk into Purnell's in Birmingham you begin to smile because this quirky Anglo-French restaurant, situated in the centre of a city best known for its baltis, is a culinary house of fun. And that's down solely to its chef-proprietor, Glynn Purnell, who, when he opened his self-titled eatery in 2007, doubled the number of great fine-dining places in his home city in an instant.

Glynn himself is something of a singularity in the food world. His palate is not one of classical notes honed only to crave the taste of Perigord truffles or the silky foie gras of Les Landes. Glynn's is a unique palate, an English palate, a Brummie

palate. He grew up on one of the city's council estates, the son of a factory worker and a mum who was a practical cook on a tight budget. Every Saturday morning Glynn and his mother would visit a butchers in the old Bull Ring to buy the week's meat and if they spent over £30 the butcher would chuck in some pig's trotters for free. These would be put in the pressure cooker for a whole day and Glynn remembers vividly the thrill of tucking into them, sitting on the couch in his pyjamas with his brother and two sisters as they watched *Blind Date*. 'Our arms would be covered in all this sticky, meaty juice as we just ate and ate. I thought it was great!'

Those first innocent joys of eating helped Glynn decide what he wanted to do in life. At the age of 14 he got himself work experience and then an evening job at the Birmingham Metropole hotel, initially mopping floors before graduating to its small side-kitchen making baguettes and omelettes. His ambition then was just to make it into the full service kitchen but his father had other ideas. Purnell Senior saw Glynn's catering work as just a hobby that filled in the time between his other passions of football and running. His dad's opposition was the spur that Glynn needed. He vowed never to work in a factory and got himself an apprenticeship at the Metropole.

By the time he was 18, he had moved into cooking for the hotel's à la carte menu and had been encouraged to try his luck in the world of culinary competitions. Taking part in one contest, he was introduced to Andreas Antona, who owned the only restaurant of note in the Birmingham area at that time – Simpson's, in nearby Kenilworth, which was recognised as a beacon of modern classic French cuisine.

Glynn got himself some work experience with Andreas, and after two days in the Simpson's kitchen he was offered a job. By the age of 24 he was sous chef (second-in-command behind the head chef and Andreas), and an important part of the team that secured the restaurant a Michelin star, a longed-for goal of chefs all over the Europe. When he had time off from the kitchen, Glynn used it to grow his culinary knowledge, shooting off to do more *stages* (work experience to you and me) with the pioneers of British food at that time: people like Alastair Little and Gordon Ramsay. Eventually he took the plunge and headed off to France for his first taste of authentic French fine-dining. His Midlands accent perplexed his French colleagues, but they soon began to appreciate his skills and he won them over. No mean feat that.

His quest for knowledge took him, in 1999, on another working holiday to San Sebastian in Spain; to a restaurant called Zaldiaran, which opened his eyes to the world of sous vide, foams, and emulsifiers. The modern Spanish approach to fine-dining excited him because it combined cutting-edge modern techniques with Basque culinary traditions. He decided to seek out a chef in the UK who combined modernism with a nod to the past – preferably not too far from his beloved Birmingham. In the end, he gravitated westwards to Ludlow, in 2002: to the kitchen of Claude Bosi. The Anglophile Frenchman's food was modern, liberating. At Hibiscus, you could serve savoury trifles for starters and vegetables for dessert.

Nine months later Glynn got an opportunity to head home thanks to Birmingham entrepreneurs Keith and Diane Stevenson, who were looking for an investment opportunity in the city. The couple teamed up with Glynn to open a restaurant called Jessica's. It was an immediate hit and by 2005 it had won the AA Restaurant Guide's Restaurant of the Year for England award and a Michelin star. Reviewers were drooling over its food and it put Glynn's name on the culinary map – so much so that two years later he had the confidence to strike out on his own.

It was a leap of faith, but in July 2007 he opened the doors to Purnell's and hasn't looked back, even netting in 2009 the same AA restaurant award as Jessica's did four years previously. The restaurant is housed in a corner-sited ex-furniture showroom in the financial district of Birmingham. The building's Victorian and the dining room has high vaulted ceilings with plenty of light. Giant globular lampshades hang from the ceiling, casting shifting shadows on walls adorned with photos of the city. One wall sports a scowling acrylic painting of Glynn in the kitchen – just to remind you who is in charge.

Despite the scowling painting, Glynn is a likeable man whose Midlands tones rise and fall when he talks, at breakneck speed, about his food. He lives life at a frenetic pace and his food reflects this. He often gets bored with dishes and ingredients and is constantly looking for ways to tweak or reinvent them. And his love affair with his home city and childhood constantly informs his menus. Just look at the dish inspired by the smoked haddock and eggs his mum used to make. She used to poach haddock in milk until it almost disintegrated, and Glynn swears the milk

always tasted better than the fish, so he's made the milk the star of his modern version of the dish – using it to form the basis of an airy, haddock-tasting foam which nestles around a delicately poached egg yolk to produce an apparent fried egg. The dish also has a rumour of curry oil as a nod to Birmingham's Indian heritage and, best of all, a sprinkling of cornflakes. Yes, cornflakes. 'I was always nipping back to the cereal box for a handful during the day when I was a kid.'

Stories flow from Glynn about his early years if you get him talking (not hard to do). The family always ate well, despite

not having much spare cash: rabbit and barley casseroles, ox hearts, pig's ears were all devoured with gusto by everyone. Glynn's father had an allotment which produced rhubarb and other treasures, while a contact at the local pub regularly donated boxes of chicken's eggs. The way Glynn describes it, his council estate sounds more like a village rather than the biggest concentration of subsidised housing in Europe.

But he draws from the present as well, be it a trip to a child's birthday party or a well-known London landmark. Each time his dishes arrive at the table there is a chortle, a giggle then a sigh as diners clock witty illusions like the fried egg lookilike. Glynn's cooking is a culinary adventure. His food is like your first two-wheeled bike ride: after months of plodding along on stabilisers you are suddenly free to roam the playground on a voyage of discovery. Who would have thought Birmingham could deliver such an explosion of culinary fun?

Purnell's
55 Cornwall Street, Birmingham B3 2DH
Phone 0121 212 9799 **www.purnellsrestaurant.com**

BRILL POACHED IN COCONUT MILK, TOFFEE CARROTS WITH PASSION FRUIT, CARROT VINAIGRETTE

My mum used to always cook fish in milk when I was growing up and I like to do the same, but because I'm from Birmingham I like to use Indian spices and ingredients. That's why I poach the brill in coconut milk. The idea to make toffee carrots was a complete accident – one day I had some cooking over a low heat and just noticed how their natural sugars oozed out and thought 'there's a dish in that'.

SERVES 4

For the carrot vinaigrette
2 large carrots, shredded into thin
*   strips*
8 tablespoons olive oil
2 teaspoons aged balsamic vinegar
1 lemon, zested and zest finely cut

600ml full fat coconut milk
4 x 150g brill fillets
50g caster sugar
25g salted butter, roughly cubed
1 teaspoon ground cumin
2 carrots, cut into thin wide strips on
*   a mandolin*
1 large passion fruit, halved and with
*   the flesh and seeds scooped out*
A pinch of rock salt
2 pinches of ground ginger

Place all the vinaigrette ingredients together in a bowl, mix them thoroughly until you have a smooth dressing and then put the vinaigrette to one side.

Put the coconut milk into a large saucepan, place it over a medium heat and bring the liquid to a gentle simmer. Place the brill fillets in the simmering coconut milk and cook them for 3-4 minutes, then turn off the heat but leave the fish in the coconut milk to keep warm.

Make a caramel by melting the sugar in a frying pan over a medium heat. When it starts to bubble and turn golden, add the cubed butter and cumin and, holding the pan handle, swirl the mixture until it turns into toffee. Add the wide carrot strips and stir until they're coated in toffee, then add the flesh and seeds of the passion fruit.

Serving
Using a fish slice, remove the fish fillets from the coconut milk and place them on their plates. Season them with rock salt and ground ginger. Add the wide carrot strips alongside the fish, then finish the fish and toffee carrots with the carrot vinaigrette.

ROYALE OF GOAT'S CHEESE AND PINEAPPLE ON STICKS, WATERCRESS CRISPS

About three years ago I took my son, Oliver, to a birthday party where they wheeled out a brilliantly retro cheese and pineapple hedgehog. I wanted to tap into the happy party memories that day brought back – and here's the result. My version's got cubes of creamy goat's cheese royale, pineapple jelly and air-dried pineapple (known as 'leather' in our kitchen) – it always gets a smile when a customer sees it.

SERVES 4-6

300ml double cream
115g goat's cheese, roughly crumbled
3 free-range eggs, beaten
A small handful of Parmesan or
 Cheddar cheese, finely grated
700ml fresh pineapple juice
1 leaf of gelatine
½ large pineapple, peeled
250g salted butter, melted

For the garnish
300ml vegetable oil, for deep frying
A small handful of fresh watercress
Salt and freshly ground black pepper

Preheat the oven to 220C/gas mark 7. Pour the cream into a small saucepan and bring it to the boil over a high heat. Add the goat's cheese and season with salt and freshly ground black pepper. Pour the mixture into a bowl, whisk in the beaten eggs and pass through a sieve into an ovenware dish and finally sprinkle the top with the grated Parmesan or Cheddar cheese. Place the dish into a roasting tray and fill this with boiling water until it reaches half-way up the sides of the dish. Put the tray into the oven and cook the sauce for 25-30 minutes. Once the mixture has set, but still has a bit of a wobble, take it out of the oven and cool down. Then, once firm, cut it into 2.5cm squares.

Heat 200ml of pineapple juice in a small saucepan over a medium heat. Place the gelatine leaf into a small bowl, cover with cold water and leave until softened. Drain off the water, squeeze out the excess and add the soaked gelatine leaf to the hot pineapple juice. Remove from the heat and leave to dissolve for 1-2 minutes. Stir well and then pour the jelly into a square tub to set in the fridge for 50 minutes. Once set, cut into 2.5cm squares.

Reduce the oven temperature to 130C/gas mark 1. Submerge the pineapple in the melted butter in a small baking tray and gently cook it in the oven, turning frequently, for 10 minutes or until the fruit is tender, then remove it from the oven. Once cool cut into 2½cm squares.

Pour 500ml of pineapple juice into a saucepan and simmer over a medium heat for 5 minutes or until it has reduced to a syrup. Take off the heat and cool, then strain it through a fine sieve. This should make around 200ml of syrup.

Pour the vegetable oil into a large saucepan or deep fat fryer and heat it up to 180C/gas mark 4 or until a small cube of bread turns golden in 30 seconds (remember not to leave the oil unattended as it can easily catch fire). Once the oil is hot enough, carefully drop the watercress into it and fry it for 1 minute until it is crisp. Remove with a slotted spoon and drain on kitchen paper.

Serving
Reheat the pineapple syrup gently. Take the squares of goat's cheese royale and place them on top of the pineapple squares. Next, place the jelly squares on top of these and stick a cocktail stick through the middle to secure everything. Serve two goats' cheese sticks per person on individual plates, pouring over some pineapple syrup and topping with deep-fried watercress.

TAIL FILLET OF BEEF IN LIQUORICE CHARCOAL, JAPANESE BLACK RICE, TAMARIND, LIQUORICE PUREE, SALSIFY, GREEN BEANS

I'm not a big fan of beef fillet because it doesn't have the flavour of other cuts, but tail fillet's got a little bit more fat in it and the taste is better because of that. The liquorice idea came about when I thought of all those barbecues when you accidentally drop the meat into the charcoal but you eat it anyway and it has that really charcoal-y taste. I wanted that in a more sophisticated form.

SERVES 4

For tail fillet
4 x 350g tail fillets of beef, lightly trimmed of fat
25 liquorice roots, roasted until blackened and ground to a powder
Rock salt, to taste
Ground ginger, to taste
300ml veal gravy, to serve

For the tamarind jam and liquorice purée
15 tamarind fruit, pods removed
½ a lime, juiced
15-20 pieces of Pontefract cake (plain liquorice)
Splash of water

For the black rice
55g butter
175g glutinous Japanese black rice
568ml strong veal stock
A pinch of ground ginger
Rock salt and freshly ground black pepper

For the beans, rocket and salsify
150g green beans
50g butter
150g wild green or red rocket leaves
2 peeled salsify roots, 1 of them cut into logs
Salt and freshly ground black pepper
300ml vegetable oil, for deep frying

Beef
Roll the fillets in the liquorice powder and seal in bags with a Vac Pac machine. Pour hot water into a large pan, heat to 62C, add the fillets and boil for 20 minutes. Remove from the water and rest for 5 minutes. If you haven't got a Vac Pac machine, rub a little oil on the fillets, then cook them slowly in the oven for 20 minutes at 180/gas mark 4.

Tamarind jam and liquorice purée
Place the tamarind fruit into a saucepan, add the lime juice and enough water to cover the tamarinds and then simmer them over a medium heat until softened. Drain and then pass them through a sieve to remove the stones and then blend to a smooth purée with a hand blender or in a liquidiser.

Place the liquorice into a small saucepan, add a splash of water and place over a low heat until melted. Remove from the heat and blend it with a hand blender or in a liquidiser until smooth, then pass it through a sieve.

Japanese rice
Melt half of the butter in a saucepan, add the rice, stirring it to coat the grains in the butter. Add the veal stock and simmer it over a medium heat, stirring frequently, until the rice is tender and sticky. Drain the rice through a sieve over a bowl and keep the stock. Season the rice with ground ginger and rock salt. Place the remaining stock in a saucepan over a medium-high heat and reduce it by a third, then whisk in the remaining butter and season the sauce with salt and freshly ground black pepper.

Beans, rocket and salsify
Bring two large saucepans of salted water to the boil. In one, drop in the beans and blanch them for 2-3 minutes, then drain and refresh them in iced water, before finely chopping them. At the same time, drop the salsify logs into the other saucepan and blanch for 2-3 minutes. Drain and dry the salsify well.

Finely slice the second salsify root on a mandoline. Heat the vegetable oil a medium-sized saucepan until it is hot enough to turn a small cube of bread golden in 30 seconds. Carefully drop the salsify discs into the hot oil and deep fry until golden-brown, then remove from the oil with a slotted spoon and dry them on kitchen paper. Season with salt and freshly ground black pepper.

Melt 25g of butter in a small saucepan, add the blanched salsify logs and gently fry them until they are softened and turning golden-brown. Season well with salt and freshly ground black pepper. Melt the remaining 25g of the butter in a saucepan, add the chopped beans and rocket and stir until the rocket has wilted. Season with salt and freshly ground black pepper.

Serving
Warm the veal gravy over a medium heat and, if necessary, the tamarind jam and liquorice purée. Remove the beef fillet from the plastic Vac Pac bags, dry it off in kitchen paper and caramelise the outside with a mini-blowtorch to give it a charcoal flavour. Season the outside of the veal with rock salt and ground ginger and slice the meat. Put some tamarind jam and liquorice purée onto your serving plates, then add a line of rice, beans and salsify, top with the sliced veal and finish with some cooked rocket and green beans. Drizzle over a little veal gravy and serve.

POACHED EGG YOLK, SMOKED HADDOCK MILK FOAM, CORNFLAKES, CURRY OIL

You'll need an iSi soda siphon for this dish to create the foam (they're not expensive). It's one that I daren't take off the menu and it goes all the way back to when I was a kid and my mum gave us haddock and poached egg. I don't like egg whites much, though, so my 'egg white' is a milk foam made from milk that's had fish cooked in it. Actually, that's down to my mum, too – her eggs used to be flavoured with haddock because she poached them in the same milk she cooked her fish in.

SERVES 4

For the curry oil
300ml sunflower oil
2 tablespoons medium curry powder

For the haddock
400ml milk
250g undyed smoked haddock, skinned
½ tablespoon xanthum gum
4 free-range egg yolks
20 cornflakes

Curry oil
Place the oil and curry powder into a small saucepan over a very low heat and heat gently for one hour, then remove it from the heat and allow the oil to cool before straining it through a fine sieve or muslin cloth.

Haddock milk
Place the milk into a wide, deep saucepan over a low heat and bring it to a gentle simmer. Add the smoked haddock and poach it until the fish begins to flake and the milk has taken on the flavour of the fish. Now remove the fish from the heat and strain the haddock and milk through a fine sieve into a bowl, squeezing as much moisture from the haddock as possible. Transfer the milk to a clean saucepan over a low heat. Discard the haddock (or use in other dishes, such as kedgeree) then add the xanthum gum to the milk and whisk until it is dissolved and the milk thickened. Pour the milk into an iSi soda siphon, then place the siphon into a jug or bowl of hot water to keep the milk mixture warm.

Serving
Bring a saucepan of water to the boil over a medium heat, then poach the egg yolks in gently simmering water for 1 or 2 minutes. Remove them with a slotted spoon.

While the yolks are poaching, pipe out a circle of the thickened milk from the siphon into each serving bowl. Place an egg yolk into the centre of the milk (so the milk and yolk resemble a fried egg) and then place or sprinkle the cornflakes over the milk (5 per bowl). Finally drizzle the curry oil over the egg in a zig-zag pattern

WARM DARK CHOCOLATE MOUSSE AND DARK CHOCOLATE TORTE, MANGO AND ROSEWATER SORBET, MANGO LEATHER

We're a milk chocolate nation in the UK but you need to use chocolate that has 70% cocoa solids for this – my attempt at creating a warm, chocolate Angel Delight! It's one for the ladies which I first put on the menu when I was at Jessica's and has always been really popular. I think that's because although it uses dark bitter chocolate the mousse just lightens the taste a little.

SERVES 6-8

Chocolate mousse
200g dark chocolate
150g double cream
150g egg white

Mango and rosewater sorbet
2 mangos, cut into small cubes
Stock syrup (500ml water, 200g caster
    sugar, boil and leave aside)
1 tablespoon of rosewater

Chocolate crumble
90g plain flour
10g cocoa powder
50g butter
25g sugar

Mango leather
250g mango, cut into strips
25g sugar
Splash of water

Chocolate mousse
Bring a saucepan of water to the boil over a medium heat. Once simmering gently, place a bowl over the top, but make sure this doesn't touch the water. Melt the chocolate and cream in the bowl, stirring occasionally. Remove from the heat and whisk in the egg white. Put the mixture into an iSi soda siphon and charge with three canisters, then keep warm in the saucepan of hot water.

Mango and rosewater sorbet
Place the mango into a Pacojet ice-cream container and cover with stock syrup. Add the rosewater essence and process to a sorbet. If you haven't got a Pacojet ice-cream machine, then heat the mango and stock syrup in a saucepan over a medium heat until it begins to break down, remove it from the heat, add the rosewater essence and blitz in a liquidiser. Pass through a sieve, then place the mixture in a shallow dish and put this in the freezer, taking it out every few minutes to stir. When the sorbet is slushy leave it in the freezer to set completely.

Chocolate crumble
Preheat the oven to 230C/gas mark 8. Put all the crumble ingredients into a bowl and rub together until they resemble a fine breadcrumb texture. Place this onto a baking tray and pop in the oven for about 12 minutes to crunch up, taking it out to mix the crumble every 3-4 minutes to prevent it from clumping together.

Mango leather
Put the sugar and a splash of water into a saucepan over a medium-high heat and dissolve the sugar to a soft ball. Add the mango and cook until soft. Remove the fruit from the heat and spread it evenly onto a soft silicone mat or silicone paper then place it above a hot oven to dry it out.

Serving
Squirt some chocolate mousse from the iSi soda siphon into glasses, pop a scoop of mango and rosewater sorbet on top and then sprinkle some chocolate crumble over the sorbet. Finish with a bit of dried mango.

THEO RANDALL

Every so often the food world throws up an anomaly. Twenty years ago it was a young Yorkshireman who'd never been to France cooking some of the finest classical French cuisine the UK had ever seen (a certain Marco Pierre White). Today, another English chef is cooking phenomenal food from a different, but equally revered, European gastro giant. The chef is Theo Randall, the cuisine he excels in is Italian. And it's the considered opinion of many that Theo cooks some of the best Italian food west of the Adriatic at his restaurant in the InterContinental Park Lane hotel in London. But to see how a boy from Kingston-upon-Thames in Surrey got to strut his stuff on equal terms with his Italian-born counterparts, we have to look to his childhood.

From the age of six onwards, Theo holidayed regularly in Italy, thanks to the work his architect father had on the go in Tuscany. His father and his mother, an artist, would pile

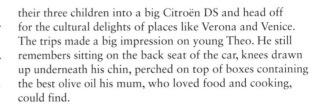

their three children into a big Citroën DS and head off for the cultural delights of places like Verona and Venice. The trips made a big impression on young Theo. He still remembers sitting on the back seat of the car, knees drawn up underneath his chin, perched on top of boxes containing the best olive oil his mum, who loved food and cooking, could find.

One particular moment on a holiday in Venice sparked his subsequent love affair with Italian food. The family had hired a boat for the day to tour the islands in the city's lagoon, and when lunchtime came the boatman lit an impromptu barbecue on board. He layered it with fennel sticks and threw three giant sardines on to the grill, then proceeded to produce a hunk of fresh bread and a glass or two of Frascati wine for everyone. 'They were the fattest, juiciest sardines you've ever seen. I'll never forget the taste.'

It wasn't just on holidays that Theo enjoyed Italian cuisine. Back in England his mother packed him off to school every day with Gorgonzola sandwiches: and had delicious delights straight from Elizabeth David's classic Italian cookery book waiting for him when he came home for tea.

Yet despite all of this, when he left school he toyed with the idea of being an artist and an affinity with the school forge nearly led to a career as a blacksmith. Luckily for us his love of food soon asserted itself and after a few temporary jobs as a pot washer he got his first gainful culinary employment as a chef with Max Magarian at a restaurant called Chez Max in Surbiton. Max's menu was classic French and there were just the two of them in the kitchen, which meant they worked liked dogs, tirelessly turning out dish after dish to Max's loyal diners. They did their own butchery and made all their own stocks and it was Max who first taught Theo the benefits of getting good produce and treating it with respect.

After four years with Max, Theo heard of a recently opened Italian restaurant in Hammersmith called the River Café. Its owners, Ruth Rogers and Rose Gray, were making waves on the London food scene with their simple brand of Italian cooking. Their reputation rested on using the very best ingredients, no matter how expensive, and utilising minimal cooking techniques, thereby allowing their produce, always, to take centre stage. Intrigued, Theo applied for a job at the River Café – and, at 21, soon became their right-hand man. And there he stayed, apart from a year-long sabbatical in the early 1990s, until he left to set up Theo Randall at the InterContinental in 2006.

That sabbatical was hugely important for Theo. It was spent working in California at San Francisco's famous Chez Panisse with the legendary American chef Alice Waters and her equally famous head chef Paul Bertolli. The experience underlined what Max, Ruth and Rose had already instilled in him – that produce is everything – and Theo became obsessed with sourcing the best ingredients to cook with and doing them justice without fuss or frippery. The obsession is still with him today and it helped the River Café, after he had returned to it from America, to gain an iconic status and a Michelin star.

Theo was at the River Café for nearly 17 years in total, eventually becoming a shareholder and partner in the restaurant. But there comes a time when a chef has to strike out on his own. He opened his eponymous restaurant, with Ruth and Rose's blessing, three years ago and was soon creating one of the tastiest menus in the capital.

There are so many tantalising temptations on Theo's menu it makes it damn hard to choose what to eat. You could go for a starter of pan-fried squid, seasoned with a hint of chilli and anchovy, served on tender, slow-cooked borlotti beans. That would lead you towards the ambrosia of ricotta, spinach and marjoram ravioli bathed in a simple sage and butter sauce – nothing less than pasta pillows of golden Mediterranean sun. Then again, you could try the 'little hats' of cappelletti stuffed with slow-cooked veal and pancetta; or maybe skip the pasta (but you'll regret it) and go straight to Anjou pigeon roasted on crunchy bruschetta in a wood-fired oven (see recipe, page 215) – absolutely delicious – or a veal chop the size of Sicily supported by portobello and porcini mushrooms and a little salsa verde.

You see what I mean? It's like Stendhal Syndrome, a psychosomatic illness that occasionally afflicts visitors to Florence whose senses get so overwhelmed with visual beauty that they cannot cope. Choosing your dishes at Theo Randall is similar – you are in danger of being swept away on a tidal wave of greed. But if you succumb to 'Randall Syndrome' before the dessert finale, you'll be missing something very special; several things, actually, but two in particular.

A blood orange sorbet that is as delicate, sweet and light as an Italian breeze blowing through the orange groves; and Theo's lemon tart. The latter is the stuff of dreams, with a gossamer pastry so crisp and thin that a mere raised voice would snap it – and a filling made with the finest Amalfi lemons. When he reviewed Theo Randall in 2006 the *Observer*'s restaurant critic Jay Rayner, declared it, 'quite simply the best tart I've ever eaten'.

The tart is sublime not only because of Theo's technical expertise but also because it is led by its main ingredient, the Amalfi lemons – regarded by all chefs as the best you can get. His passion for great ingredients in their season, when their taste is at its best, is something that Theo never

compromises on. Unlike so many city-based chefs, who write a menu before ringing up their producers, he sees what he can get his hands on then starts to think about what he can cook. And he's always tracking down new suppliers. He takes regular trips to Italy and hunts down the best that Britain has to offer, too. Such detailed attention to sourcing means that Theo totally understands his ingredients and translates their unique flavours into beautifully balanced dishes, where everything used has a chance to shine. And it's this that sets this 41-year-old chef's food apart from that of his peers. His cooking is not just a series of steps, it's a complete dance.

Like his food, the look of Theo's restaurant is, at once, both simple and sophisticated. The basement dining room is open and modern with grey slate floors, chocolate browns and touches of pale, cool green. Some have said it has a monastic feel but this is perhaps appropriate. Theo Randall, the restaurant, is a place in which to worship food. Forget about its lack of windows, there is Italian sunshine enough to spare in the food. Who cares about Stendhal Syndrome? Embrace Randall Syndrome.

Theo Randall at the InterContinental
1 Hamilton Place, Park Lane, London W1J 7QY
Phone 020 7 318 8747 **www.theorandall.com**

MONKFISH WITH PROSCIUTTO, ARTICHOKES, CAPERS, PARSLEY AND CHARLOTTE POTATOES

The great thing about this dish is that everything is cooked in one pan which means that all the flavours seep through into the potatoes and the fish picks up the saltiness from the prosciutto. Always buy Cornish monkfish if you can, caught by day boat and not by trawlers, as fished this way it doesn't drown in the net and lose the quality of its firm, dense – almost meaty – flesh.

SERVES 2

4 Roman artichokes, trimmed and
    topped
75ml olive oil
1 garlic clove, halved and one half
    finely chopped
2 teaspoons chopped parsley
½ glass of white wine
2 x 160g fillets of monkfish
300g boiled charlotte potatoes, sliced
1 tablespoon small capers
100g prosciutto, sliced
Splash of lemon juice
Salt and pepper

Preheat the oven at 200C/gas mark 6. Scoop out the choke of the artichokes, then, using a potato peeler, peel down their stems until you hit the tender centres. Put the olive oil in a saucepan over a medium heat, add the artichokes head-downwards together with half a garlic clove and 1 teaspoon of the chopped parsley. Put the saucepan lid on and cook for 25 minutes, until the artichokes are tender. Take them off the heat, cool down and then slice them lengthways.

Salt and pepper the monkfish. Heat a splash of olive oil in a large metal-handled, heavy-based frying pan and seal the monkfish fillets on one side over a medium heat until golden. It should take about 2 minutes. Turn the fillets over and seal the other side, then take out of pan.

Cook the potatoes for 1 minute or so in the same pan that you have fried the fish in. Make sure they are a light golden colour on all sides. Replace the monkfish in the frying pan on top of the potatoes, add in the sliced artichokes, capers, remaining parsley and the half clove of chopped garlic. Cover with the prosciutto slices and pop in the oven to cook for 6-8 minutes.

Serving
Remove the fish from the oven, add a splash of lemon juice and a dash of olive oil. Serve the monkfish on top of the potatoes and then top the fish with the artichokes and prosciutto.

RISOTTO DI PEPERONI

I had this risotto when I was visiting Verona once and it was unbelievable, so as soon as I got back I started playing around with it and came up with my version. The key to getting it right is to char-grill the peppers and allowing their sweetness to really comes through the rice. The riper the peppers the better.

SERVES 4

2 red peppers
2 yellow peppers
1 red onion, finely chopped
3 sticks celery, finely chopped
300g risotto rice
½ glass of white wine
2 litres chicken stock
4 ripe plum tomatoes, skinned, deseeded and finely chopped
150g Parmesan, grated
A handful of fresh basil
75g unsalted butter
Olive oil, for cooking
Salt and pepper

Set the grill on to its highest setting, then char-grill the red and yellow peppers under it until they turn black and begin to blister. Next, place them in a bowl and cover it with clingfilm. Leave to one side for 15 minutes, then peel off the black skin from the peppers. Deseed them by rinsing under running water, finely chop and set aside.

Heat a little olive oil in a large saucepan over a medium heat, add the onion and add celery and cook until they are soft and the onion is translucent. Add the rice, cook it for 5 minutes, then add the white wine and gradually ladle in the stock, stirring continuously, until the rice has absorbed all the liquid.

Serving
When the rice is almost ready, add in the chopped peppers, tomatoes, and Parmesan, some torn basil leaves and the butter. Stir vigorously to obtain a lovely creamy consistency and season with a little salt and pepper. Ladle on to plates and serve.

FISH STEW

This is a substantial dish, inspired by a Ligurian fish stew – and should really be cooked for four to six very hungry people! The addition of porcini mushrooms may seem strange but they provide an incredible background flavour which seasons the broth beautifully. You can use any dense white fish – monkfish is great, but John Dory or sea bass are fine.

SERVES 4

1 medium lobster
2 x 25g red mullet
1 x 1kg monkfish tail (or 200g other white fish)
3 litres water
1 stick of celery
10 black peppercorns
1 bay leaf
A small bunch of parsley
1 teaspoon olive oil
½ small onion, finely chopped
½ carrot, finely chopped
½ fennel bulb, finely chopped
1 teaspoon fennel seeds
2¼ garlic cloves, finely chopped
20g dried porcini mushrooms, soaked in hot water for 8 minutes
500g fresh very ripe plum tomatoes, deseeded and roughly chopped
200g Roseval potatoes, cut into 1.5cm pieces
A pinch of saffron
250g clams
100ml white wine

For the garnish
1 tablespoon chopped parsley
½ clove garlic

Bring a large saucepan of salted water to the boil, then cook the lobster in it for 5 minutes. Remove from the heat and refresh the lobster under cold running water for a few minutes.

Scale and fillet the red mullet and monkfish, keeping the bones (but remove the eyes and gills from the red mullet first). Place the fish bones in a large saucepan with 3 of litres water, 1 stick celery, the black peppercorns, bay leaf and parsley stalks. Put the saucepan over a medium heat and bring the water to the boil, then simmer for 30 minutes, remove from the heat and strain over a bowl. Discard the fish bones.

Break the lobster up by removing its head, claw and tail. Put to one side, then add the head to the fish stock and return the stock to the heat and simmer over a medium heat for 8 minutes. In a separate saucepan heat a teaspoon of olive oil over a medium heat, then add the onion, carrot, fennel, fennel seeds and garlic (keeping back a little garlic for dressing the soup). Roughly chop the mushrooms and add these in, together with the tomatoes. Cook for 20 minutes until the tomatoes start to break down.

Meanwhile, strain the fish broth through a sieve into a separate container, retaining the lobster head. Put the lobster head into a saucepan with 2 ladles of the fish stock and bash the lobster head with a rolling pin until it is broken up, then strain through a sieve and add this strained liquid to the tomato mixture. Next add the fish broth to the tomatoes and continue cooking for 20 minutes. Remove from heat, taste and season with salt and black pepper if necessary, then purée,

ideally with a stick blender or in a food processor.

Meanwhile, bring the potatoes to the boil in saucepan of salted water together with a pinch of saffron. Take them off the heat once the boil has been reached, drain and keep to one side. Split the lobster tail in half, remove the entrails and crack the lobster claws. Wash the clams thoroughly under running water.

Heat a small amount of olive oil in a large, shallow saucepan with a tight-fitting lid over a high heat. Add in the clams, red mullet and monkfish and 100ml of white wine, cover firmly with the lid and cook for 1 minute. Jiggle the pan – this will open up the clams. If any are not open after 1 minute, throw them away.

Next, add the tomato fish broth and the saffron potatoes. Cover with the lid, bring to the boil again and then add the lobster meat. Reduce the heat, cover with the lid again and simmer the stew for a few minutes.

Serving
Mix the chopped parsley with a little finely chopped garlic (not too much). Ladle some soup into bowls, sprinkle a little of the parsley mixture over the top and serve.

SPATCHCOCK PIGEON ROASTED ON BRUSCHETTA WITH PORCINI AND PORTOBELLO MUSHROOMS AND PANCETTA

Marinating pigeon in Marsala wine means that when you cook it you get a very rich, sweet caramelised skin. Don't be tempted to use anything but sourdough bread – it not only soaks up the lovely juices soaking down from the pigeon, creating a nice, doughy centre, but crisps up beautifully around the edges. If you can't get fresh porcini mushrooms, use a mixture of dried porcinis and portobello mushrooms.

SERVES 4

4 x squab pigeon
½ glass of Marsala wine
2 cloves garlic, thinly sliced
1 sprig of thyme
200g fresh porcini mushrooms,
4 slices of sourdough bread
6 slices pancetta
½ lemon
Olive oil, for cooking
Salt and pepper

Take 1 pigeon and, using a sharp knife, cut down its back bone and force both sides of the bird away from each other. Turn the pigeon over, place on a chopping board and push down onto breasts with the palm of your hand to flatten it (the flatter it is, the more evenly the bird will cook). Repeat the process with the three remaining birds.

Put the Marsala wine, 1 thinly sliced clove of garlic and the thyme sprig into a bowl to make a marinade. Place the pigeons in and marinate them for 1 hour.

Preheat the oven to 180C/gas mark 4. Clean the porcinis. Heat up a little olive oil in a frying pan over a medium heat and fry a sliced clove of garlic in it. Add in the porcini mushrooms and cook for 3-4 minutes.

Heat a little olive oil in a metal-handled heavy-based frying pan over a medium-high heat. Pop in the pigeons and seal them on both sides for 1 minute. Add the slices of sourdough (bruschetta) and pancetta and then place the frying pan in the oven for 6 minutes. Remove from the oven and place the pigeon on top of the bruschetta, skin-side up and cook for a further 3 minutes.

Serving
Remove the pigeons from the bruschetta and slice. Put the bruschetta on your serving plates, place the sliced pigeon on top and scatter over some porcini mushrooms. Add a dash of Marsala wine to the cooking juices in the frying pan and then pour some over the pigeon and finish with a squeeze of lemon juice.

AMALFI LEMON TART

Unwaxed Amalfi lemons are one of life's treats. They have an incredible aroma and the juice has an almost sweet edge to it. If your greengrocer or supermarket doesn't stock them you can buy them through www.natoora.co.uk. I have to confess the original recipe for this tart came from Chez Panisse in San Francisco, but I've adapted it over the years and it's an incredibly popular dessert at the restaurant, a signature dish if you want.

SERVES 6

For the pastry
250g plain flour
75g icing sugar
180g butter
3 egg yolks

For the filling
7 Amalfi lemons, zested and juiced
300g sugar
300g butter
6 eggs
9 egg yolks

For serving
Crème fraîche

Pastry
Place the flour, icing sugar and butter in a food processor and mix until it resembles fine breadcrumbs. Add two of the yolks and pulse for 10 seconds. Pour the mixture into a bowl and bind it together by hand. Wrap the pastry in clingfilm and leave to rest in the fridge for 1 hour. Roll out the pastry and press into a deep 25cm loose-bottomed tart tin. Leave to rest again for a further 30 minutes while you preheat the oven to 150C/gas mark 2.

Remove the tin from the fridge and line the pastry with greaseproof paper and baking beans (or if you haven't got beans, some rice) and bake blind until golden. It should take 15-20 minutes. Remove the baking beans and paper and return to the oven for an extra 5 minutes. Lightly beat the remaining egg yolk and brush the pastry with it as soon as you take it out of the oven. This will form a seal to keep the pastry crisp.

Lemon filling
Place the lemon juice and zest, sugar and butter in a bowl, mix them together then place this over a saucepan of gently simmering water until the butter has melted, making sure that the bowl does not touch the water. Whisk the eggs and egg yolks together and add them to the rest of the ingredients, stirring constantly with a wooden spoon. Continue to cook – and stir – over a medium heat, until the mixture thickens to a lemon curd consistency. Pour this into the pastry shell, stirring as you do so. Preheat the grill on its highest setting and place the tart under it until black dots appear on top (this sets the custard). Watch it like a hawk – the pastry must not burn. Remove and cool down.

Serving
Divide the tart equally and serve with a little crème fraîche.

SHAUN RANKIN

Thanks to its lenient tax laws, Jersey is known as a millionaire's hideaway. But for anyone with a nose for food, the island is much more intriguing than just a playground for the mega rich. The truth is, Jersey is a veritable Garden of Eden of culinary delights. This small nine-by-five-mile island has fantastic seafood, wonderful dairy produce and is home to the princely Jersey Royal new potato – a soil-covered gem of a vegetable. Loved by chefs all over the world, this shining symbol of Jersey food, these days, has an official champion. Shaun Rankin, the island's most celebrated chef, is the 'face of the Jersey Royal'. Being tagged with that moniker may sound like an affliction from a Dennis Potter play, but Shaun – who's the executive chef at St Helier's award-winning Bohemia restaurant – is a

passionate advocate of Jersey's famous spud and, indeed, of all the island's produce. In fact, he's often said that he thinks of Jersey as his own nine-mile kitchen garden. With a sentiment like that you'd think Shaun was born-and-bred in Jersey. You'd be wrong, though. This 37-year-old was brought up in North-East England, in the town of Ferryhill, County Durham.

If you talk to him, you'll soon discover he's retained a soft Geordie lilt even though he's lived in Jersey for nearly 16 years. It's particularly noticeable when he speaks with passion about his food and menu. About the local red mullet, partridge and venison that autumn brings to his kitchen door; about the scallops, the Jersey clotted cream, the summer berries; about spring's Jersey Royals, naturally. The passion for Jersey produce has, of course, been imbued in Shaun since he moved to the island in 1994, but the passion for food and cooking started way back in Ferryhill, thanks to his mother, who treated Shaun and his younger brother to some fine home cooking during their childhood.

Pies of all sorts and 'amazing ham hock' soups were often on the dinner table, Shaun recalls. His mother's enthusiasm for cooking was infectious and it wasn't long before Shaun was helping to prepare the Sunday lunch and picking up the basic skills that 30 years later helped him to create the best treacle tart in the UK. Its pasty is light and crisp and snaps like glass when you bite into it; and the treacle filling is unctuous and sweet with a touch of salt to rein back the taste buds. It is, simply, perfect.

Having been bitten by the cooking bug, Shaun announced that he was going to be a chef when he was just 14-years-old and as, soon as he left school, he headed south to train at the highly regarded Thames Valley College in Slough (now Thames Valley University). His catering course incorporated day-release practical work at the Mayfair InterContinental hotel and at first he was conscious of the north-south divide, but that soon dissipated. 'I was a little Northerner with a chip on my shoulder. It soon got knocked out of me when I came to London!'

Nevertheless, three years in London were enough for Shaun and when, in 1992, he was offered a job at North Yorkshire's Black Bull Inn in Moulton he headed northwards again. The restaurant consisted of two converted original Pullman coaches and was a Yorkshire culinary legend. It gave Shaun his first real taste of classical French cooking and inspired him to master its huge array of fish dishes. After two years in Yorkshire, though, he was ready for another move and jumped at the chance to work at Longueville Manor, a one star Michelin kitchen, in St Saviour, Jersey. That, as they say, was that. Shaun immediately fell in love with the island. He worked at Longueville for five years under its head chef Andrew Baird before transferring for three years to its sister restaurant, Suma's, as head chef. Longueville had a kitchen garden and, while there, Shaun began to learn the value of easy access to home-grown produce. It was a lesson that was to prove very useful when he accepted an offer to head up a brand-new restaurant on the island, Bohemia, which opened in April 2004.

There was a hiatus, however, between leaving Suma's and the opening of Bohemia and Shaun took himself off to do a *stage* (work experience, to the rest of us) at the internationally fêted Charlie Trotter's restaurant in Chicago. Working here, Shaun experienced an epiphany. 'The produce was off the wall. We were getting white alba truffles the size of baby's heads and I also got my first sight of micro herbs. When I got back I knew I didn't have any of these things and I wanted them – so that became my mission.'

Returning to launch Bohemia, Shaun knew there was tremendous potential in Jersey's raw produce and rich farming land, but getting a consistent supply of local, sometimes modern, ingredients into the kitchen was another matter – the supply infrastructure was lacking. So he set about working directly with suppliers and farmers, getting them to grow new ingredients especially for him, encouraging them to try out new farming techniques. Now he has an array of local produce at his fingertips to work his culinary magic on and creates exciting menus that are a triumph of Jersey fare.

Among his starters is a dish of lightly poached local oysters on linguine with a beurre blanc and a sprinkling of sevruga caviar. It's a taste of the seashore so light and effervescent that if you close your eyes you can almost hear the waves rolling in on the rocks. The *Independent*'s then restaurant critic Terry Durack named it a highlight of his entire food year in 2006 and called Shaun one of the 'most highly gifted and polished chefs' cooking in the UK.

Of course, Shaun does allow some non-Jersey ingredients on to his plates, but the rule is they have to be better than he can get at home or something that isn't available at all on the island. So you'll see luxury truffles and foie gras – and a piece of Welsh lamb listed, too. The lamb often comes with some Sainte Maure de Touraine goat's cheese beignets and a chunk of local honeycomb to take the edge off the cheese and enhance the sweetness of the meat.

The dish is a good example of Shaun's contemporary, chic Anglo-French style of cuisine and sits well in the Art Deco-esque luxury of Bohemia's dining room and bar, with its Mondrian-style lattice windows and burnt orange walls.

It's hard to beat the sophistication of either the restaurant or Shaun's cooking and the two have drawn plaudits and awards aplenty, including a prestigious Catey award in 2006 from *Caterer and Hotelkeeper* magazine (regarded by many as a hospitality industry 'Oscar'), a Michelin star in 2005 and four AA rosettes.

The restaurant itself is part of the Club Hotel and Spa situated in the heart of St. Hellier, a stone's throw from the beach and in the shadow of Fort Regent, a defence put up during the Napoleonic wars. In Jersey, it's hard to get away from reminders of the island's sometimes turbulent past: a past that includes ownership, 900 years ago, by Norman France and invasion by the Nazis in WWII. Its history has forged Jersey's national character and, in a way, Shaun's food mirrors the island's personality. It's British at heart, with the style of a Parisian woman, and a fierce sense of self – a self linked inextricably to the fine island produce that he's had such a hand in spotlighting. It's hard not to think that it was a happy day for all concerned when the boy from County Durham made the hop over the water to the Channel Islands, and in doing so proved that Jersey is an island for foodies, not merely millionaires.

Bohemia Bar & Restaurant, Green Street, St Helier, Jersey JE2 4UH. **Phone:** 01534 880588. **www.bohemiajersey.com**

LIGHTLY POACHED JERSEY ROYAL BAY OYSTERS WITH SAFFRON LINGUINE, SEVRUGA CAVIAR AND LEMON BUTTER SAUCE

You have to be careful not to muck around with the delicate taste of oysters too much, especially when the oysters are as fantastic as the Jersey ones. That's why gently – and quickly – poaching them works so well. The dish has actually been on the menu since Bohemia opened and it's always been popular – it's very much a signature dish now. If you don't fancy making your own pasta you can, of course, buy some fresh pasta instead and you can also use other types of pasta, too – like tagliatelle.

SERVES 4

For the pasta
600g pasta flour
3 eggs
6 egg yolks
3 tablespoons saffron infusion
1 teaspoon olive oil
Pinch of salt

(Note: you make a saffron infusion by heating up 100ml water, adding a good pinch of saffron and infusing it for 10 minutes)

For the butter sauce
300ml white wine
6 black peppercorns, crushed
1 sprig of thyme
1 bay leaf
1 shallot, finely chopped
2 tablespoons of double cream
250g unsalted butter, cut into cubes
½ lemon, juiced
Salt and freshly ground black pepper

12 oysters
1 cucumber, peeled and cut into small batons
4 teaspoons sevruga caviar
2 teaspoons of chopped chives
A small handful of micro celery leaves

Pasta
Sieve the flour and the salt together into a food processor along with the eggs, egg yolks, saffron infusion and olive oil, and then process until the mixture comes together. Stop the machine, tip the ingredients onto a board and knead well until you have a firm smooth ball of dough. Wrap the dough in clingfilm and put it in the fridge to rest for at least 30 minutes.

Lightly flour a working surface and divide the dough into 4 equal pieces. Take one part of the dough and roll out with a rolling pin to a rectangle approximately 5mm thick. Feed the dough through a pasta machine several times, starting off on the thickest setting and adjusting down a notch each time until you finish with the thinnest setting. Then, using the linguine attachment, run the dough through. Let the linguine hang over a wooden pole to dry before cooking in a large saucepan of boiling salted water over a medium heat. Once cooked, drain the linguine through a colander and refresh it in iced water. When it has cooled, drain again and toss it in a little olive oil. Set aside until needed.

Butter sauce
Put the white wine, peppercorns, thyme, bay leaf and chopped shallot into a small saucepan and bring to the boil over a medium heat, then simmer for 10 minutes until the liquid is reduced by half its volume. Take off the heat and strain through a fine sieve into a clean saucepan. Add the cream, replace on the heat and bring back to the boil then pull the pan to the edge of the stove and, while it is warm, slowly add the cubed butter, a little at a time and whisking to emulsify it,

making sure the sauce does not boil. Add the lemon juice, season with salt and freshly ground black pepper and keep warm until needed.

Oysters
Carefully open and cut out the oysters over a bowl so that you catch their juices, adding them to the bowl with the juices as you go along.

Serving
Bring a large saucepan of salted water to the boil over a medium heat and quickly reheat the linguine in it for about 10 minutes. Drain the pasta and, twisting it round a carving fork, make three little bobbins for each plate. Meanwhile, take out the oysters from their juices, transfer the juices to a saucepan and warm them up over a medium heat. When hot, drop the oysters in for about 8 seconds, then spoon them out onto some kitchen paper and drain well. Place three oysters on top of each pasta bobbin and top them with some cucumber batons and a teaspoon of caviar. Add the chives to the warm lemon butter sauce, then spoon some sauce over the oysters and noodles. Finish with a little micro celery.

LINE-CAUGHT JERSEY TURBOT WITH PARSLEY RISOTTO, CLAMS AND RED WINE SAUCE

Being an island, fish and shellfish are a big thing on Jersey. and the seafood we get here is superb, so I'm always looking for ways to show it off on the menu. One of the things I like to do in my dishes is to use classic cooking techniques and recipes and just put them together in modern way. Here, I've done exactly that to frame a lovely, meaty fillet of turbot. You'll have more parsley purée and red wine sauce than you need – but the surplus can always be used in other dishes.

SERVES 4

For the parsley purée
1 shallot, finely sliced
2 cloves garlic
2 sprigs of thyme
500ml stock
150 ml double cream
900g curly parsley, stalks removed
A splash of olive oil
A pinch of salt

For the red wine sauce
8 banana shallots, finely sliced
2 garlic cloves
2 sprigs of thyme
1 bay leaf
1 tablespoon sherry vinegar
2 bottles Cabernet Sauvignon wine
10 button mushrooms, washed and sliced
1 litre reduced chicken stock
A splash of olive oil

For the clams
900g clams, in their shells
2 parsley stalks
50ml white wine
1 tablespoon butter
1 shallot, finely chopped
1 tablespoon sherry vinegar

For the risotto and fish
500ml vegetable stock
25ml olive oil
1 onion, finely chopped
1 garlic clove
A sprig of fresh thyme
1 bay leaf
200g carnaroli or arborio rice
125ml white wine
100ml parsley purée, for risotto base (see above)
A good pinch of chopped parsley
60g unsalted butter, cubed
4 x 110g turbot fillets, skinned
½ lemon, juiced
A few sprigs of micro parsley
4 baby leeks, sliced and braised in salted water and butter
Salt and freshly ground black pepper

Parsley purée

Heat a splash of olive oil in a saucepan over a medium heat, add the shallot, garlic and thyme and gently cook until the shallot is soft and translucent, but not coloured. Next, add the chicken stock and reduce its volume by half, then add the cream and bring the mixture to the boil. Add the parley and cook until it is tender, then transfer the mixture to a blender or food processor and blitz it until you have a smooth, bright green parsley purée. Check the seasoning and add a pinch of salt if necessary. Strain the mixture through a fine sieve.

Red wine sauce

Heat a splash of olive oil in a saucepan over a medium heat, add the shallots, garlic, thyme and bay leaf and cook gently until the shallots are soft and translucent, but not coloured. Add the sherry vinegar and once it has thickened, add the red wine and sliced mushrooms and continue to cook until the liquid is syrupy, then add the reduced chicken stock and bring the sauce back to a simmer. Continue to cook for about 20 minutes, skimming the sauce to remove any impurities that come to the surface, then remove it from the heat, strain through a fine sieve and cool.

Clams

Heat a heavy-based saucepan over a high heat and when it's very hot add the fresh clams and parsley, then pour over the white wine and quickly cover the saucepan with a lid. Cook the clams for about 1 minute, or until the shells open, then take off the heat and cool. Once they are cold, carefully remove the clam meat from the shells, discarding any clams that haven't opened.

Risotto and fish

Heat the vegetable stock up in a saucepan over a low heat and once it is warmed through remove it from the heat and leave to stand. Heat the olive oil in a heavy-based saucepan over a medium heat, add the onion, garlic, thyme and bay leaf and cook until the onion is soft and translucent but not coloured. Add the rice and cook for 1 minute, then stir-in the white wine. Once the wine has evaporated, add the hot stock, one ladle at a time, making sure you wait until the stock has been absorbed before you add each ladle. Keep adding stock until the rice is cooked – it should be soft but have a bit of bite. Add a little salt and pepper if necessary. Remove the bay leaf. Finally, add 100ml parsley purée to the rice and finish off with the chopped parsley and 30g of butter.

(Continued on page 226)

(Continued from page 225)

Heat 1 tablespoon of olive oil in a non-stick frying pan over a medium heat. Add the turbot fillets and cook until golden brown on one side, then finish with the remaining 30g of butter and a splash of lemon juice, spooning the butter over the fish to help cook the fillets through.

Serving
Heat up 1 tablespoon of butter over a medium heat. Once the butter starts to foam, add the clams and cook for 1 minute. Remove the clams, add in the shallots and once they have softened add the sherry vinegar and reduce it to a syrupy glaze.

Warm the leeks through and, if necessary, reheat the risotto and red wine sauce. Spoon some risotto on to your serving plates, then add the braised leeks and some warm clams. Drizzle some of the reduced cooking liquor from the clams around the risotto, drain the turbot well and place it on top. Pour a little red wine sauce around the plate and finish with a few leaves of micro parsley.

WARM BUTTERED JERSEY LOBSTER TAIL WITH FENNEL AND CRAB CEVICHE AND LOBSTER MACARONI

It would be unthinkable to leave lobster off the Bohemia menu. The waters around Jersey are so clean and clear that they produce some of the sweetest-tasting lobster meat you're ever likely to find. That goes for crabs, too. This recipe combines the two in a jazzed-up lobster salad. By the way, chancre crab is the big, flat crab you get off the coast of the UK . In the restaurant we use a lot of scallop velouté as the basis for our fish sauces, so make large quantities in one go – you can leave it out if you want to and just use lobster stock as the basis for your sauce.

SERVES 2

For the scallop velouté
500g scallop skirts
150ml white wine
2 litres whipping cream
2 lemons, juiced
Salt and white pepper

For the lobster
2 x 450g lobsters
1.2 litres water
1 carrot, finely chopped
4 banana shallots, finely chopped
1 leek, finely chopped
2 parsley stalks
8 black peppercorns
1 bay leaf
100g butter

For the lobster stock
2 x lobster shells and heads
6 tablespoons of olive oil
1 onion, finely chopped
2 carrots, finely chopped
1 celery stick, chopped
1 garlic clove, crushed
2 lemongrass stems, crushed
1 pinch of saffron
2 teaspoons Cognac

200ml Noilly Prat
1 litre fish stock
3 plum tomatoes, roughly chopped
1 teaspoon tomato purée
2 basil leaves
2 sprigs of tarragon
2 sprigs of parsley
1 bay leaf
Sea salt and freshly ground black pepper

For the lobster sauce
300ml lobster stock
600ml scallop velouté
1 tablespoon red wine sauce
2 teaspoons lime juice
A pinch of chopped chives
A pinch of chopped chervil
A pinch of chopped tarragon
A pinch of dill

Salt and freshly ground black pepper

For the saffron macaroni
720g pasta flour
5ml olive oil
7 egg yolks
20ml saffron reduction
(see oyster recipe xx)
3 whole eggs, beaten
A pinch of salt
A splash of olive oil

For the crab
1 x 1kg chancre crab
1 lemon, juiced
2 parsley stalks
Cold water, enough to just cover crab

For the fennel ceviche
4 bulbs baby fennel
A pinch of chopped chives
A pinch of chopped chervil
A pinch of chopped tarragon
A pinch of dill
1 lime, juiced
Salt and pepper

Scallop velouté
Heat a saucepan over a medium heat, add the scallop skirts and cook them for 3-4 minutes but do not colour them – you don't need any oil. Add the white wine and when it has reduced its volume to almost nothing add the cream, bring the liquid to the boil and cook out for 2 minutes. Remove and strain through a fine sieve, then season with the lemon juice and a pinch of salt and white pepper.

Lobster
Place the lobsters in the freezer for 10-15 minutes to comatose them, then remove and pull the heads away from the bodies quickly, break off the claws, wrap the tails around a butter knife and tie with string to keep them straight. Keep the heads.

Meanwhile, put the water, carrots, shallots, leek, parsley stalks, peppercorns and bay leaf into a large saucepan and bring to the boil over a medium heat. Simmer for 3 mintues, then pop in the lobster tails. After 3 minutes add the claws and continue cooking for a further 4 minutes. Once the lobster meat is cooked, remove both claws and tails from the broth and plunge them into iced water. Once cold, crack the shells and extract the meat, making sure you keep the tails whole. Cube all the claw meat and put it in the fridge. Place the lobster tails in a Vac Pac bag together with 10gms of butter, seal and put in the fridge. If you haven't got a Vac Pac machine, then just place them in a sealable freezer bag.

(Continued on page 228)

(Continued from page 227)

Lobster stock
Finely chop up the heads and bodies of the lobsters, keeping all the soft tissue for flavour. Heat half the olive oil in a large heavy-based saucepan over a medium heat, add the lobster shells from the head and body and cook for 5 minutes, then remove them from the saucepan and set aside. Heat the remaining olive oil in the same saucepan, then add the chopped vegetables, garlic and lemon grass and cook for about 5 minutes until softened. Add the saffron and cook for a further 30 seconds. Next, add the Cognac, and once it has absorbed the juices and evaporated a little, add the Noilly Prat and simmer the mixture until its volume reduces by half. Now, return the lobster shells, add the fish stock, tomatoes, tomato purée and herbs, bring the stock to the boil and simmer for 20 minutes. Remove from the heat and strain the stock through a large fine sieve into a clean saucepan, pressing the shells with the back of a spoon to extract as much flavour as possible.

Lobster sauce
Put the lobster stock, scallop velouté and red wine sauce into a saucepan over a medium heat and bring to the boil. Season with 1 teaspoon of lime juice and, if necessary, a pinch of salt and freshly ground black pepper.

Saffron macaroni
Put the flour, salt and olive oil in a food processor. Switch on and slowly pour in the egg yolks and saffron reduction, and once a dough has formed remove it, wrap it in clingfilm and rest it in the fridge for at least 30 minutes.

Divide the pasta dough into 4 equal pieces. Feed one portion of dough through a pasta machine several times, starting off on the thickest setting and adjusting down a notch each time until you finish with the thinnest setting. Lightly flour a work surface, transfer the pasta sheet on to it and, with a sharp knife, cut out a rectangle 10cm x 4cm. Next, using a pencil, roll the pasta rectangles around the pencil to form the macaroni shape, seal the pasta with the beaten egg and blanch it in boiling salted water until tender. Refresh the pasta in iced water. Once cold, drain it and set aside. Repeat the process with the other pieces of dough until you have enough macaroni.

Chancre crab and ceviche
Put the crab into a saucepan and cover it with cold water. Add the lemon and the parsley stalks and bring to the boil over a medium heat. Once the boil is reached, cook the crab for 2 minutes, then remove from the saucepan and cool under cold, running water. Once the crab is cold, remove the claws and crack the shells. Take out the crab meat and put to one side.

Make a ceviche by trimming the base of the baby fennel and, using a mandolin, finely slicing the bulb into a bowl. Add in the ceviche herbs, lime juice and a pinch of salt and freshly ground black pepper, then pop in the white crab meat and mix well.

Serving
Pop the Vac Pac lobster tail meat in a water bath at 62C for 10 minutes to warm slowly in the butter (or put it into a large saucepan of simmering water, heated to 62C for 10 minutes). Put a line of ceviche in the middle of your serving plates – form it into the same shape as the lobster tails. Remove the lobster tails from the bag and, using a sharp knife, slice each tail into 6 even pieces and arrange on the fennel and crab ceviche – one tail per person. Bring the lobster sauce to the boil over a medium heat, add in the cooked macaroni and spoon some into serving bowls. Finish the sauce with some finely chopped herbs and a little extra lime juice.

TREACLE TART WITH CLOTTED CREAM AND FRESH RASPBERRIES

This dish is fit for so many occasions, from a sumptuous dinner with friends to a family Sunday lunch – even with a good cup of tea. It works whether you dress it up or leave it simple, but no matter how you serve it, it will always bring back childhood memories – and people will always want more! Just a word of warning, you need to be very precise when you salt the treacle filling.

SERVES 8

For the pastry
518g plain flour
202g icing sugar
67g ground almonds
250g butter
4 eggs
1 tablespoon milk

For the treacle filling
92g unsalted butter, cubed
3 eggs
70ml double cream
2 level teaspoons of salt
720g golden syrup
165g brown breadcrumbs

For the raspberries
260g raspberries
½ lemon, juiced
1 tablespoon icing sugar
A pinch of freshly ground black
   pepper
Clotted cream, to serve

Pastry
Preheat the oven to 180C/gas mark 4. Put the flour, sugar, almonds and cubed butter in a large bowl and mix together, using your finger tips, until you get a fine breadcrumb texture. Add 2 eggs, beating them lightly first, mix well and bring the ingredients together to form a pastry dough. Cover the dough with clingfilm and put it in the fridge for 30 minutes to rest. Then, roll it out to approximately 2mm thick and line a 26cm tart ring, letting the pastry hang over the sides, then put some baking beans in the middle and bake blind for about 20 minutes until the pastry is cooked through and lightly golden. Remove from the oven. Beat the remaining eggs lightly with the milk in a bowl, then brush the tart shell completely with it to seal the pastry. Put the tart back in the oven for a further 3 minutes to set the egg wash, then remove the tart case and let it cool down.

Treacle tart filling
Preheat the oven to 160C/gas mark 3. Melt the butter in a saucepan over a medium heat until it starts to foam and begins to turn brown. Remove the butter from the heat and strain it through a fine sieve to remove any sediment. Mix the eggs, cream, and salt in a bowl and heat the golden syrup in a saucepan over a low heat. When the treacle is hot, remove it from the heat and add the 'brown' butter to it, stirring to incorporate the butter thoroughly – you'll know when this is done because the mixture will go cloudy. (It's very important that you mix the treacle and butter together while they are both still hot – and that you mix them before adding any other ingredients, because this will stop the mixture from separating.)

Next, stir in the cream, then add the breadcrumbs, making sure you mix them in well. Then pour the mixture into the cooked tart base and cook in the oven for 25 minutes before turning the heat down to 140C/gas mark 1 and cooking for a further 20 minutes. Remove and cool on a wire rack for about 2 hours. Once the tart is cold, the top should be chewy, the middle soft and moist and the pastry crisp. Don't forget to trim the pastry overflow at the sides of the tart.

Raspberries
Place the raspberries in a bowl, add the lemon juice and icing sugar and mix well, then add the cracked black pepper and put to one side.

Serving
Warm a knife in hot water and use it to cut the tart. Put a slice of tart on each serving plate and scatter some dressed raspberries over and around, it. Serve with a dollop of clotted cream.

JERSEY LAVENDER PANNA COTTA AND STRAWBERRY SALAD

Jersey has a fantastic lavender farm at St Mary's, and wonderful strawberries, and together they make a classic flavour combination which I've used as the basis of this dish. People order this dessert expecting just a bowl of strawberries; on seeing it they get a big 'wow' factor. Ab-Zorbit powder is a type of maltodextrin: when added to olive oil, the oil becomes a powder, which then transforms back into a liquid when put in the mouth. Isomalt is a very dry type of sugar which helps to keep biscuits – or tuilles – nice and crisp for longer. You can buy both ingredients on-line at www.msk-ingredients.com.

SERVES 6

For the strawberry tuilles and powder
500g strawberry purée
100g isomalt

For the strawberry sorbet
1.1 litres strawberry purée
477ml water
313g sugar
100ml liquid glucose
2 lemons, juiced

For the lavender panna cotta
650ml whipping cream
120g caster sugar
10g fresh lavender
2 gelatine leaves

For the strawberry purée and
strawberry mousse
800g strawberries
2 lemons, juiced
5 gelatine leaves
150ml stock syrup
450ml double cream, semi-whipped

For the strawberry jus, foam and jelly
400g strawberries

1 tablespoon icing sugar
1 tablespoon lemon juice
4 gelatine leaves

For the olive oil shortbread
450g butter
400g sugar
800g flour
200g ground almonds
1 teaspoon salt
½ teaspoon baking powder
1 vanilla pod, split and seeds removed
9 egg yolks, lightly beaten
150ml olive oil

For the olive oil powder
100g Ab-Zorbit powder
50ml good-quality olive oil

For the doughnut dough
350g strong flour
½ teaspoon salt
25g sugar
2 lemons, zested
17g fresh yeast
1 egg, lightly beaten
150ml milk
45g soft butter
A jar of strawberry jam
Sprinkle of cinnamon sugar (ground
    cinnamon and caster sugar)

For the garnish
2 lavender flowers
12 strawberries

Strawberry tuilles and powder
Preheat the oven to 50C/gas mark ¼. Put the strawberry purée into a saucepan over a medium-low heat and, once hot, add the isomalt, stirring until it is dissolved. Continue stirring as the purée reduces – the aim is to evaporate the water out of the fruit, it should take about 3 minutes – then remove from the heat and pour it on to a silicone baking mat or into a shallow baking

tray lined with silicone paper. Put in the oven and bake slowly overnight. The next morning, remove from the oven and, while it is still pliable, peel the strawberry tuille off the mats and cut into 2.25cm x 2.25cm squares, keeping the leftovers to make the strawberry powder. Place the square tuilles back in the oven and dry until brittle, then take out and cool. Once they are completely cool, store the tuilles in an airtight container. Place the leftovers in a plastic bag and crush them with a rolling pin until you get a powder, then pop this into the freezer.

Strawberry sorbet
Put the strawberry purée in a bowl. Next, make a syrup. Put the water, sugar, glucose and lemon juice into a saucepan over a medium heat and bring to the boil, stirring occasionally to help dissolve the sugar. Once it reaches the boil, take the syrup off the heat and pour it over the purée, stirring as you do so. Continue to stir until the purée and syrup are fully combined and then strain the mixture through a fine sieve or muslin cloth. Chill in the freezer overnight, then use a Pacojet to make the sorbet. If you don't have a Pacojet, either churn in an ice-cream machine in the normal manner, or place the mixture in a shallow dish in the freezer, taking it out every few minutes to stir. When the sorbet is slushy put it into a freezer-proof bowl and put it in the freezer to set completely.

Lavender panna cotta
Put the cream, sugar and lavender in a saucepan over a medium heat and bring to the boil, then remove from the heat. Meanwhile soak the gelatine leaves in cold water for 1-2 minutes

(Continued on page 232)

(Continued from page 231)

until they become soft. Remove them from the water, squeeze out the excess water and add them to the hot cream mixture. Stir well until the gelatine has dissolved and then pass the mixture through a fine sieve or muslin into a bowl. Chill over a bowl of ice. When cool, pour the mixture into martini glasses and put in the fridge to set.

Strawberry mousse

Cut the tops off the strawberries. Put them in a blender or food processor and blitz until you get a purée, then strain this through a fine sieve or muslin cloth to remove the seeds. Put the 600ml of fresh strawberry purée and the lemon juice into a bowl. Put the stock syrup in a saucepan over a medium heat and bring to the boil. While you're waiting for the syrup to reach the boil, soak the gelatine leaves in cold water for 1-2 minutes, and once they are soft remove them from the water, squeeze to get rid of excess water and add the leaves to the boiling syrup, stirring until the gelatine has dissolved. Add the syrup to the purée and chill the mixture over a bowl of iced water until cold and slightly firm. Fold the whipped cream into the purée mixture; pour into a clingfilm-lined large square dish, or small individual clingfilm-lined moulds, and put in the fridge for 1-2 hours to set.

Strawberry jus and foam and jelly

Put the strawberries, icing sugar and lemon juice into a bowl. Place the bowl over a saucepan of boiling water and heat slowly. When the juice has seeped out of the strawberries, take off the heat, remove the strawberries with a slatted spoon and discard them. Strain the juice through a fine sieve or

muslin cloth into a clean saucepan, then put 500ml in a clean saucepan and reheat slowly over a low heat. Meanwhile, soften the gelatine leaves in some cold water for 1-2 minutes and once soft add them to the strawberry juice and stir until dissolved. Remove from the heat and divide the liquid in half. Pour one half into a small cone-shaped mould or a small shallow container and put in the fridge for 2 hours to set. Place the second half of the liquid into a soda siphon.

Olive oil shortbread

Preheat the oven to 180C/gas mark 4. Put the butter and sugar in a bowl and beat them vigorously together until light and fluffy. Add the flour, ground almonds, salt, baking powder and vanilla seeds and mix until the ingredients start to combine. Next, slowly add the egg yolks and olive oil to make a wet dough. Wrap the dough in clingfilm and put in the fridge to firm up overnight. The next day, roll out the pastry to 1.5cm thickness, transfer to a baking sheet and cook in the oven until it is just starting to brown. Take out of the oven and cut into rectangles 9cm x 3cm. Place the biscuits back in the oven and bake until they turn golden brown.

Olive oil powder

Put the Ab-Zorbit powder into a blender. Switch on and slowly add the olive oil until a fine, dry powder is formed.

Doughnuts

Mix the flour, salt, sugar, lemon zest and yeast together in a bowl. Add the eggs and milk, mix well and then add the butter and draw everything together to make a pliable dough. Divide and then roll the dough into small balls and pop these onto a floured tray and cover

with a damp cloth and leave them to prove in a warm place for about 20 minutes. Once proved, deep fry the doughnuts for a few seconds in a fat fryer until just starting to brown. Remove and drain on kitchen paper.

Serving

Make a line of strawberry powder down the middle of your serving plates and put two lavender flowers on the side of each plate in line with the powder. Cut 6 pieces of shortbread in half and sprinkle 6 of the cut pieces with some of the olive oil powder. If you have set the mousse in one dish, take a 3cm pastry cutter and cut out 6 circles of the mousse and place these on top of the sprinkled shortbread – or if the mousse is individual moulds, turn it out on to the shortbread. Next, put the mousse-topped shortbread on to your plates, on one side of the strawberry powder line. Using the same 3cm cutter, make a circle of finely cubed strawberry on each plate, below the mousse. Cut the top off a strawberry and cut in half, put on the plate on the opposite side of the line to the mousse. Spoon some strawberry jelly onto the plate (or tip out of the moulds) opposite the cubed strawberry. Make a small hole in each doughnut and pipe in a small amount of strawberry jam. Quickly deep fry the doughnuts until brown, then drain on kitchen paper to take off the excess oil and roll them in cinnamon sugar. Put on the plates between the mousse and cubed strawberry. Squeeze some foam between the jelly and the fresh strawberry, place a scoop of sorbet onto the cubed strawberry and a strawberry tuille on top of the mousse. Take the martini glasses with the panna cotta out of the fridge, sprinkle with some strawberry powder and serve with the strawberry plate.

MATT TEBBUTT

You know you are off the beaten track when roads narrow down to single lanes and every other car you pass has mud on its skirting. Judged by these criteria, the village of Nantyderry is well off the track. It lies just across the border from England in Monmouthshire between Abergavenny and Usk – and is tiny and picturesque. To get to it you have to drive through Chain Bridge, though, thankfully, no longer over one. Nevertheless, the journey's a bit of an adventure. But an adventure well worth having, because Nantyderry houses a gastronomic dynamo called Matt Tebbutt, the chef-proprietor of a piece of Welsh gold, the Foxhunter pub.

Matt has been blazing a trail in this sleepy Welsh village ever since he and his wife, Lisa, bought the former station master's-house-turned-local-hostelry in 2001. Together they completely transformed it, restoring its Welsh flagstone floors, putting in log-burning stoves and leather sofas, hanging food-related artwork on the walls – and implementing Matt's culinary mission of serving fresh, seasonal, no-frills food. Food full of confident flavours and strong, hearty combinations. Dishes like locally sourced chicken, roasted and served with soft braised oxtail, or braised organic mutton with Jersey cream mash and roast marrow. There's no place for foams and jellies in Matt's food – he scratches his head at the mere idea of them. He's a hungry man's chef.

His honest style of cooking has won Matt favour with foodies and drawn awards and plaudits from many organisations, including the AA (gongs for the restaurant and its wine list) and a golden True Taste of Wales stamp of approval from the Welsh Development Agency. Yet though he's now well-ensconced in Nantyderry and was brought up in South Wales, this 35-year-old only classes himself as an 'honorary Welshman'. The reason? He was born in High Wycombe in Buckinghamshire, only moving to Newport with his family when he was six months old!

He grew up in Newport wanting to be a pilot. But despite learning to fly with the University Air Squadron when he was at Oxford Brookes university, he decided life in the RAF wasn't for him and opted instead to take a one-year diploma course in London at the famous Leith's School of Food and Wine. It wasn't such a drastic change of direction as it might seem on paper. When he was a child, Matt's parents took the family caravanning around Brittany, and six-year-old Matt developed a passion for fish soup with little bits of gruyère and croûtons. His culinary curiosity developed from then onwards and he cooked throughout his childhood and teenage years.

Graduating from Leith's in 1996, he went on to do tours of duty in the kitchens of several landmark London restaurants, starting off with perhaps the hardest of them all – Marco Pierre White's Oak Room at the Criterion hotel in Piccadilly. Stints at Chez Bruce, Alastair Little and Clarke's followed but like all passionate and individual chefs Matt dreamed of a place of his own and began to think of moving back home to Wales. Both Lisa and he knew the area around Abergavenny from childhood, so they targeted the Welsh Marches for their search and eventually found the Foxhunter.

Between them, they've turned the pub into the kind of place you fantasise about reaching after a long day's journey into night in the depths of winter or autumn. A dream of a chocolate box building, all stone walls and cosy windows, with a glimmer of candles twinkling through the panes inviting you to push open the doors and be welcomed by warm friendly staff, a toasty fireside seat and, most enticingly of all, the promise of good food.

And it is very good, indeed. Matt is in the lucky position of having a good network of local suppliers so he's able to change his menus twice a day to reflect the treasures that turn up at his kitchen door. That can be anything from local game, to wild ingredients like St George's mushrooms, samphire or sorrel. Foraging is one of Matt's hobbies and he's often to be found out on ingredient-scouting walks or fishing in the River Usk, which flows close by Nantyderry. Such is his obsession that he runs foraging trips for interested guests who stay in the pub's adjoining cottages.

However, Matt isn't slavishly tied to Welsh, or even UK, produce. At the end of the day, his menu is driven by his palate and he'll happily use ingredients sourced around the world if he thinks they are worthy of being on his menu – Iberico ham or honeycomb from Germany, for instance. Most of the foreign imports come from the Mediterranean, a reflection of the influence that working with Alastair Little had on him.

Little cooked within the traditions of Italian cuisine, a style that's famously simple. And it is the simplicity of Matt's own cooking that is so wonderful. His dishes have no heavy sauces or tricksy garnishes; he even flinches at the idea of sieving purées! He'd rather serve a nice bit of longhorn steak, or a roast chicken, or some butcher's offal, like sweetbreads. His skill is shown not in clever modern techniques but in his faultless sense of ingredient matches. Steak comes with a few succulent oysters, chicken with ox cheek for added oomph. 'Food for me isn't about temples of fine dining with very intricate dishes; it is about the simple joys of eating great fresh ingredients,' he says.

That's not to say that Matt doesn't appreciate what other chefs do. He admires the intricate cutting-edge cooking of people like Jason Atherton and avidly follows the UK food scene, both through the newspapers and through presenting his own show on UKTV Food. It seems he's just as comfortable in the bright lights of the media as in his own kitchen – and his chiselled good looks and conspiratorial grin certainly go down well with viewers.

But the Foxhunter remains his culinary sweetheart and he is there more often than not. He and Lisa, after all, have their names above the door and treat it like an extension of their home. In fact, until recently, it was their home and they and their son, Henry, used to sleep above the kitchen. They moved out only when the imminent arrival of their daughter, Jessie,

meant that they needed more family living space. The pub still retains many personal touches though, like the bookshelf full of great cookery tomes by the likes of the legendary food writer Elizabeth David and her latter-day counterpart, Nigel Slater.

The joys of the Foxhunter don't end with its dining room, either. Next door to the pub is a row of cottages, two of them owned by Matt and Lisa. One consists of two rooms plus a cosy sitting room, the other (an old stable block) has a mezzanine floor with a sofa bed. Both come with a fridge full of glorious breakfast goodies and fresh coffee on tap. Staying in one of them is the most wonderful bookend to one of Matt's hearty dinners.

Imagine tucking into plates of delicious food, quaffing a bottle or two from the brilliant wine list and rectifying all the troubles in the world late into the night. Then rolling the 20 yards from the Foxhunter to the cottage's front door, through the coal-black Welsh night, and collapsing on to a lovely, soft, bed fit for the Prince of Wales himself. Do that, and you'll get a sense of the euphoria that a stay at the Foxhunter engenders. There is only one drawback – remembering to leave enough room to enjoy a fry-up of locally laid eggs, or pots of French yoghurt, the next morning.

The Foxhunter
Nantyderry, Abergavenny, Monmouthshire NP7 9DN
Phone 01873 881101 **www.thefoxhunter.com**

GROUSE WITH CHICORY AND ORANGE TART

This is an elegant starter full of some wonderful autumnal colours and flavours, such as walnuts and grouse. If you can't get hold of grouse, partridge or pheasant are great substitutes.

SERVES 2

100g puff pastry
2 heads of chicory
60g unsalted butter
4 tablespoons caster sugar
1 teaspooon coriander seeds, crushed
1 star anise, crushed
2 oranges, juiced
Splash of Cointreau or Grand Marnier
1 tablespoon olive oil
1 grouse, breasts removed
1 clove of garlic, crushed
2 sprigs of thyme
Red chicory leaves, to serve
2 tablespoons extra virgin olive oil
1 orange, segmented
2 tablespoons of wet walnuts, toasted and roughly chopped
Salt and freshly ground black pepper

Preheat the oven to 180C/gas mark 4. Begin by making the tarts. Roll out two pastry discs big enough to fit a 10cm blini or frying pan. The pastry needs to be just less than the thickness of a pound coin. Once it's rolled out, place the rounds on two plates, cover with clingfilm and chill in the refrigerator.

Cut the chicory lengthways and lay it in a roasting tray that is just large enough to hold it. Dot with 40g of the butter and sprinkle over 3 tablespoons of the sugar, the coriander seeds and star anise, and then pour over the orange juice and Cointreau or Grand Marnier. Now cover the chicory with some kitchen foil and roast it in the oven for 25-30 minutes until tender, then remove and put it to one side.

Take two individual blini pans, divide 10g of the butter equally between the two pans then sprinkle the rest of the sugar over it. Arrange the cooked chicory cut-side down in the pans, then lay the pastry discs over it, making sure to tuck the pastry in around the edges to keep each tart snug and tight. Cook for about 15 minutes in the oven until the pastry is a golden colour.

Meanwhile, heat the olive oil in a saucepan over a medium-low heat. Season the grouse breasts with a little salt, pop them in the pan and gently cook them, skin-side down, for 4-5 minutes. Turn over the breasts and continue cooking them for a further 2 minutes, ensuring they remain pink in the middle. Be careful not to overcook them as they can dry out very quickly. Add the rest of the butter, garlic and thyme to finish, then remove the breasts from the heat, baste and allow them to rest in the pan.

Serving
Quickly and carefully turn out the tarts. Slice the grouse breasts (not too thin) and place one breast on each tart. Accompany with some red chicory leaves dressed with extra virgin olive oil and the orange segments. Season with salt and pepper if necessary, then top with the walnuts. Finally, pour over some of the cooked chicory juices.

POACHED CHICKEN AND CHICKEN LIVERS, SMOKED BACON DUMPLINGS AND TOMATOES

This dish encompasses everything I love about cooking – beautiful ingredients which pack a punch in flavour, simply prepared. What could be better than that? The secret is always to use the best raw product you can – liver from organic free-range chickens, the freshest herbs, freshly made stock. You can use baby plum tomatoes, if you like (cut in half and deseeded) instead of a larger kind.

SERVES 2

4 rashers of good-quality smoked
    bacon
1 tablespoon olive oil
2 shallots, finely chopped
1 garlic clove, finely chopped
1 small bunch of fresh basil
500ml white chicken stock
2 bay leaves
2 chicken breasts, boned and with the
    skin removed
4 fat chicken livers, veins removed and
    thickly sliced
4 tomatoes, deseeded and diced
A handful of baby spinach leaves

First make the dumplings. Remove the rind from the bacon, keeping it to use later, then mince the bacon in a food processor. Heat the olive oil over a medium heat in a small saucepan, add the shallots and garlic and fry until they are soft and translucent. Remove from the heat and allow everything to cool. Destalk and shred the basil, keeping the stalks and a few leaves aside to use later. Put the minced bacon, shallots and garlic into a bowl. Add the basil and mix well, roll the mixture into small balls (about the size of a 2 pence coin) and put into the fridge to firm up.

Put the chicken stock in a saucepan together with the bay leaves, basil stalks and bacon rind and bring it to the boil over a medium heat. Simmer for 20 minutes to allow the herbs to infuse, then strain through a fine sieve into a clean saucepan and discard the herbs and rind. Replace the strained stock over a medium heat, drop in the chicken breasts and simmer them very gently for 10 minutes. Now add the dumplings and continue cooking for a further 5-7 minutes, adding the chicken livers and tomatoes after about 3-5 minutes. Do not allow the stock to boil or the chicken and the livers will toughen.

Serving
Place some of the raw spinach leaves into two bowls, top with the chicken breasts, livers and dumplings. Ladle over the stock and tomatoes, and garnish with the remaining basil leaves.

ROAST HAKE WITH PARSLEY, ALMOND AND MUSSEL VINAIGRETTE

Hake is one of my favourite fish – and its soft, delicate flesh means it is always best cooked on the bone. Sherry, saffron, almonds and mussels are a perfect accompaniment for hake and they also bring back many memories of trips to Spain, where hake is used a lot in traditional dishes, particularly in the Basque region of northern Spain.

SERVES 2

400g fresh mussels
1 small glass of fino sherry
4 tablespoons extra virgin olive oil
1 splash of sherry vinegar
1 pinch of saffron
2 tablespoons light olive oil
2 x 200g hake steaks, cut through the
   bone
10g unsalted butter
12 spears of asparagus, woody ends
   removed and cut in half at an angle
1 tablespoon of chopped fresh parsley
2 tablespoons of whole almonds,
   toasted and chopped coarsely
1 big handful of wild bittercress or
   watercress
Salt and freshly ground black pepper

Preheat the oven to 180C/gas mark 4. Prepare the mussels by washing and cleaning them thoroughly in fresh, cold water. Heat a large saucepan over a high heat until it's very hot, then add in the mussels and the sherry. Put on the lid and allow the shellfish to steam for 3-4 minutes, giving the pan a shake from time to time, then take them off the heat and strain through a colander over a bowl so that you catch the cooking juices. Pour the mussels into a deep-sided tray to cool. Then, once cooled, remove the meat from the shells, discarding any mussels that have not opened. Strain the cooking juices through a fine sieve into a clean saucepan, then bring this to the boil over a medium heat and simmer until you have reduced its volume by half. Remove from the heat, add the reserved mussel meat and leave to one side.

In a bowl, whisk together the extra virgin olive oil and sherry vinegar. Add the saffron and allow to infuse. Now, add enough of the mussel liquor, about 100ml, to flavour the sherry vinaigrette.

Heat the light olive oil in a metal-handled saucepan. Season the hake steaks and add to the pan. Cook over a moderate heat, flesh-side down, for 3-4 minutes until golden. Then turn them over and place the saucepan in the oven for 8-10 minutes, depending on the thickness of the fish. Remove from the oven, add the butter and baste the fish as it melts. Leave to one side, keeping the hake warm, for 2 minutes.

Meanwhile, bring a saucepan of salted water to a rapid boil over a high heat and add in the asparagus. Cook for 2 minutes until just tender. Remove immediately from the heat and drain.

Serving
Add the parsley and toasted almonds to the vinaigrette. Divide the asparagus up between two plates, place a hake steak on each and drizzle with some mussel vinaigrette. Pour the mussels and reduced liquor around the steaks and finally scatter on some wild bittercress or watercress.

LAMB IN SALT CRUST, PARMESAN CREAMED CANNELLINI BEANS AND FRESH HERBS

Wrapping lamb in a salt crust is an old-fashioned method of sealing in all the wonderful flavours of the meat. Needless to say, the lamb you use must be of the highest quality. We are very lucky here as we use the beautiful Welsh lamb which is raised on the fields surrounding the restaurant. I like to use fresh cannellini beans but if you can't get these substitute them with dried ones – and cook these according to the instructions on the packet.

SERVES 4

2 tablespoons olive oil
1 x 3kg leg of lamb
1kg plain flour
200g coarse sea salt
400g fine sea salt
2 eggs, beaten
500ml warm water
2 tablespoons Dijon mustard
1 bunch of fresh parsley, chopped
1 bunch of fresh thyme, chopped
1 bunch of fresh mint, chopped
1egg and 1egg yolk, mixed lightly
    together for a glaze
600g fresh cannellini beans
500ml chicken or lamb stock
250ml double cream
150g Parmesan, freshly grated
100g samphire, blanched for 2
    minutes and refreshed in iced water
Salt and freshly ground black pepper

Preheat the oven to190/gas mark 5. Heat the olive oil in a saucepan over a medium heat. Season the lamb with salt and black pepper, then cook it in the saucepan for about 10 minutes, until nicely golden all over. Take it off the heat and set aside to cool a little.

Meanwhile, make the salt crust by mixing in a large bowl the flour, the two salts, the 2 beaten eggs and enough of the water to bind the mixture into a dough. Now cover it with clingfilm and chill for up to 1 hour in the fridge.

Brush the lamb with the mustard, then roll it in the herbs, reserving a tablespoon of each herb to use later.

Now, roll the salt dough out to 1cm thick. Lay it over the lamb, covering the meat completely, then seal the dough edges with water. Brush it with the egg glaze and place on a wire rack in a roasting tray. Cook in the oven for 40-50 minutes until pink, or longer if so desired. Remove the lamb from the oven and allow it to stand for at least 30 minutes before serving.

Place a large pan of water over a medium heat, add in the fresh cannellini beans and bring to the boil, then simmer for 30-40 minutes until tender. Allow the beans to cool in the water before draining them in a colander. In a clean saucepan, bring the chicken or lamb stock to the boil over a medium heat and reduce its volume by half. Add in the cream and return to the boil, then simmer for 5 minutes until slightly thickened. Stir in the beans and the Parmesan cheese. Season with salt and pepper and add the reserved herbs and the samphire.

Serving
To serve, remove the salt crust from the lamb and thinly slice the meat, sharing it equally between your four plates. Add some of the creamed cannellini beans and serve.

SPICED POACHED PEAR WITH GORGONZOLA AND HONEYCOMB

This dessert is a wonderful combination of delicious flavours which all come together in perfect harmony. Alongside the delicate poached pears there is the rich red wine, salty and pungent Gorgonzola and the oozing honeycomb. It really is a very simple dish and always sells well in the restaurant. Everybody likes it because it's fresh and zingy, with a richness provided by the honeycomb and cheese.

SERVES 2

1 bottle of fruity red wine
100g of sugar or more to taste
3 cloves
1 teaspoon black peppercorns
1 star anise
1 small cinnamon stick
1 orange, zested
2 Williams or conference pears
200g Gorgonzola cheese
120g of good-quality honeycomb
Toasted bread or biscuits, for serving

Place the wine, sugar, cloves, peppercorns, star anise, cinnamon and orange zest in a saucepan over a medium heat and bring to the boil. Simmer for 30 minutes to allow ingredients to infuse, then remove from the heat and transfer everything to a bowl to cool down.

Peel and core the pears, leaving them whole. Add the pears to the cooled red wine syrup, ensuring they are totally covered. Cover with clingfilm and allow to marinate overnight in the fridge.

The next day, transfer the pears and red wine to a saucepan, place over a medium heat and bring up to a gentle simmer, then poach them until they're tender. The length of time will depend upon the size and ripeness of the pears. Remove from the heat and allow the pears to cool in the liquor.

Serving
Place a pear on each plate, together with a generous lump of Gorgonzola cheese and some honeycomb. Serve with either toasted bread or biscuits.

MARCUS WAREING

For some people aiming for excellence is not enough and perfection is the only acceptable goal. Marcus Wareing is one such man. Just the mention of his name can cause chefs to check their shoes and reach for a clean white jacket lest they come under his laser-blue gaze. Step into his eponymous restaurant, nestling in one corner of London's Berkeley hotel, and you'll see at once how that eye for detail translates into reality. For here, Marcus has created one of the most polished dining experiences in Britain.

Marcus Wareing at the Berkeley runs with infinite ease: like a Swiss watch, it has an exact rhythm. Nothing is ever out of place or left to chance, either out front or in the kitchen. In fact, Marcus' attention to minutiae is akin to the obsession of a great painter like Canaletto, so precise is his cooking, so perfect the placement of tables, glasses and cutlery. Everything is in focus, nothing, not the smallest thing, is blurred. Having a meal in Marcus' restaurant is like pampering yourself in a luxury spa. You just sit back and lap up the treat with a sigh of utter contentment. His food combines the highest level of technical ability with a passion for seasonal British ingredients; it's delicate, clean as a whistle on the palate and pretty as a picture on the eye. A meal might begin simply with an *amuse-bouche* of something like pumpkin soup with an airy flavour-pocket of Parmesan foam, then quickly enter the world of the sublime with the likes of scallops and confited cod with cauliflower and macadamia nuts.

Marcus, of course, wasn't born with extraordinary cooking and restaurateuring skills, he learned them. And his childhood in the Merseyside town of Southport was quite unextraordinary. His father was a potato and vegetable supplier and Marcus often used to help out delivering orders. Through the business, Marcus imbibed a passion for the best of British produce and an understanding that you don't get anywhere in life without hard graft. His first glance of chefs' whites, though, came thanks to his older brother, Brian, who worked at a local steakhouse. His father used to supply the restaurant and Marcus would sometimes do the delivery. Hanging around waiting for orders to be checked, he began to learn the language of the kitchen. And he was intrigued.

So much so, that when he failed his school exams, he put his name down for catering college. He soon found out he was a natural cook and as he trained began entering, and winning, culinary competitions. One competition brought him to the attention of Anton Edelmann, the executive chef of London's famous Savoy hotel, and soon he was putting his feet on the first rung of the culinary ladder to stardom with a job as a trainee chef under Anton's watchful eye. He stayed at the hotel for nearly two years, devoting himself wholeheartedly to the task of learning his craft.

Moving from a provincial northern seaside town to the vastness of London was a culture shock and at first 18-year-old Marcus felt homesick, but work filled the void and out-of-hours he kept himself fit in the gym. His hard work soon paid off, and in 1990 he made the move from the Savoy to Albert and Michel Roux Jr's legendary Le Gavroche

– perhaps the most famous restaurant in London – and it was while in their kitchen learning the precise ways of classical French cuisine that he met a certain Gordon Ramsay. Like Marcus, Gordon was a fiercely hardworking young chef with an eye for detail and a desire for success. Although their paths would diverge temporarily a couple of times, from that moment their careers became entwined for the next 18 years and their culinary partnership would eventually help Gordon establish an international restaurant empire.

Before then, though, Marcus spent over two years in the Roux fold – working not only at Le Gavroche but also at restaurants in New York state and Amsterdam where Albert had consultancies. Returning to the UK in 1992, he did stints at Gravetye Manor in West Sussex (where he met his wife, Jane) and, briefly, with Pierre Koffmann at the latter's legendary La Tante Claire in London. But fate came knocking in the form of Gordon, who was given a chance to open a new restaurant in Chelsea called Aubergine. He invited Marcus, 23, along for the ride as his second-in-command.

Aubergine proved to be one of the toughest kitchens in Britain, but it was an incredible experience. The cooking was exciting and there was a sense of theatre in the dining room. But it was unrelenting in its demands and after a couple of years at the hobs Marcus handed his notice in. He needed a rest.

That rest took in working at famous eateries in New York and Paris but Gordon lured him back in 1996, initially to set up L'Oranger in St James as a sister restaurant to Aubergine and eventually, when he launched his own company, to open a new restaurant, Pétrus. It quickly garnered plaudits, including a Michelin star, and it wasn't long before Marcus' role in Gordon Ramsay Holdings expanded to encompass a highly successful relaunch of his former workplace, the Savoy Grill.

In the same year that the Savoy project got underway, Pétrus relocated to the Berkeley hotel and four years later, in 2007, Marcus netted a much longed-for second Michelin star for the restaurant. Sadly, by that time his working relationship with Gordon was beginning to break down and, amid much bitterness and recrimination in the media and under the eye of a whole bunch of expensive lawyers, Marcus and the management at the Berkeley hotel took

over the site of Pétrus. From September 2008 it relaunched as Marcus Wareing at the Berkeley.

The split from Gordon sent shock waves through the industry but painful though it was, the 'divorce' energised Marcus and the restaurant really took flight. Since he launched under his own name, magazines and food guides have been queuing up to hand over gongs to both Marcus and the restaurant: the AA, Harden's, the Good Food Guide, GQ and Michelin among many.

The pats on the back are thoroughly deserved. Marcus's menu is without doubt one of the most perfect examples of modern British cuisine in the country, although I doubt Marcus would even consider his food to be British. But it is. In spite of its

obvious debt to French culinary traditions, it has a British spirit about it with just the right amount of derring-do.

You can see it in his slow-poached wild sea bass with wild herbs, sweet golden beets and a sauce made of sea urchin and vermouth, which is as frothy and invigorating as sea spray; in the matching of tender British salt marsh lamb and rose veal with sea purslane and Dorset snails. And in the many humble British staples like flapjack, custard tart or ice cream and jelly, which have been transformed into things of wonder on the restaurant's dessert menu. 'My food is my palate. It's about how I taste and how I feel. A chef's job is to create his own individual combination from millions of possible ingredients. It's about putting yourself into the equation and adding your own spice,' he says.

The 39-year-old chef has certainly added his own spice to his restaurant, which these days runs as a family concern with Jane taking charge of back-room business like bookings as well as looking after their own young family of three children. Between them, Marcus and Jane have created a bespoke dining experience to satisfy their bespoke-suited clientele. A culinary masterpiece, no less. And if you get a front row seat at the chef's table in the kitchen, you will be left in no doubt that you are witnessing the brushstrokes of a true master chef.

Marcus Wareing at The Berkeley
The Berkeley Hotel, Wilton Place, London SW1X 7RL
Phone 020 7235 1200 **www.marcus-wareing.com**

FOIE GRAS WITH HONEY AND ALMOND, APRICOTS, AMARETTI AND BLACK OLIVE

This is a fabulous dish for summer, utilising sweet and flavoursome apricots and beautiful almonds which perfectly complement the richness of the foie gras.

SERVES 4

For the black olive crumble
50g pitted black olives

For the honey and almond meringue
100g blossom honey
2 egg whites
1 teaspoon almond essence

For the tea syrup
3 tablespoons sugar
250ml water
1 tablespoon Lapsang Souchong tea

For the apricot compote
6 ripe apricots, finely chopped
25ml amaretto liqueur
60g caster sugar

For the foie gras
1 tablespoon vegetable oil
240–280g foie gras, cut into 4 pieces
½ teaspoon table salt

For the garnish
Amaretti biscuit, crumbled
Fresh almonds, sliced

Black olive crumble
Preheat the oven to 50C/gas mark ¼. Put the olives on to an oven tray and dry overnight in the oven. Chop roughly when dry to make a crumble to garnish the dish with later.

Honey and almond meringue
Place the honey in a small saucepan over a low heat and bring to the boil. Meanwhile, put the egg whites into a bowl and whisk until stiff, then slowly pour the hot honey into the egg whites, continuing to whisk until the bowl is cool to the touch. Add the almond essence then place the uncooked meringue into a piping bag and put it in the fridge.

Tea syrup
Put the sugar and water in a saucepan over a medium heat and bring to the boil, then add the tea and boil for 5 minutes. Remove from the heat and strain the infusion to get rid of the tea leaves, then replace on the heat, bring to the boil again and simmer until it has reduced to a thick syrup.

Apricot compote
Put half of the apricots in a bowl with the amaretto. Cover with clingfilm and put in a warm place for 1 hour. Next, make a jam by placing the remaining apricots in a saucepan with the sugar over a medium heat, bring to a rolling boil and simmer gently until thick. Put the jam into a blender or food processor and blitz until you get a purée, then pass the mixture through a fine sieve.

Foie gras
Heat the oil in a large frying pan. Season the foie gras with the salt, then brown it all over in the pan and allow to cook until slightly soft to the touch. Remove and allow to rest in a warm place for 2 minutes before serving.

Serving
Put the apricot jam and the amaretto-infused apricots into a saucepan over a low heat and warm through. Meanwhile, pipe a small circle of meringue into the plate and smear it a little with a spoon to create a swipe. Using a culinary blow torch lightly colour the meringue, then sprinkle it with the amaretti and black olive crumble. Place the warm compote on the plate alongside the meringue and top this with the foie gras. Sprinkle the foie gras with the almonds, then drizzle the tea syrup around.

ROASTED HALIBUT WITH SWEETCORN, CHORIZO AND LEEKS

SERVES 4

Halibut is a flat fish which has a creamy yet meaty texture. It lends itself well to rich accompaniments like sweetcorn and chorizo. When fresh sweetcorn is unavailable, try substituting with a mushroom purée and sautéed mushrooms.

For the sweetcorn
30g butter
400g fresh sweetcorn kernels
½ teaspoon table salt
200ml chicken stock
50ml cream
100g chorizo, finely chopped

For the leeks
2 tablespoons vegetable oil
2 leeks, white part only and cut in half
*   lengthways, then widthways*
¼ bunch of thyme
25g butter
100ml chicken stock
Table salt and freshly ground black
*   pepper*

For the leek and thyme salad
80g leeks, white part only and finely
*   sliced*
1 tablespoon olive oil
½ teaspoon white wine vinegar
1 tablespoon thyme leaves, stalks
*   removed*
A pinch of table salt

For the fish and garnish
4x 100g halibut fillets
2 tablespoons vegetable oil
25g unsalted butter
½ teaspoon table salt
Chorizo trimmings, baked in the oven
*   and finely chopped*

Sweetcorn
First, make a purée. Put 25g of the butter into a saucepan over a medium-low heat. Once it is hot enough, add 200g of the sweetcorn and ½ teaspoon of salt and cook gently for a few minutes without colouring it. Add the chicken stock and continue cooking until the corn is tender. Remove from the heat, add the cream then blend until smooth. Pass the purée through a fine sieve into a clean saucepan and cover until needed.

Now put the remaining butter (approximately 1 tablespoon) into a small saucepan over a medium heat. Melt it until it browns lightly, then add the remaining 200g of sweetcorn and cook for 1 minute before adding the chorizo and cooking for a further 2 minutes.

Leeks
Heat the oil in a large frying pan over a medium heat. Season the leek pieces with salt and freshly ground black pepper then place them flat-side down in the pan together with the thyme. Brown lightly then add the butter and stock and cook until tender.

Leek and thyme salad
Put the sliced leeks together with the salt, olive oil, vinegar and thyme into a bowl and mix well.

Halibut
Heat the oil in a non-stick frying pan over a medium to high heat. Season the fish then gently place it into the hot oil. Brown the fish on one side, then turn it over and add the butter. Reduce the heat and cook for a further 2 minutes until the fish is cooked through, but be careful not to overcook it. Remove from the heat

and allow it to rest for 2 minutes.

Serving
If necessary, warm the sweetcorn purée, sweetcorn and chorizo and braised leeks. Put a spoonful of warm sweetcorn purée on the plate. Place 2 pieces of braised leek on the plate, then the sweetcorn and chorizo and sit the fish on top. Then place a spoonful of the leek and thyme salad over the fish. Finish with the crispy chorizo trimmings.

SMOKED BABY BEETROOT, MASCARPONE AND TARRAGON SALAD

SERVES 4

The sweetness of the beetroot is enhanced by smoking it with the Lapsang Souchong – itself a smoked black tea. The result is a perfect match with the mascarpone and tarragon. The toasted walnuts add texture to the dish to create a great autumn salad.

1 tablespoon Demerara sugar
1 tablespoon rice
½ tablespoon Lapsang Souchong tea leaves
250g cooked, lightly pickled baby beetroot
25g unsalted butter
100g walnuts
8 tablespoons balsamic vinegar
4 tablespoons extra virgin olive oil
150g mascarpone
½ bunch tarragon leaves, all stalks removed
Maldon sea salt and freshly ground black pepper

Mix the sugar, rice and tea together. Line a large roasting dish with kitchen foil and place the tea mix inside. Arrange the beetroot on a rack on top of the tea mix. Cover the entire dish with some more kitchen foil, ensuring there are no gaps for any smoke to escape through, and place over a moderate heat for 8 minutes. Remove from the heat and allow to sit for 30 minutes without removing the foil. Once it has cooled, cut the beetroot into 1cm cubes.

Heat the butter in a saucepan over a medium heat until foaming, then add the walnuts, season well with a good pinch of table salt and allow them to colour evenly, stirring continuously. When they are nicely golden, pour into a colander to allow the excess butter to drain off.

Place the balsamic vinegar in a small saucepan and bring to a gentle simmer over a low heat until it has reduced by two thirds, then add the oil and swirl to combine.

Place a large spoonful of mascarpone on each of your 4 serving plates and smear it along the plate with the back of the spoon. Place the diced beetroot over the mascarpone and scatter with the tarragon, walnuts and a good pinch of sea salt and freshly ground black pepper. Finish with a drizzle of the balsamic dressing.

CHAR-GRILLED BANANAS WITH BITTER CHOCOLATE AND TOASTED MARSHMALLOW ICE CREAM

SERVES 4

This is my restaurant take on bananas with marshmallow! We had this dish on the lunch menu for quite some time as it was a great favourite of our customers. It's a great winter comfort dish and is a winner with all ages.

For the marshmallow ice cream
4 large scoops of your favourite vanilla ice cream
8 marshmallows

For the bananas
50g caster or granulated sugar
25g butter
2 tablespoons dark rum
3 under-ripe bananas, halved lengthways
1 tablespoon vegetable oil
A splash of water

For the chocolate ganache
40g single or double cream
50g dark chocolate

8 marshmallows and some cocoa nibs (or cocoa Grue), for garnishing

Marshmallow ice cream
Take the vanilla ice cream out of the freezer and allow to soften slightly. Lightly toast the marshmallows – either with a culinary blow torch or by popping them under the grill – then mix them into the ice cream. Put the ice cream back into the freezer to set.

Bananas
Put the sugar into a saucepan over a moderate heat and swirl until a caramel forms. Once this has happened, whisk in the butter and rum. Add a little water to create a thick syrup and put to one side. Heat a char-grill frying pan until smoking. Rub the banana flesh with the oil, then place them on the char-grill until blackened grill marks appear. Remove, cut in ½ again and submerge the bananas in the syrup.

Chocolate ganache
Put the cream into a saucepan over a medium-low heat and bring to the boil, remove from the heat and pour it over the chocolate. Allow to sit for 2 minutes until the chocolate has melted, then whisk together.

Serving
Put the bananas in their caramel syrup into an ovenproof dish and gently heat in a low oven for 2 minutes. Spoon a dollop of chocolate ganache into each serving bowl and swish up the side using a spoon. Place 2 marshmallows in each bowl and caramelise with a culinary blow torch until golden. Arrange 3 banana halves around the marshmallows and serve with the ice cream on the side.

MACERATED ENGLISH STRAWBERRIES, FROMAGE FRAIS AND ROSE MERINGUES

SERVES 4

This is just a take on a classic strawberries and cream. It's the perfect summer pudding – sweet yet light. The rose adds a distinct perfume to the dish, which enhances the strawberries' flavour and the strawberry 'leather' is another layer of fruit texture. We make our own in the kitchen by slowly drying out strawberry purée on a flat sheet but you should be able to find some in health food shops.

400g ripe English strawberries
200ml water
25g sugar
1 vanilla pod
100ml strawberry liqueur (crème de fraise)
1 tablespoon rose water
100g fromage frais, for garnishing
A small handful of basil leaves, finely shredded
Strawberry leather to garnish

For the rose meringues
2 egg whites
50g caster sugar
50g icing sugar
1 teaspoon rose water
½ teaspoon crystallised rose petals, finely chopped

For the strawberry chantilly
100ml double cream
½ vanilla pod
2 tablespoons strawberry liqueur (crème de fraise)

Hull the strawberries, then prick them all over with a sharp knife. Split the vanilla pod open and scrape out the seeds. Put the water and sugar in a saucepan over a medium heat, bring to the boil and simmer for 4 minutes. Take off the heat, then add the vanilla pod and seeds, strawberry liqueur and rose water. Allow to cool slightly then add the strawberries, cover and leave to macerate for at least 5 hours in the fridge.

Rose meringues
Preheat the oven to 90C/gas mark ¼. Put the egg white into a bowl and whisk until stiff then add in the caster sugar and whisk until thick and glossy. Mix in the icing sugar and rose water, then transfer the mixture into a piping bag and pipe individual meringues (about 1cm across) onto a tray lined with parchment paper. Sprinkle the raw meringue with the chopped rose petals, then place the tray in the oven and turn it off. Leave the meringue in the oven for 1 hour, then remove and scoop out the inside using the end of a spoon.

Strawberry chantilly
Put all the ingredients in a bowl and whisk together until stiff. Transfer the mixture to a piping bag and just before serving pipe the cream into the meringues and stick two together end to end.

Serving
Put a spoonful of fromage frais into each serving bowl and spread up the side of the bowl with a spoon. Remove the strawberries from the marinade and place into the bowls. Add the meringues then finish with some finely shredded baby basil leaves and squares of strawberry leather. Pass the marinade through a fine sieve and serve on the side for your guests to pour over the strawberries.

EMILY WATKINS

It doesn't get more Cotswoldy than the village of Kingham. Honey-coloured stone houses line every street, hugging narrow pavements, winding their way towards a wide, picturesque green and the dining room of a certain Emily Watkins housed in the local inn, the Kingham Plough. It's one of those pubs which everybody dreams about living round the corner from. Imagine being within walking distance of one of the most talked-about steak and chips in the UK; or of an evocative comfort treat like beef shin dumplings with Cheltenham beetroot. Even the bar menu reads like the score of a much-loved culinary composer – scotched quail's eggs, potted rabbit, Cotswold rarebit and sourdough soldiers. But, unlike a classical music score, Emily's menus are not set in stone, they're constantly evolving and changing – so much so, she often creates a new dish, teaches it to her staff in hours and has it on her menu on the same evening.

This whirlwind creativity is not surprising when you remember that Emily spent almost two years before she opened the Kingham Plough working with the Caractacus Potts of the food world, Heston Blumenthal, at the award-winning Fat Duck in Bray, Berkshire. Heston is constantly inventing new ways of looking at ingredients, always searching for the essence of what makes a favourite dish popular, continually improvising on a theme – and you can see echoes of the same spirit in Emily. The stint in Bray, though, exhausted her and she left to recuperate, briefly, in London working as a private chef ('the pay's good and you get to cook what you like!') before setting about creating her Cotswold culinary Camelot in 2007. She enlisted local suppliers as her knights, established her court in the kitchens of Kingham's old coaching inn and championed Cotswold food with chivalric zeal at regular Sunday farmers' markets in the pub's car park.

Her suppliers are a key inspiration for Emily, constantly bringing her the freshest of ingredients and often experimenting with new produce at her request. Sometimes it's a slow battle to convince them to grow something new, but Emily gently bends them to her will and, fittingly, she pays credit to her suppliers on her menu. People like Alan Cox (the leek man) and Roger Crudge (the cheese man) are now as familiar to Kingham Plough diners as Emily herself – or her husband Miles Lampson, who's responsible for bagging the pigeon that wends its way to the dining room tables. So great is Emily's faith and respect for her suppliers and their beautiful produce that she changes her menus instantly to showcase what comes through her door; she changes them daily, sometimes more than once – her office is awash with menus!.

The inn itself has a warm, homely feel with tables spread out over the whole ground floor, some by the bar and some in quieter nooks and crannies. There's a life-sized stone pig sitting by the fire in the bar and during colder months people can park themselves by its side and roast chestnuts if they so wish. And there's plenty to keep you occupied while you wait for your meal – trinkets and reading material dotted all over the dining room and the hubble-bubble of Cotswolds life being recounted around you. Best of all, the pub has seven comfortable bedrooms – cool and calming, practically chintz-free – where the travel-weary foodie can sleep off lunch or dinner. Time has a habit of melting away, here.

Though the Kingham Plough is quintessentially English there is a resonance of Italy in the way that Emily operates; in the way she and the local suppliers interact – in the habit that people have of bringing produce to her, the great local cook, anxious to see her translate it into mouth watering dishes. And, in fact, she spent two years working in Florence straight after leaving university, ditching without a backward glance the years she had spent studying politics and economics at university. Perhaps that was inevitable; as a girl, she grew up in south Dorset and her mum, who ran a country house hotel, was always cooking and often took Emily and her sisters out mushroom-picking and foraging. They would turn whatever they found into lunch, maggots and all. 'Mum always said that maggots never hurt anyone,' she remembers.

Given Emily's stint with Heston Blumenthal, you'd expect her food to be uber modern, but her menu is surprisingly simple and unfussy: Dorset roots and Italian connections seem to have won out. So you'll see Mr Cox's leeks turned into a soup with potato and topped with a crispy duck egg fried in breadcrumbs. And she uses her freshly shot pigeon to make a pastry-bound Wellington served with Jerusalem artichokes. But you can't keep the Fat Duck experience down and she cooks the pigeon breasts, like most of her meat, very slowly, sealed in a bag and popped into a bath of water, as she believes this is the only way to allow the true taste of the animal to come through.

Emily does all her butchery on site at the pub, which allows her to celebrate some of the less obvious parts of many beasts. The lamb sweetbreads (see recipe, page 265) are a good example. She cooks them with a handful of hay, before breadcrumbing and deep frying them. They come out golden and crispy on the outside and soft on the inside: simply wonderful!

There's one dish that's already become a signature at the Kingham Plough: the aforementioned steak and chips. And it's something to behold. It's about the size of an old vinyl LP record (that's 12 inches wide to any of you too young to remember) and is cooked, initially, sous vide then caramelised off in the pan. The sirloin is Emily's cut of choice and she leaves a little extra juicy fat on the steak to enhance its flavour. And the crunchy, soft-centred chips it comes with are thrice cooked (a nod to Heston) and perfect. It's not a dish for the diet-conscious – there should be a prize awarded to anyone who manages to clean their plate.

There has been effusive praise for this gargantuan steak andchips in our national press, but Emily struggles with high-handed praise about her cooking and her transformation of the Plough. At heart she loves to feed people and her pleasure comes from the smiles on her diners' faces as they wipe their plates clean with her homemade bread. Having achieved success in such a short time, it would be easy for her to settle on a safe, reliable, unchanging pub menu, sell her local beers, relax and watch the money roll in. But that's not the path this softly-spoken, somewhat enigmatic 31-year-old wants to tread. She is passionate about evolving the Kingham Plough and prefers

to push ahead trying out new ideas. There's always something afoot, whether it's air-drying and smoking her own ham in the chimney or making cheese down in her cellar; or planning a working herb garden.

The endearing thing about Emily, though, is that she believes her Camelot isn't – and doesn't need to be – unique. Every part of Britain, she thinks, has a culinary identity and a food history to be proud of. Nevertheless, the locals of Kingham and the Cotswolds are lucky to have the Kingham Plough on their doorstep and to have a food champion of the calibre of Emily Watkins in their midst. And now you know where they both are, you can share a little of that luck, too!

The Kingham Plough
The Green, Kingham, Chipping Norton, Oxfordshire OX7 6YD
Phone 01608 658 327 **www.thekinghamplough.co.uk**

HODGE PODGE PUDDING WITH POACHED DUCK EGG AND FRESH BROAD BEANS

SERVES 6

Hodge podge is the Cotswolds version of black pudding, but it's baked in the oven rather than poached. It's much lighter in texture than a traditional black pudding and is made with a different range of spices – and when you eat it, you don't feel as if you're eating something that's made with blood! I love it – but I loathe black pudding, so if you're the same, give it a try. It goes well with any type of beans or peas, just adapt your garnish to whatever's in season.

500g beef fat
450g pearl barley
80g salt
35g black peppercorns
10g coriander seeds
10g paprika
½ medium-sized loaf of stale white bread, crust removed and finely chopped
1 litre pig's blood
1 litre milk
100g oats
750g beans
6 duck eggs
Splash of white wine vinegar
1 small bunch of chives
Butter and vegetable oil for cooking

Set the oven to 180C/gas mark 4. Grate the beef fat with a cheese grater. Wash the barley and transfer it to a saucepan with enough water to cover it. Cook over a medium high heat on the boil until it is soft – it should take about 15-20 minutes. Once cooked, remove and drain the barley.

Crush all the spices in a pestle and mortar until they are well ground, then put these together with the suet, barley, salt, breadcrumbs, pig's blood, milk and oats into large bowl and mix well. Leave this pudding mixture to stand for 30 minutes for the bread to soak up the liquid – it should end up like a wet risotto in texture. Now, line a baking tray with baking parchment and pour the mixture onto it, then cook it in the preheated oven for 45 minutes until it's firm to the touch. Remove it from the oven and allow it to cool at room temperature. While the pudding is cooling, pod the broad beans. Put a saucepan with water over a medium high heat and bring to the boil, then drop in the podded beans and quickly blanch them – it should take about 30 seconds. Drain them and once cool, pop the beans out of their soft white skins.

Place a saucepan of water over a medium heat, add the white wine vinegar and bring the liquid to the boil. Take a spoon and spin the water, crack open a duck egg and drop it into the water while it is still spinning and poach it. You can drop in another couple of eggs at the same time, just remember to keep the water spinning. Repeat the process with the three remaining eggs.

Meanwhile, cut the hodge podge pudding into cubes (it's up to you how chunky you make them) and place a non-stick frying pan over a medium high heat. Add a knob of butter and a little oil to the pan (the oil will prevent the butter from burning) and place 6 cubes of the hodge podge in the fat to fry until just crisp. Don't forget to keep checking the eggs – they are cooked when just firm to the touch but the yolks are still runny.

Serving
Gently reheat the beans and dress them with a little bit of butter and some cut chives. Scatter some beans at the bottom of each plate, put a piece of the fried hodge podge pudding on top of them, and finally perch the poached duck egg on the pudding.

CRISPY LAMB SWEETBREADS AND GANDPA'S CABBAGE

SERVES 5

My grandad used to cook cabbage this way for us when I was a growing up in Dorset and I love it – the sweetness of the shallots balances perfectly with the crisp bacon and freshness of the Savoy cabbage. Using hay to cook the sweetbreads gives them an edge of meadow sweetness: if you live in the country get the hay from your local farmer, otherwise you buy it from pet shops.

1kg lamb sweetbreads
1 handful of clean hay, washed
1 bunch of thyme
A splash of white wine vinegar
15g yellow mustard seeds, crushed
1 litre water
A little plain flour, for dusting
2 eggs, beaten
300g fresh breadcrumbs
2 tablespoons butter, for frying the
    sweetbreads
Sea salt

For the cabbage
1 Savoy cabbage, finely shredded
100g bacon, roughly chopped
4 large banana shallots, finely sliced

For the mustard sauce
400ml double cream
1 large tablespoon Pommery mustard
Salt and pepper

Sweetbreads

Soak the sweetbreads in cold water for 10 minutes, then peel away and discard the membrane. Place the hay in a saucepan with the thyme, vinegar and mustard seeds. Put the sweetbreads on top of the hay and cover with the water. Bring to the boil over a medium-high heat, but once the boil has been reached turn down the heat immediately and simmer the sweetbreads for 15 minutes until just firm.

Lift them out of the pan with a slotted spoon and place them on a plate to cool. When they're completely cool, breadcrumb them – roll each sweetbread lightly in the salted flour, then dip them in the beaten eggs and finally roll them in the breadcrumbs until they are evenly coated. Replace them on the plate and put in the fridge to cool for 10 minutes until you're ready to cook them.

Grandpa's cabbage

Bring a saucepan of water to the boil over a high heat and quickly blanch the Savoy cabbage in it for 1 minute. Drain the cabbage and refresh it in iced water. Heat a frying pan over a medium-high heat and once it's hot pop in the bacon and sauté it until crisp. Turn the heat down a little, add the shallots and cook them until they're soft and translucent – then take the pan off the heat.

Mustard sauce

Place the double cream in a saucepan over a medium heat and bring it to the boil. Add in the mustard and reduce the sauce by a third. Season it with a little salt and pepper to taste.

Serving

Heat a non-stick frying pan over a medium-high heat. Add and melt the 2 tablespoons of butter and when it is foaming, drop in the sweetbreads and cook them until they're golden, continuously turning them and basting them with the butter. Meanwhile, place the shallots and bacon back on the stove over a high heat. Add in the Savoy cabbage and sauté it until soft but do not colour. In another saucepan, warm up the mustard sauce. Remove the sweetbreads from the pan and dry them on some kitchen paper and season with sea salt. Place the cabbage on your plate, then put the sweetbreads over this. Finally dress with some mustard sauce. It goes well with creamy mashed potato.

PHEASANT SAUSAGE WITH PHEASANT AND BARLEY BROTH

SERVES 4-6

Living in the Cotswolds we're surrounded by game and it's not unusual during the shooting season for me to turn up at the restaurant in the morning to find that a kind neighbour has left a brace of pheasants over the garden fence. This recipe has both a rich, clear pheasant broth made with the bird's brown body meat and a sausage made with its breast meat. I like to use lardo (cured pork fat) in the sausages, but if you can't get it, you can substitute salt and pork fat.

2 good-sized pheasants
2 carrots, roughly chopped
1 large onion, roughly chopped
2 leeks, roughly chopped
1 bay leaf
1 bunch of sage
2 litres chicken stock
Splash of brandy, to finish
250g pearl barley, soaked

For the sausage
400g pheasant breasts taken off the
   bird, lightly trimmed of sinew
150g lardo (cured pork fat)
1 tablespoon thyme leaves
25g fresh breadcrumbs
50ml milk
1 egg
2 litres water
1 bay leaf
1 bunch each of sage and thyme

Pheasant broth
First of all you need to butcher your pheasants. Remove the breasts off the birds and place to one side to use for the sausages. Now, remove the thighs and drumsticks and roast these and the carcasses in the oven with a little oil until they are golden. It isn't necessary to season them.

Take a large heavy-based saucepan, add a little oil and butter and place it over a medium heat. Sweat the vegetables and herbs in a large stock pot until soft and golden, then add the bones from the breasts and legs. Cover with the chicken stock and bring to the boil and simmer for 2 hours to reduce the stock down by a third and then add enough water to cover everything again. Bring the stock back to the boil, then reduce the heat a little and simmer for a further 2 hours, skimming off any impurities. Strain the broth through a fine sieve, then place it back on the stove over a high heat and reduce it down by a third. Add a splash of brandy, taste the broth and season with salt if necessary.

Pheasant sausage
Chop the pheasant breasts and lardo into dice, then place them with all the other ingredients for the sausage in a food processor and pulse them until they are thoroughly mixed. Don't over-process, you're aiming for a coarse rather than smooth texture. Put the sausage mixture onto some clingfilm and roll it into a sausage shape, tying up the ends. Put the 2 litres of water in a saucepan together with the bay leaf and bunches of sage and thyme. Bring the water to the boil, then add the sausage and simmer it gently for 15 minutes before removing from the poaching liquor.

Serving
Wash the barley well, bring the pheasant broth to the boil over a medium heat, add the barley and cook it until soft. Melt a little butter with some oil in a frying pan over a medium-high heat. Add the sausage to colour it. To serve, ladle some broth and barley into bowls and place a pheasant sausage on top.

POTTED RABBIT

SERVES 10

This is a great snack to make in autumn when wild rabbits are abundant and the breeding season is over. I like to use ferret-caught rabbits rather than ones that are shot – the taste is very different, much less gamey, and they are much more tender than those hunted with a gun. Also, there's no danger of the rabbit's delicate bones being shattered. The hay adds another sweet, aromatic layer of taste underlining those of the herbs.

2 medium-sized rabbits
Vegetables for a mirepoix (carrot, onion, celery, garlic, leeks), roughly chopped
250ml dry white wine
2-3 litres chicken stock
1 tablespoon green peppercorns
1 bunch of parsley and thyme, finely chopped
1 handful of clean hay, washed
100g clarified butter, melted
Salt and pepper
Vegetable oil for cooking

Preheat the oven to 150C/gas mark 2. Quarter the rabbits and season the meat well. Heat a little oil in a heavy-based saucepan with metal handles, or a casserole pot, over a medium-high heat and seal the rabbit quarters in it until they are lightly coloured. Remove the rabbit from the saucepan and keep to one side. Now place the mirepoix vegetables in the same saucepan and sauté gently until they're soft. Replace the rabbit back in the saucepan, add the white wine and deglaze the pan by boiling it for 1 minute. Now add enough chicken stock to cover the rabbit, and bring the liquid to the boil. Add half of the pepper and herbs and the whole of the hay and pop on the saucepan or casserole lid, then place in the oven for about 4-5 hours – until the rabbit is completely tender. Once the rabbit is done, remove it from the oven and leave the rabbit to cool down in its cooking juices.

Once it is cool, carefully pick all the meat from the bones and pour the cooking juices through a fine sieve. Place the cooking juices back in a saucepan and reduce them by about a third over a high heat until you have a gelatinous, very rich sauce. Crush the remaining peppercorns and mix them with the remaining herbs and rabbit meat. Taste a little bit and, if necessary, add a pinch of salt and pepper. Put the rabbit meat into some ramekins, pour over enough of the hot, reduced sauce to cover the meat and put them in the fridge to cool for about 12 hours. When the sauce is completely cool, pour over a thin layer of melted, clarified butter and chill in the fridge for 30 minutes.

Serving
The potted rabbit is best eaten at room temperature so take it out of the fridge in good time and serve it with three thick slices of toasted, brown sourdough bread.

COTSWOLD MESS

SERVES 6

All my dishes are modern takes on traditional fare – this is my version of Eton Mess, and it's a great favourite with diners at the restaurant. Traditionally, Eton Mess is made with strawberries, but in early spring and early autumn I'm lucky enough to have a plentiful supply of local raspberries, so I use these instead. When strawberries are around, I revert to tradition – and in September when our damson tree is laden I substitute these lovely old-fashioned plums in the recipe.

4 eggs, separated
320g caster sugar
200ml elderflower cordial, preferably homemade
200ml water
6 leaves gelatine
500g fresh raspberries
400ml double cream

Preheat the oven to 100C/gas mark ¼. Place the egg whites in a bowl and whip them to soft peaks, then gradually add 8 tablespoons of the sugar and continue to whisk until the mixture is firm and glossy. Pipe the meringue in little rosettes onto a baking tray lined with greaseproof paper and then cook them for about 3 hours in the oven until the meringue is firm but not coloured. When cooked, remove the meringues from the oven and cool them down.

Measure out 100ml of the elderflower cordial and make up to 400ml with water. Soften 4 leaves of the gelatine in some cold water for about 5 minutes and warm up a small amount of the cordial and water mixture. Take the softened gelatine out of the water, squeeze the leaves to remove excess moisture and add them to the warm cordial, stirring until the gelatine has completely dissolved. Now add the rest of the cordial and water mixture to this, stirring as you do so until it is thoroughly incorporated. Pour the mixture into 6 tumblers and drop 3 raspberries into each glass. Place the tumblers in the fridge until the jelly has set.

Meanwhile make some raspberry mousse. Place 300g of the raspberries and 80g of caster sugar into a deep bowl and make into a purée, using a stick blender if you have one. If you prefer a sharper tasting purée, just put in a little less sugar – if you have a sweet tooth, add a little more. Once the purée is done, pass it through a fine sieve to remove the pips. Soften the remaining 2 leaves of gelatine in some cold water for about 5 minutes. Put the egg yolks into a bowl, then place this over a saucepan containing simmering water, making sure the bowl does not touch the water. Whisk the yolks together with 150g of caster sugar and a splash of water until it increases its volume by 4 times and is stiff and pale. Take the gelatine out of the water, squeeze the excess water out of the leaves and add them to the whisked yolks.

Whisk 150ml of the double cream to firm peaks. Fold the egg mixture and the raspberry purée together and then fold through the double cream. Remove the elderflower jellies from the fridge and pour some mousse into each tumbler over the set jelly. Return the tumblers to the fridge to set the mousse.

Whisk the remaining 250ml of cream and 100ml of elderflower cordial together until you get firm peaks. Transfer the mixture to a piping bag.

Serving
Remove the jellies from the fridge and pipe some of the cream and elderflower mixture into each one, covering the layer of raspberry mousse. Sprinkle some meringue over the top and decorate with the remaining raspberries.

BRYN WILLIAMS

To say Bryn Williams is passionate about his food is a huge understatement. But then what do you expect from a chef who grew up surrounded by the rolling hills of North Wales, with a fabulous cook for a mum and a dad who was always bringing home game for the family table? His home town of Denbigh boasts one of the finest bakeries in Wales and he was able to witness and learn, first hand, the wonderful artisanal skill of kneading and folding that produces pillows of yeasty bread. And let's not forgot the influence of his very first head chef at a restaurant in Colwyn Bay, Carl Swift, whose gentle encouragement and belief in Bryn pushed him out of the land of the dragon and into the bright lights of London and the kitchens of its great chefs.

These days, the 32-year-old is still in the capital – in the exclusive North London 'village' of Primrose Hill on the edge of Regent's Park – at Odette's restaurant, which numbers pop stars, writers and fashionistas among its residents. A local legend for 31 years, Odette's welcomed Bryn as its head chef in 2006. It was the first time he had headed up a kitchen, but now, a mere two years later, he jointly owns this little neighbourhood hotspot having successfully pulled it out of its culinary comfort zone into the tasty world of modern dining.

Under Bryn's leadership the food has been updated and the restaurant given a make-over. That said, he's been careful to embrace Odette's colourful past and it retains its pull as a romantic destination (legend has it Liam Gallagher got down on one knee and proposed to actress Patsy Kensit at table 12), thanks to a mish-mash layout of mezzanines and conservatories that provide secretive corners for the shy or famous.

The current luxurious design – full of flowing yellows, turquoise and thick French wallpaper – is down to trailblazing interior designer Shaun Clarkson. The ground floor dining room is airy with lots of natural light, while downstairs there is a very cool bar and private dining space with alcove seating fiercely fought over by the great, the good and the downright bad. It is the perfect environment for mischief but the fact is the most likely topic of conversation these days is Bryn's food.

One dish, in particular, is endlessly discussed. A certain fish dish. The one that allows Bryn to stand shoulder-to-shoulder with the great chefs of his era. The fish dish that was considered so good it was chosen to be the fish dish on the menu of the Queen's 80th birthday lunch at the Banqueting House in 2006, an event filmed as part of BBC2's *Great British Menu* series. The dish is, of course, pan-fried turbot with braised oxtail, cockles and salsify. It's a prime bit of Welsh surf 'n' turf – and it's hard to beat. The beef is meltingly soft, the turbot firm enough to hold its shape but flaking easily under the merest hint of a fork; the whole is dish underpinned by the essence of the seashore in the cockles and the earthy land in the salsify. It's a majestic dish, one that everyone should demand on their own birthday.

Bryn's turbot dish showcases his immense technical ability and keen nose for flavour. The importance of the latter was instilled into him when he worked for Michel Roux Jr at London's legendary Le Gavroche. Michel drove his chefs (and still does) to appreciate every aspect of an ingredient's flavour and to underpin it by proper seasoning. To underline the standard of cooking he wanted from his chefs, he would bang his knife on his board and shout out to the young team that Bryn was part of, 'are you a Ferrari or a tractor, boys?'. The reply, always, was, 'Ferrari, chef.'

Today, Bryn's diners can see the benefit of his time at Le Gavroche in dishes like fois gras served with orange confit, where the citrus is able to cut through the richness of the liver and lift its essential flavour onto a higher plane. And in the crème brûlée he learnt under Michel, whose richness he also offsets and enhances with a gentle punch of acidity imparted via a delicate apple sorbet. Odette's desserts, in fact, are not to be missed – from the rich chocolate fondant with a deliciously light yoghurt ice cream, to a wickedly sharp lemon curd parfait.

Michel, of course, isn't the only chef to have influenced Bryn: the Welshman is the sum of all the chefs he has worked under over the years, including his very first mentor Carl Swift, who took the young Bryn under his wing at Colwyn Bay's Café Nicoise when Bryn worked at the restaurant as part of his culinary course at Llandrillo College (Coleg Llandrillo Cymru) at Rhos-on-Sea. Carl gave him the sound technical base and confidence that enabled Bryn, at 20, to land his first London job, as a junior chef with the great Marco Pierre White at MPW's Criterion restaurant. Three years with Marco followed by another three with Michel at Le Gavroche – a chef could hardly have a better launch to his career. Stints in France, at a Paris patisserie and an award-laden hotel in Nice, and four years as André Garrett's second in command at London's well-regarded Orrery and Galvin at Windows restaurants made Bryn the complete chef-proprietor package – ready, and infinitely able, for the challenge of Odette's.

This superb training means Bryn has a great bag of culinary tricks at his fingertips and he uses them in an exciting way. He loves matching different culinary styles with British flavours: for instance, the gamey taste of wood pigeon is spiced with pepper and contrasted with a soft and creamy sweetcorn panna cotta and wild earthy mushrooms. It's a dish packed with flavour which reaches back to his home country and childhood – the wild pigeon is shot by his father in Wales for Bryn, continuing the tradition he established for his family when Bryn was a boy.

When he was young, Bryn would accompany his father on shooting trips and then watch his mother or grandmother cook whatever they had bagged. His grandparents had a farm and the house had a larder. Often there would be beef or lamb hanging in it as well as game. The family would consume each animal from the bottom up because the carcasses were too heavy for his slightly-built grandmother

to lift down and fully butcher in one go. Chops – a favourite of Bryn and his two brothers – would always follow leg joints. The legacy of those days exists at Odette's now, as Bryn still does his butchery in-house and is slowly training his small team of five chefs to do the same.

His father's game donations aside, Bryn is always searching for quality Welsh produce to champion at his restaurant – be it the very best salt marsh lamb or delicious coastal samphire – because he's keen to show the wider world what his homeland is capable of producing. He's been so successful at doing this that he's regarded as something of a national treasure back in Wales. Bryn may have left Wales years ago, but his home country is still an integral part of him – he's even taught his chefs a few words of Welsh.

Of course, you wouldn't classify Odette's as a 'Welsh' restaurant – the links are much more incidental than forced and Bryn's classical training puts him firmly in the Anglo-French camp. However, with Bryn at the helm of Odette's the place is going places. Head to Primrose Hill and you'll see what all the fuss is about for yourself.

Odette's
130 Regent's Park Road, London NW1 8XL
Phone 020 7586 8569 **www.odettesprimrosehill.com**

PAN-FRIED TURBOT WITH COCKLES AND OXTAIL

SERVES 4

I can't go anywhere without being asked about this dish, which I created for the *Great British Menu* series on BBC2 and cooked for the Queen's 80th birthday lunch at the Banqueting House. For me, it's the essence of Wales, from sea to hills: turbot from the sea, cockles from the shore, oxtail from the countryside. I love cooking it – and I'm sure it'll be inscribed on my tombstone!

1kg Welsh black beef oxtail
1 litre red wine
1 large onion, roughly chopped
1 large carrot, roughly chopped
2 bay leaves
50g plain flour, seasoned with salt and
  freshly ground black pepper
2 litres chicken stock
1 litre veal stock
400g cockles
1 glass of white wine
1 tablespoon olive oil
350g sea beet, stalks removed
Nutmeg, for seasoning
A splash of lemon juice, for seasoning
4 x 120g turbot fillets, skinned
2 tablespoons crème fraîche
Vegetable oil, for cooking
Olive oil, for cooking
Sea salt and freshly ground black
  pepper
Butter, for finishing

Place the oxtail, red wine, chopped onions, carrots and 1 bay leaf in a bowl and cover with clingfilm, then leave to marinate for 24 hours.

The next day, preheat the oven to 140C/gas mark 1. Strain off the red wine from the oxtail and vegetables and place it in a saucepan over a medium heat. Bring it to the boil, skimming off any froth that rises to the surface.

Meanwhile heat a little vegetable oil in a heavy-based saucepan with metal handles over a medium heat. Dust the oxtail in seasoned flour, then colour in the saucepan until golden brown on all sides. Remove it from the saucepan and set to one side. Add the marinated vegetables to the same saucepan and cook until nicely caramelised. Add the hot red wine to the pan and reduce it by half, then return the oxtail to the red wine sauce, add the chicken stock and veal stock and bring to the boil. Skim, cover with a lid and cook in the oven for 2½ hours. When cooked, remove from the oven and cool.

Once cooled, remove the oxtail and take the meat off the bone, retaining it in large pieces. Strain the liquid into a large saucepan, put it over a medium heat and reduce its volume by half.

Warm a saucepan over a medium heat, add in the cockles with a glass of white wine. Immediately cover with a lid and cook over a high heat for 1-2 minutes, or until the shells have opened. Strain the cockles through a colander over a bowl so that you catch the cooking liquor, then pick the cockle meat from their shells, discarding any that haven't opened. Reserve a few in their shells.

Heat some olive oil in another saucepan, add the sea beet and cook until it is wilted – about 30 seconds – seasoning with salt, pepper, nutmeg and a splash of lemon juice. Remove from the heat.

Finally, heat a little olive oil in a non-stick frying pan over a medium-high heat and put in the turbot fillets. Cook until the undersides are brown, then turn them over and lower the heat. Add a knob of butter to finish, spooning it over the turbot once melted.

Serving
Warm up the oxtail jus if necessary. Place some wilted sea beet on each plate, arrange the cockles and oxtail around it and drizzle over some oxtail jus. Put the turbot on top of the sea beet. Bring the cockle liquor to the boil and whisk in the crème fraîche, then pour some on to the plates and serve immediately.

Bryn's turbot dish showcases his immense technical ability and keen nose for flavour. The importance of the latter was instilled into him when he worked for Michel Roux Jr at London's legendary Le Gavroche. Michel drove his chefs (and still does) to appreciate every aspect of an ingredient's flavour and to underpin it by proper seasoning. To underline the standard of cooking he wanted from his chefs, he would bang his knife on his board and shout out to the young team that Bryn was part of, 'are you a Ferrari or a tractor, boys?'. The reply, always, was, 'Ferrari, chef.'

Today, Bryn's diners can see the benefit of his time at Le Gavroche in dishes like fois gras served with orange confit, where the citrus is able to cut through the richness of the liver and lift its essential flavour onto a higher plane. And in the crème brûlée he learnt under Michel, whose richness he also offsets and enhances with a gentle punch of acidity imparted via a delicate apple sorbet. Odette's desserts, in fact, are not to be missed – from the rich chocolate fondant with a deliciously light yoghurt ice cream, to a wickedly sharp lemon curd parfait.

Michel, of course, isn't the only chef to have influenced Bryn: the Welshman is the sum of all the chefs he has worked under over the years, including his very first mentor Carl Swift, who took the young Bryn under his wing at Colwyn Bay's Café Nicoise when Bryn worked at the restaurant as part of his culinary course at Llandrillo College (Coleg Llandrillo Cymru) at Rhos-on-Sea. Carl gave him the sound technical base and confidence that enabled Bryn, at 20, to land his first London job, as a junior chef with the great Marco Pierre White at MPW's Criterion restaurant. Three years with Marco followed by another three with Michel at Le Gavroche – a chef could hardly have a better launch to his career. Stints in France, at a Paris patisserie and an award-laden hotel in Nice, and four years as Andre Garrett's second-in-command at London's well-regarded Orrery and Galvin at Windows restaurants made Bryn the complete chef-proprietor package – ready, and infinitely able, for the challenge of Odette's.

This superb training means Bryn has a great bag of culinary tricks at his fingertips and he uses them in an exciting way. He loves matching different culinary styles with British flavours: for instance, the gamey taste of wood pigeon is spiced with pepper and contrasted with a soft and creamy

sweetcorn panna cotta and wild earthy mushrooms. It's a dish packed with flavour which reaches back to his home country and childhood – the wild pigeon is shot by his father in Wales for Bryn, continuing the tradition he established for his family when Bryn was a boy.

When he was young, Bryn would accompany his father on shooting trips and then watch his mother or grandmother cook whatever they had bagged. His grandparents had a farm and the house had a larder. Often there would be beef or lamb hanging in it as well as game. The family would consume each animal from the bottom up because the carcasses were too heavy for his slightly-built grandmother

BRYN WILLIAMS

To say Bryn Williams is passionate about his food is a huge understatement. But then what do you expect from a chef who grew up surrounded by the rolling hills of North Wales, with a fabulous cook for a mum and a dad who was always bringing home game for the family table? His home town of Denbigh boasts one of the finest bakeries in Wales and he was able to witness and learn, first hand, the wonderful artisanal skill of kneading and folding that produces pillows of yeasty bread. And let's not forgot the influence of his very first head chef at a restaurant in Colwyn Bay, Carl Swift, whose gentle encouragement and belief in Bryn pushed him out of the land of the dragon and into the bright lights of London and the kitchens of its great chefs.

These days, the 32-year-old is still in the capital – in the exclusive North London 'village' of Primrose Hill on the edge of Regent's Park – at Odette's restaurant, which numbers pop stars, writers and fashionistas among its residents. A local legend for 31 years, Odette's welcomed Bryn as its head chef in 2006. It was the first time he had headed up a kitchen, but now, a mere two years later, he jointly owns this little neighbourhood hotspot having successfully pulled it out of its culinary comfort zone into the tasty world of modern dining.

Under Bryn's leadership the food has been updated and the restaurant given a make-over. That said, he's been careful to embrace Odette's colourful past and it retains its pull as a romantic destination (legend has it Liam Gallagher got down on one knee and proposed to actress Patsy Kensit at table 12), thanks to a mish-mash layout of mezzanines and conservatories that provide secretive corners for the shy or famous.

The current luxurious design – full of flowing yellows, turquoise and thick French wallpaper – is down to trailblazing interior designer Shaun Clarkson. The ground floor dining room is airy with lots of natural light, while downstairs there is a very cool bar and private dining space with alcove seating fiercely fought over by the great, the good and the downright bad. It is the perfect environment for mischief but the fact is the most likely topic of conversation these days is Bryn's food.

One dish, in particular, is endlessly discussed. A certain fish dish. The one that allows Bryn to stand shoulder-to-shoulder with the great chefs of his era. The fish dish that was considered so good it was chosen to be the fish dish on the menu of the Queen's 80th birthday lunch at the Banqueting House in 2006, an event filmed as part of BBC2's *Great British Menu* series. The dish is, of course, pan-fried turbot with braised oxtail, cockles and salsify. It's a prime bit of Welsh surf 'n' turf – and it's hard to beat. The beef is meltingly soft, the turbot firm enough to hold its shape but flaking easily under the merest hint of a fork; the whole is dish underpinned by the essence of the seashore in the cockles and the earthy land in the salsify. It's a majestic dish, one that everyone should demand on their own birthday.

SEARED SCALLOPS, BRAISED CHICKEN WINGS, JERUSALEM ARTICHOKE PUREE, HAZELNUT JUS

SERVES 4

I do quite a lot of what chefs call surf 'n' turf – putting meat and seafood together in one dish – and scallops are great for this because their flavour stands up well. This was my first attempt at a surf 'n' turf starter and I wasn't sure how it would go down. But within 2 months I knew I'd never be able to take it off the menu because it was so popular. You can change the purée, depending on the time of year. Onion or celeriac work well in the autumn.

100g butter
8 chicken wings, tips removed
1 medium carrot, finely chopped
1 medium onion, finely chopped
1 bunch of thyme, stalks removed
100ml white wine
1 litre chicken stock
300g Jerusalem artichokes, sliced
150ml double cream
10ml olive oil
8 medium scallops, shelled and coral
    roe removed
1 lemon, juiced
Salt and pepper
50g hazelnuts, roughly chopped
2 tablespoons of thyme leaves

Heat up a heavy-based saucepan and add half the butter. Season the chicken wings and place skin-side down into the melted butter and fry until golden. Remove from the saucepan and keep to one side. Add the carrot and the onion to the same saucepan and cook them until soft and golden, then add the bunch of thyme and white wine, and reduce the liquid by half. Place the chicken wings back in the saucepan on top of the vegetables, then cover with 500ml of chicken stock and simmer for 30 minutes, then remove the saucepan from the heat and allow to cool. When the wings have cooled, take them out of the saucepan and remove the wing bones, then place them in the fridge to firm up. Strain the braising liquor through a sieve into a clean saucepan, replace over a medium heat and simmer until you have reduced it to a nice sauce.

Melt the remaining butter in a heavy-based saucepan. Add the Jerusalem artichokes, season with salt and pepper, cover with the remaining chicken stock and cook until soft and the stock has evaporated. Add the cream, then transfer everything into a food processor and blend until you get a smooth purée.

Heat up a frying pan until very hot and add the olive oil. Pop in the scallops and cook for 1 minute, then turn them over for 30 seconds, making sure they are undercooked in the centre. Remove from the frying pan, season with salt and a splash of lemon juice.

Serving
Warm the sauce up over a low heat. Crisp up the chicken wings in the same frying pan in which you have cooked the scallops. Put 2 decent tablespoons of the Jerusalem artichoke purée at the bottom of your serving plates or bowls, then 2 scallops per person on to the purée and the chicken wings to the side. Finish the sauce with the some thyme leaves and hazelnuts and pour it over the chicken wings.

ROAST LOIN AND BRAISED SHOULDER OF SALT-MARSH LAMB WITH CAPER JUS

These days you can get lamb for most of the year because different parts of the country produce new-born lambs at different times. Personally, though, I prefer to use it only in spring and summer when grazing is best and the meat sweeter. Up until June I always use Welsh hill lamb, but when it finishes I move on to salt marsh lamb reared on the Welsh coast. The meat is a little denser and firmer because of the salt in the grazing, which dries it out. I'm from Wales, so I use Welsh salt marsh lamb – but any coastal-reared lamb is fine.

SERVES 4

1 shoulder of salt marsh lamb
1 large onion, roughly chopped
2 medium carrots, roughly chopped
A large sprig of rosemary
250ml white wine
2 litres chicken stock
2kg desirée potatoes, finely sliced
2 tablespoons chopped rosemary
1 large rack of lamb
1 teaspoon capers
200g of seasonal vegetables (such as broad beans, courgettes, peas)
100g mushrooms
Olive oil for cooking
Salt and pepper

Heat the oven to 140C/gas mark 1. Heat a splash of oil in a large metal-handled heavy-based saucepan over a medium heat and seal the shoulder of lamb in it. You won't need much oil because the meat is fatty. When the shoulder has coloured, remove it from the saucepan. Now add the chopped onions, carrots and sprig of rosemary into the saucepan and cook them until they are golden brown. Add the white wine and reduce it by half. Put the shoulder of lamb back into the saucepan on top of the vegetables and cover with the chicken stock. Bring the stock to the boil, then remove the saucepan from the heat and place it in the oven for 1 hour.

When the lamb is cooked, remove it from the oven and cool the meat down. Then remove the meat from the bone and shred it into small pieces. Strain the stock into a clean saucepan, discarding the vegetables, and bring it back to the boil over a medium heat, skimming off any grease and impurities.

Meanwhile, place a thin layer of potatoes in the bottom of a casserole dish. Season with salt, pepper and the chopped rosemary. Add a layer of the shredded lamb shoulder, then build up 2 further layers of potato and lamb. Next, cover the layers with some of the skimmed lamb stock (keeping at least 200ml back for cooking the seasonal vegetables) and then put the casserole into the oven for 30 minutes, or until the liquid has been absorbed. Remove it from the oven and keep warm.

Turn the oven up to 180C/gas mark 4. Season the rack of lamb and then seal it with a splash of oil in a heavy-based saucepan with a metal handle. Place the saucepan in the oven for 6-8 minutes to cook the rack – it should be nicely browned around the edges but pink in the middle. Once cooked, remove the rack from the oven and rest it for 15 minutes.

Measure out 150ml of the lamb stock and reduce it in a saucepan over a medium-high heat to a sauce consistency. Add in the capers and keep warm.

Prepare the seasonal vegetables and simmer them in a little of the original lamb stock over a medium heat until tender. Pan-fry the mushrooms in a little olive oil, and season them with salt and pepper

Serving
Cut out 1 cylinder from the potato and lamb layers per person. Divide the rack of lamb equally and position the cutlets to the side of the potato cylinder. Arrange the seasonal vegetables and mushrooms around the meat. Finally pour over a little of the caper jus.

CHOCOLATE ORANGE FONDANT, YOGHURT ICE CREAM, CANDIED ORANGE

SERVES 8

I always have a chocolate fondant on the menu. This version came about because I have a friend in Wales, Toby Beevers of Kokonoir in Llandudno, who makes chocolate for me and one day he experimented by flavouring some with orange oil. We tried it out in the fondant and hit the jackpot. Chocolate and orange are a classic combination and the yoghurt ice cream just cuts through the richness of the cocoa.

For the chocolate fondant
50g cocoa powder
250g orange-flavoured chocolate
   (54% cocoa solids)
250g unsalted butter
5 eggs
5 egg yolks
125g caster sugar
30g flour
Butter, to grease the moulds

For the yoghurt ice cream
2 egg yolks
60g caster sugar
250ml milk
500g plain yoghurt
75ml double cream

For the candied orange
Zest of 1 large orange, cut into thin
   strips
100ml water
100g caster sugar
1 star anise
Caster sugar, for coating

For the chocolate tuilles
50g unsalted butter
2 egg whites
85g caster sugar
125g cocoa powder

Chocolate fondant
Butter 6 small moulds, dust them with cocoa powder, and then place in the fridge. Place the chocolate and butter in a bowl and set the bowl over a saucepan of simmering water on a low heat to melt, making sure the bowl doesn't touch the water. Meanwhile, mix the eggs, the additional yolks and the sugar in a large bowl, making sure not to capture too many air bubbles. Pour the melted chocolate mixture on to the eggs and stir well to combine all the ingredients, then fold in the flour. Tap the bowl down on the table to remove any air bubbles from the mix. Fill the buttered moulds with the mixture until they are three-quarters full and place them in the fridge to chill.

Yoghurt ice cream
Whisk the egg yolks and sugar in a bowl until thick and creamy. Put the milk and the cream in a small saucepan and bring to the boil over a medium-low heat. Pour the hot milk mixture onto the yolk mixture and stir well to create a custard base. Return this to the saucepan and stir over a low heat until the mixture thickens enough to coat the back of a spoon, then remove it from the heat, strain through a sieve and add in the yoghurt, stirring well. Allow it to cool down and then pour the mixture into an ice-cream machine and churn until frozen but not too stiff. The ice cream is ready when it holds its shape after scooping, at which point you can transfer it a container and put it in the freezer. If you don't have an ice-cream machine, place the mixture in the freezer, taking it out every 30 minutes to stir.

Candied orange
Blanch the orange zest in boiling water for 1 minute. Drain, then refresh it in iced water – and then repeat the process twice again. Bring the water, sugar and star anise to the boil over a medium heat and allow to thicken to create a syrup, then add the strips of blanched orange zest and simmer for 1 hour. Using a fork, carefully remove the zest strips from the syrup and place on a plate covered in caster sugar. Gently coat the strips with sugar, then set them to one side until needed.

Chocolate tuilles
Melt the butter in a saucepan over a low heat and, once melted, set aside. Meanwhile, beat the egg white and sugar in a bowl with an electric whisk until they form soft peaks. Reduce the speed of the whisk, add in the melted butter in a steady stream and continue to mix until it is fully incorporated. Add the cocoa powder, a tablespoon at a time, until it, too, is fully incorporated. Transfer the mixture to a clean bowl, cover and place in the fridge for 2 hours before using.

Preheat the oven to 170C/gas mark 3. Remove the tuille mixture from the fridge and line a baking tray with baking parchment. Drop teaspoonfuls of the mixture on to the tray, making sure to leave a 6cm gap between each tuille, as they will spread during cooking. Flatten each blob of mixture with a palette knife and then use a round pastry cutter to cut a circle in the mixture. Bake the tuilles for 4-5 minutes in the oven until they are crispy. Remove and form them into cylinder shapes before they cool down.

Serving
Preheat the oven at 170C/gas mark 3. Pop the fondants in to cook for 15 minutes, then take them out and leave to one side for 2 minutes to rest before carefully removing them from the moulds on to one side of a dinner plate. Place a tuille biscuit to the side of the fondant, a scoop of yoghurt ice cream on the tuille and scatter the candied orange pieces on the ice cream.

LEMON CURD PARFAIT, SABLE BISCUIT, RASPBERRIES AND RASPBERRY JELLY

SERVES 12

This summer dish plays on a classic British taste – lemon curd – and raspberries work really well against the richness of the parfait. The biscuit just gives a little extra texture. You can make most of the dish's elements the day before you serve it, but the biscuit is better made on the same day as it goes soft very quickly.

For the raspberry jelly
400g over-ripe raspberries
30g caster sugar
2 gelatine leaves
30 fresh raspberries, for decoration

For the lemon curd
100g butter
8 lemons, juiced
250g sugar
4 eggs, beaten

For the pâte bombe
100ml water
400g sugar
10 egg yolks

For the lemon curd parfait
320g pâte bombe
600g lemon curd
3 lemons, zested and juiced
325ml double cream, semi whipped

For the sablé biscuit
225g plain flour
25g cornflour
100g icing sugar
3 egg yolks
200g unsalted butter, roughly chopped
   and at room temperature
Salt

Raspberry jelly

Place the raspberries and caster sugar in a bowl and cover with clingfilm. Set the covered bowl over a saucepan of simmering water on a low heat for 1 hour until the raspberries have released all of their juices. Make sure the water doesn't touch the bowl. Remove the bowl from the heat and strain the juices through a muslin cloth and discard the pulp. Soften the gelatine leaves in cold water. Gently heat 50ml of the strained raspberry juice in a small saucepan. Remove the gelatine from the water and squeeze to get rid of excess water, then add the leaves to the warm raspberry juice and stir until dissolved. Next mix this and the remaining raspberry juice together. Line a small, shallow tray with clingfilm and pour in the juice to the depth of 1cm and put it in the fridge to set.

Lemon curd

Fill a saucepan with water and bring to a simmer over a low heat. Melt the butter, lemon juice and sugar in a bowl over the saucepan, making sure it doesn't touch the water. When the sugar has dissolved, add the beaten eggs and continue to cook the curd, stirring gently with a whisk, until it thickens. Remove from the heat, measure out 100g of the lemon curd to use when you plate up the dish, then put this and the remaining curd in the fridge to cool.

Pâte bombe

Place the water and sugar together in a heavy-based saucepan and bring to the boil at 120C using a sugar thermometer to check the temperature. Whisk the egg yolks until they double in size then pour the sugar slowly over the yolks, continuing to whisk as the mixture cools.

Lemon curd parfait

In a large bowl whisk together the pâte bombe, lemon curd (not the reserved 100g) and the juice with the lemon zest, then fold in the semi whipped double cream. Pour the mix into a lined tray then place in the freezer for 24 hours.

Sablé biscuit

Sift the flour, cornflour, icing sugar and a pinch of salt into a large bowl. Add the butter and gently work together with your fingertips until you get a fine breadcrumb consistency. Add the yolks and gradually work the mix together until you form a ball of dough, but do not overwork. Wrap the pastry in clingfilm and refrigerate it for 2 hours. Roll out the dough to a thickness of 1cm, cut it into rectangles of 2cm x 8cm, then place these on a baking tray lined with baking parchment and place in the oven at 180C/gas mark 4 for 5-7 minutes or until golden all over. Remove from, oven and cool.

Serving

Fill a small plastic squeeze bottle with the 100g of reserved lemon curd, turn out the jelly on to a clean chopping board and cut out small cylinders of jelly using a 1cm pastry cutter. Turn out the lemon curd parfait on to a clean chopping board and cut to the same size as the sablé biscuits, then carefully place it on top of the biscuits Pop this on to the centre of your plates, surround the parfait with the jellies and a few fresh raspberries, and finally dot some lemon curd between the jellies and raspberries.

INDEX

US CONVERSIONS CHART

British and American cookbooks use different measuring systems. In the UK, dry ingredients are measured by weight, with the metric system increasingly replacing the Imperial one, while in the US they are measured by volume.

WEIGHT

7g	$1/4$ ounce	200g	7 ounces
20g	$3/4$ ounce	220–225g	8 ounces
25–30g	1 ounce	250–260g	9 ounces
40g	$1^1/2$ ounces	300g	$10^1/2$ ounces
50g	$1^3/4$ ounces	325g	$11^1/2$ ounces
60–65g	$2^1/4$ ounces	350g	12 ounces
70–75g	$2^1/2$ ounces	400g	14 ounces
80g	$2^3/4$ ounces	450g	1 pound
90g	$3^1/4$ ounces	500g	1 pound 2 ounces
100g	$3^1/2$ ounces	600g	1 pound 5 ounces
110–115g	4 ounces	700g	1 pound 9 ounces
120–130g	$4^1/2$ ounces	750g	1 pound 10 ounces
140g	5 ounces	800g	$1^3/4$ pounds
150g	$5^1/2$ ounces	900g	2 pounds
175–180g	6 ounces	1kg	$2^1/4$ pounds

VOLUME

50ml	$1^3/4$ fl oz	300ml	10 fl oz
60ml	2 fl oz (4 tablespoons/$1/4$ cup)	350ml	12 fl oz
75ml	$2^1/2$ fl oz (5 tablespoons)	400ml	14 fl oz
90ml	3 fl oz ($3/8$ cup)	450ml	15 fl oz
100ml	$3^1/2$ fl oz	475ml	16 fl oz (2 cups)
125ml	4 fl oz ($1/2$ cup)	500ml	18 fl oz
150ml	5 fl oz ($2/3$ cup)	600ml	20 fl oz
175ml	6 fl oz	800ml	28 fl oz
200ml	7 fl oz	850ml	30 fl oz
250ml	8 fl oz (1 cup)	1 litre	35 fl oz (4 cups)

LENGTH

5mm	$1/4$ inch	8cm	$3^1/4$ inches
1cm	$1/2$ inch	9cm	$3^1/2$ inches
2cm	$3/4$ inch	10cm	4 inches
2.5cm	1 inch	12cm	$4^1/2$ inches
3cm	$1^1/4$ inches	14cm	$5^1/2$ inches
4cm	$1^1/2$ inches	20cm	8 inches
5cm	2 inches	24cm	$9^1/2$ inches
6cm	$2^1/2$ inches	30cm	12 inches

ACKNOWLEDGEMENTS

This book could not have happened without the passion and kindness of twenty incredible chefs. Thank you for sharing.

Huge thanks and respect to our wonderful publisher, Jon Croft (who has taught me the joys and terrible results of drinking dessert wine!) and his brilliant (sorry Jon, but it's true, they are) team, but especially Matt Inwood and Meg Avent.

I cannot ever convey here how much we owe to Joanna Wood, our incredible editor. Her tireless work and impeccable attention to detail has been inspiring.

Thank you Cristian Barnett, who has broken some kind of record for photographic food miles.

To Mr Martin, for being so much better at breakdancing than people know! Shh! don't tell them.

To Amanda Ross, for being the best general a lowly TV foot soldier could ever hope for.

To the whole *Saturday Kitchen* team, Andy, Emma, Anna, CJ and JP. And to the fantastic fellow food junkies Janet B and Michaela.

Mr Bulmer, it's been a pleasure, and we must do this again very soon!

I dedicate this tome to my whole family, and thank you Mum and Dad and Aunt Margaret for putting such great food on the table, food that even outshines anything within these pages.

Millie and Sam – I love you and remember always to make a fuss about food. One, two, tree!

Finally to my wonderful wife, Victoria, who has watched my waistline grow over the process of writing this book without complaint. I am back darling! xxx

Now, let's eat!

JAMES WINTER

Books of this type are created through an awful lot of hard work by an awful lot of people, most of it not actually overseen by the author. Therefore, I would like to reiterate Mr Winter's sentiments and offer our sincere gratitude to our publisher, the inimitable Jon Croft, and his fantastic team, and especially Matt Inwood and Meg Avent. I hope we continue to work together.

I'd also like to thank Joanna Wood, who has tirelessly battled with our inane ramblings and, through her patient, intelligent work, has created the free-flowing text in this book. It is not easy to put your thoughts clearly on paper, as we have found, but Joanna has somehow managed it.

A special note must go to the real geniuses in this book: the twenty amazingly talented chefs whose recipes I hope you enjoy as much as we have.

Thanks must also go to Cristian Barnett for bringing the food to life with his exquisite photography.

Without you Mr Winter, this book would never have happened; remaining just another drunken idea in a bar. I look forward to enjoying many more long lunches with you in the future.

A big thank you must go to the people who have assisted me in my working life and allowed me the time to indulge in this passion. My business partner and rock at MyJam Communications, Maziar Yazdanian and my 'food guru' assistant, Stuart Singer, who I'm sure one day will write a similar book.

To my beautiful partner and soon-to-be wife Kate Tully, who is a better cook than I will ever be.

And finally, thanks go to my family, Lynn, Derek and Rebecca for their unconditional love and support. Special mention must go to my father, though, who, as Editor of the Michelin Guide, has been my inspiration to explore and enjoy the fascinating world of food and drink.

JAMES BULMER